C000091215

A HISTORY OF BRITAIN

The Age of Reason and the Industrial Revolution, 1714-1832

This volume of the evolving series covers the period from the arrival on the throne of the Hanoverian King George I in 1714 to the passage of the Reform Act in 1832. The reigns of the four Georges saw the assertion – and loss to Britain – of the American colonies, but also great expansion for the Empire in India, Canada and Australia. Domestically it was a relatively stable period for the United Kingdom created by the Acts of Union in 1707. It could stand back from the devastating revolution of its neighbour, France, which it was to overcome in the war (from 1799 to 1815) to defeat the would-be master of Europe, Napoleon Bonaparte. The important revolutions in Britain in this period were, rather, agricultural and industrial, with technological innovations allowing Britain to become the world's first great manufacturing power. Victory in war reinforced Britain's position as master of the seas, and its emergence as the world's leading trading nation.

EH Carter was Chief Inspector of Schools in the 1930s and '40s. **RAF Mears** taught history at Warwick School between 1923 and 1933.

David Evans, who edits the restored series, is an historian and former Head of History at Eton College.

PUBLICATION SCHEDULE

A HISTORY OF BRITAIN

The Age of Reason and
the Industrial Revolution
◆
1714-1832

by

EH Carter & RAF Mears

edited and updated by

David Evans

STACEY
INTERNATIONAL

A HISTORY OF BRITAIN
The Age of Reason and
the Industrial Revolution

STACEY INTERNATIONAL
128 Kensington Church Street
London W8 4BH
Tel: +44 (0)20 7221 7166; Fax: +44 (0)20 7792 9288
Email: info@stacey-international.co.uk
www.stacey-international.co.uk

ISBN: 978 1906768 24 9

Original version published in 1937 by The Clarendon Press

1 3 5 7 9 0 8 6 4 2

Printed in the UAE

The Publishers of this edition of *The History of Britain*, revised by David Evans
(formerly Head of History, Eton College), give wholehearted acknowledgment to the
original work of the late E H Carter (sometime Chief Examiner in History, Board of
Education, and H M Inspector of Schools) and R A F Mears (former Senior History
Master, Warwick School), who died respectively in 1954 and 1940. The Publishers
declare that prolonged endeavours devoted to tracing whether rights to the work of
these two distinguished scholars rested with any successors or assigns have been
without avail, and that they remain ready to indemnify, as may be mutually deemed
appropriate, proven holders of such rights.

Maps by Amber Sheers

CIP Data: A catalogue record for this book is available from the British Library

Contents

List of Illustrations

Maps

Outline Summary

Georgian Period (1714-83)

1714 George I *acc*.
1715 Jacobite Rebellion
1721-42 Walpole Ministry
1739 First Methodist Society

1745 Jacobite Rebellion

1757-61 Pitt's Ministry

1760-1820 George III
1770-82 North's Ministry

1740-86 Frederick the Great (Prussia)
1740-8 War of Austrian Succession
1751 Siege of Arcot (Clive)
1756-63 Seven Year War
1757 ⚔ Plassey
1759 British take Quebec
1763 Treaty of Paris – Canada British
1775–83 American War of
     Independence
1776 Declaration of Independence
1783 Treaty of Versailles (U.S.A.
     independent)

Revolutionary Era (1714-83)

1783-1801 Younger Pitt's Ministry

1788 New South Wales
1789-97 Washington, President, U.S.A.
1789 French Revolution
1792-1815 Wars of French Revolution
1796 Napoleon in Italy
1798 ⚔ The Nile

1800 Union of Great Britain and Ireland

1804-14 Napoleon Emperor
1805 ⚔ Trafalgar
1806 ⚔ Austerlitz

1807 British Slave Trade ended

1808-14 Peninsular War
1815 ⚔ Waterloo
     Congress of Vienna

1819 Peterloo

1815-24 Congress System
1823 Monroe Doctrine

1825 Stockton and Darlington Railway
1829 Metropolitan Police Force

1830 Belgian Revolution

8

Introduction to
the Georgian Age

Between 1714 and 1837 Britain was ruled by a dynasty which originated in Hanover in North Germany. George I was offered the throne not because he was closest in blood to the previous Stuart dynasty, but because he was their nearest Protestant relative. The next three Kings, George I's descendants, were all called George. George IV, however, died without heirs in 1830 and was succeeded by his brother, who became William IV. All these Kings were also rulers of the state of Hanover in Germany, though from George III (1760-1820) onwards they were absentee rulers who identified with Britain. In the 18th century, the royal court was still a vital centre of power. The Kings helped to choose the ministers and had an important say in what policies were adopted. Only in the reign of William IV (1830-7) did these royal powers finally ebb away.

None of the Hanoverian monarchs ever challenged the role of Parliament in the way that the Stuarts had sometimes done. Utterly dependent on Parliament for finance, governments had to be able to command a majority in the Houses of Lords and Commons, which meant that the King's choice of ministers was in practice limited. The House of Lords contained the greatest landowners in the country, and because of the way in which parliamentary seats were distributed, the House of Commons too was dominated by the landed classes. Witnessing still to the supremacy of the great landed families in the Georgian era are the many great houses which adorn the English countryside, often, like Stowe in Buckinghamshire, surrounded by landscapes remodelled as parks. Another testimony to the golden age of the English landed aristocracy is the Georgian city of Bath, which was effectively a creation of the aristocratic elite who flocked there every summer to take the waters and to socialize. England's ruling classes were immensely proud of their political system. For them the rejection of the Stuarts at the Glorious Revolution of 1688 had endowed Britain with a perfect constitution. They gloried in the contrast between Britain's constitutional monarchy and the absolute monarchies of the continent. The British people, it was claimed, were endowed with all the blessings of liberty, while the unlucky Europeans endured a species of slavery. This vision of Britain's unique good fortune appealed to many who were not members of the landed classes and helps to explain why challenges to the political system were so few and unsuccessful, at least until around 1830.

The phrase *the British people* cannot be accurately used before the Georgian age. Scotland had lost its own Parliament and instead sent representatives to the Parliament at Westminster under the Act of Union of 1707, but at first the Union was merely a political device to prevent conflict between the two nations and did not signify any meeting of hearts or minds. Loyalty to the Stuart dynasty, represented by the son (James) and then the grandson (Bonnie Prince Charlie) of James II, still survived north of the Scottish border, especially in the Highlands. It was eradicated only after the defeat of Bonnie Prince Charlie's army at Culloden in 1746. Even when he was most successful in 1745, however, many Scots were far from enthusiastic about the Stuart prince. Protestant suspicion of his Catholic religion was one strong reason for their reservations. The economic interests, particularly of the towns, were another. The Scots were becoming partners with their English neighbours in the British empire. By the late 18th century they were partners in the industrial revolution too. Scotland ceased to be an impoverished land on the far periphery of Europe. Its thinkers, such as David Hume and Adam Smith, made a great contribution to the great intellectual movement in Europe known as the Enlightenment, while Edinburgh took on the appearance which it still retains of a handsome Georgian city. Prosperity and success reconciled Scots to the Union and helped to create a British identity, even if the restricted Scottish electorate of under 3,000 gave only a tiny minority of Scots a role in the political process. The Union with Scotland proved so successful that eventually the British government attempted to use the same device to reconcile Ireland to the British connection. In this case, it was not successful and the Georgian period ended with fresh crises in Ireland.

The Catholic majority in Ireland remained restive, but in England religion ceased to be an important political issue for the duration of the 18th century. Catholics in Britain too had no political rights and were discriminated against in respect of access to education, property rights and freedom of worship. Yet they formed so small a minority and anti-Catholicism was so widespread in society that they were content simply to evade attention as far as possible. Protestant Non-conformists could freely practise their religion and were willing to tolerate their exclusion from Parliament and local government, especially as the practice of occasional attendance at Anglican services enabled them to get round most restrictions. The Anglican Church enjoyed a privileged position in the English state, but that meant that it was virtually an arm of the government. Governments appointed compliant bishops who were not *enthusiasts* or, as we would say, fanatics. The Church became associated with the mere outward observance of religion. For many people in 18th century Britain, outward forms were not enough. They sought a Vital or Evangelical religion which stressed the personal, inward conversion of the individual by God's Grace. The result of their search was a great religious revival. The most famous revivalist was the preacher John Wesley, who travelled the length and breadth of England on his preaching tours and founded the Methodist movement. By the time of Wesley's death, Methodism was on the route to separation from the Anglican Church, but many who shared Wesley's basic religious ideas remained within it. With their stress on the equality of all people in God's sight and the availability of God's Grace to everyone, Evangelicals, as they were known, were often attracted to humanitarian causes such as the campaigns against the slave trade and slavery. In early 19th century Britain they were a force to be reckoned with.

The 18th century has always been recognized as a period of profound economic changes. There were important changes in agriculture, often dignified by the title 'the agricultural revolution'. In the many areas of England which had been farmed as open fields, the land was divided into individually owned compact farms enclosed by hedges or fences. This change transformed the appearance of the English countryside in many areas and made it easier to introduce new agricultural techniques designed to increase production. More food was necessary because the population had begun to increase very rapidly, much of it accommodated in growing towns. In the Midlands and in the North, the towns were often products of the industrial revolution. This is the label given to a series of changes which became evident in the fifty years 1780 to 1830. Transport of people and goods became much cheaper and more rapid as roads were improved and canals built. By the 1820s the first railways made their appearance. Manufactured goods themselves became cheaper and more plentiful as larger and more sophisticated machines powered by water and later by steam partially replaced human labour. New sources of power made it necessary to concentrate production in purpose-built factories instead of carrying it on in the workers' houses. Factories in turn called for the growth of large centres of population in towns. By the 1820s as many Englishmen lived in towns as in villages. England was ceasing to be a primarily agrarian society.

Britain's emergence as the workshop of the world was facilitated by the wealth that accrued from the development of trade and empire in the course of the 18th century. Britain already possessed useful colonies in the West Indies, which produced sugar by means of the labour of black slaves imported from West Africa. The colonies on the North American mainland steadily expanded, furnishing markets for English manufactures. In the Seven Years' War (1756-63) the British consolidated their grip on North America by depriving the French of Canada. At the same time the foundations of what was to be the Indian Empire were laid. The key to British success was the Royal

Navy, which was almost invariably superior to its rivals, and especially to the French in both size and technology. Only at one point in the century did this superiority falter, during the American War of Independence of 1775-83, when Britain's American colonies broke away from the empire. Temporary control of the sea enabled the French to assist the rebels to win a decisive battle at Yorktown in 1781. The British kept hold of the rest of their empire, which soon began to expand into new areas, such as Australia and South Africa. Essentially, their continued imperial successes depended on the rapid recovery of control of the sea, assisted by an ever-expanding chain of naval bases round the world.

The period 1714 to 1815 is sometimes described as a second hundred years' war between Britain and France. The century was punctuated by a series of major conflicts between the two powers: the War of the Austrian Succession (1740-8), the Seven Years' War (1756-63), the American War of Independence (which was an international conflict from 1778 to 1783), the Wars of the French Revolution (1792-1802) and finally the War against the Napoleonic Empire (1803-15). Throughout this period the British regarded the French as the national enemy and the only other power which they regularly fought was Spain, ruled by a junior branch of the same Bourbon dynasty which reigned in France till the Revolution. The British were aware that they could easily lose to France in the war for overseas empire, given that France had a national population three times that of Britain and national wealth in 1714 perhaps twice as great. Yet France had one serious weakness: it was vulnerable on land in a way in which Britain was not. What British statesmen had to do was to ensure that the French could never put all their efforts into the war at sea. Could they do so, they might very well triumph. Britain had to make sure that France always faced a threat on land serious enough to force them to divide their resources between their army and their navy. In such circumstances, Britain might stand a good chance of defeating them. There were three continental states powerful enough to pose a threat to France: the Habsburgs of Austria, who usually bore the title of Holy Roman Emperor; the militarily strong kingdom of Prussia in North Germany; and the Russian Empire, which had begun to play a major role in international affairs.

Only once during the Georgian age did Britain fight France without a continental ally. In the American War, France was able to concentrate its forces against its British rival and it is no accident that this was the only major conflict in which Britain lost. The most difficult and costly of all Britain's struggles against France was the almost uninterrupted period of hostilities following the French Revolution. Yet Britain's empire was never seriously menaced. The revolutionaries and then Napoleon neglected the navy by which alone Britain could be defeated. At the same time, they persisted in an attempt to dominate Europe which kept providing Britain with fresh allies against them. Victory in the conflict with Napoleonic France was dearly bought, but French power was never again a serious threat to Britain. French superiority in population waned in the course of the 19th century. Atlantic ports such as Bordeaux never regained their 18th century prosperity and the French navy could no longer hope to rival the British one.

The French Revolution had an enormous impact on British foreign policy. It also had major repercussions on English domestic affairs. In 1789 bankruptcy forced King Louis XVI to summon a representative assembly of his kingdom. Perhaps the most sensational of the events which followed was the storming of the Parisian fortress of the Bastille by the Paris mob. The fortress was used as a prison, though it was almost empty of prisoners, and served as a convenient symbol of royal absolutism. The Assembly proceeded to end absolutism and to establish a constitutional monarchy. Thus far the French seemed to be copying the English model and many of their neighbours across the Channel heartily approved. Some Englishmen felt that Britain too should embark on a process of reform. It soon became clear, however, that this was not a limited and respectable revolution on the model of the changes in England in 1688. The revolutionaries went on to destroy the aristocracy and reconstruct the Church. The monarchy was abolished and in a reign of terror in 1793 the King and later Queen Marie Antoinette were guillotined. At the same time, the new regime in France revealed that it had shed none of the most objectionable features of the old regime. It was even keener on invading its neighbours and was more successful than French Kings had ever been at grabbing ports in the Rhine delta from which British security and trade could be threatened. In the circumstances, admiration for the French faded rapidly and the government was able to crack down on already enfeebled reforming groups within Britain. By 1799 sanguinary revolutionaries were no longer in power in France, but Bonaparte, the military dictator, was another very appropriate hate figure for the British public. The net effect of the dramatic changes in France was to make the British ruling classes reluctant to effect any changes in their own political system lest they escalate out of control as had happened in France. Among the members of the British public, reforming ideas were discredited for thirty years and when they began to revive, it was emphatically British, not French traditions that they drew on.

I

THE RULE OF THE WHIGS

I. Hanoverians and Jacobites

THE Elector of Hanover, who became King George I of England in 1714 at the age of fifty-four, was not an attractive personality. Like William of Orange, this German prince had been summoned to the throne of England on religious and political grounds. Like William, he lacked all personal charm; his coldness, said a wit, would freeze his surroundings. Like William, he was a foreigner, and he had not troubled to learn even a smattering of English. Inevitably, some Germans came over with the King and acted as his advisors, thereby arousing English xenophobia. The King's private life was scandalous. He had quarrelled with his wife, Sophia Dorothea of Celle, and shut her up for thirty years in a German castle for an affair with a Swedish count till she died. Her son George, created Prince of Wales (1714), was on such bad terms with his father that the King tried to prevent his succeeding to the electorate; quarrels between father and son were unfortunately traditional in the Hanoverian family. Lacking a Queen, George I brought with him from Germany the fat Countess of Kielmansegge, his half-sister, and the thin Countess of Schulenberg, nicknamed in England the 'Elephant' and the 'Maypole'.

George I 1714-27

During the last years of Queen Anne, George had not formed a good opinion of the Tories, who had deserted their allies, including Hanover, to make a separate peace with France and were unenthusiastic about his accession. Even so, he hoped to have a mixed ministry of Whigs and moderate Tories, but Tory non-co-operation made this hope impractical. The Tories placed their hopes in the results of the general election due in 1715, which they expected would give them a majority and force the King to come to terms with them. In fact, the election overturned a large Tory majority and gave a

The Hanoverians and the Whigs 1714-60

comfortable majority to the Whigs. Crown influence doubtless played a part in the achievement of this result, but the Whigs did well in seats with large electorates, which is evidence of their popularity and of the acceptability to most people of the new dynasty. Fearing that the Whigs would take vengeance upon him for the policies he had followed under Anne, the Tory leader Bolingbroke fled abroad, while another leader, the Earl of Oxford, was impeached for treason by the Whig-dominated House of Commons. The Tories were excluded from the entire administrative machinery and from the lord lieutenancies in the counties and even the Justices of the Peace (JPs) were purged. There was to be no Tory ministry in the reigns of the first two Georges.

'The Fifteen'
Preston and
Sheriffmuir
1715

Even the Whigs could not pretend to feel any affection for King George I, while to some of the Tories his occupation of the throne was an outrage. A Jacobite (a label derived from the Pretender's name, *Jacobus* in Latin) plot was hatched in France to overthrow the Hanoverian succession, and place Prince James Edward, the Old Pretender, on the throne. It was fatal to its chances of success that France, exhausted after the long War of the Spanish Succession, was unwilling to intervene. Yet Scotland seemed a promising point of attack on account of the supposed loyalty of the Highland clans to the Stuart cause and also because the Union of 1707 with England was known to be unpopular. There, in September 1715, the Jacobite Rebellion broke out. It was led by the Earl of Mar, an unsteady personage known as 'Bobbing John'. Mar raised the Highlands, occupied Perth, and proclaimed James III and VIII King. A Jacobite force crossed the border into England, but the government had already been busy arresting Jacobites in England. The invaders picked up some support from English Catholics, but were surrounded and taken prisoner at Preston on 14th November. On the same day occurred an engagement between Mar and the Duke of Argyll, acting for the government, at Sheriffmuir, rendered famous by the story (not without some foundation) that both sides ran away. After the battle Mar retired to Perth, and enthusiasm for the rebellion died down. It was not increased by the arrival of the Old Pretender in Scotland in December, for he was a man of cold and unsympathetic manner, a hopeless leader for a failing cause. His loyalty to his religion – which he refused to change to become King of Great Britain – made it unlikely that many except Highlanders would join him. After a few months he returned to France, to spend the wandering life which earned him the name of 'Roving Jamie'. The rebellion was an ignominious failure, and its collapse strengthened the hands of the government. Seven Scottish peers were captured at Preston and found guilty of treason. Many Tories demanded mercy for them, which led to the ejection from the government of the last Tories and finally ensured that for many years the name Tory should be synonymous with Jacobite, and Jacobite with traitor. This was far from just. But the very accusation was enough to discredit the Tories.

The Whigs were thus firmly established in power in 1715. They proceeded to pass the Septennial Act, which laid it down that general elections needed to be called only every seven years. The Act made the Whigs less dependent upon swings in popular opinion. The Whig leaders were Lord Sunderland, Marlborough's son-in-law; James, Earl Stanhope, the soldier who had captured Minorca in the last war; Charles, Viscount Townshend (the 'Turnip Townshend' of agriculture), and Sir Robert Walpole. Townshend and Walpole quarrelled with their colleagues, and were dismissed in 1717; and Stanhope became the leading minister for the next four years, 1717-21. It was during this time that the foundations of the Whig oligarchy were firmly laid; Walpole, who ruled England for twenty years, carried on the same traditions of government.

The Whig Leaders

The rule of an 18th century Prime Minister depended on two things, the favour of the King and control of the House of Commons. The first Hanoverian Kings had no possible alternative to a Whig ministry, but the Whigs remained a united party only so long as the Tories remained a threat to them. With the eclipse of the Tories, the Whigs fragmented as early as 1717. This meant that the King had a

The Whigs and the Crown

19

real choice of ministers. His choice depended not just on his personal likes or dislikes, but also on the willingness and ability of particular ministers to get the King's business done. George I never spoke much English, but he could communicate with ministers in French and he certainly made clear what he wanted, especially in foreign affairs. The centre of his interests was Hanover, but his Hanoverian interests could be secured only if he could make use of the superior resources of his new Kingdom. Hence his ministers did not have a free hand. They had to do what he wanted. In return the King gave them an essential weapon for ruling England, control of the patronage of the Crown. Ambitious men in the Church, the Army and Navy, and the legal profession knew that they could rise to the highest posts only by supporting the King's ministers; civil servants in government pay were chosen and promoted on the same principle. Skilful deployment of royal patronage was an essential factor in the achievement of political stability in the 18th century.

The Whigs and the House of Commons

In the 18th century Prime Ministers could not survive in office unless they could command majorities in the Houses of Parliament. The House of Lords was less of a problem than the Commons. It was much smaller. Many courtiers sat in it. Many Lords coveted honours such as membership of the Order of the Bath, which could be awarded to those who loyally voted as the ministry wished. Certain groups were particularly dependent on the government, such as the 26 Anglican bishops who owed their places to the ministers and whose hopes of promotion to richer sees depended on ministerial favour. Few Lords' votes could be depended upon in all circumstances, but the ministry could usually rely on obtaining a majority.

Ministers had to work hard to keep a majority in the House of Commons. About a quarter of the Commons – sometimes nearly a third – could be accounted for by 'placemen', that is, Members of Parliament who held minor posts in return for which they were expected to vote for the government. The number of such posts was large, and the duties attached to them often small; but the Whigs thought that the more posts – and votes – there were the better. The loyalty of the placemen was in the first place to the King rather than to his ministers; so if the King's support for a set of ministers became doubtful, the placemen might begin to desert. This account of the voting behaviour of the placemen assumes that they could more or less take their electorates for granted. In the 18th century large numbers of MPs sat for seats where public opinion counted for little. Most of them were elected by the English boroughs and the electorates were frequently small, either because the population had declined, or because the vote was limited to very few people. In some places an individual was so powerful that he could in effect nominate the MPs (the nomination or pocket boroughs). This political dominance could even be bought and sold. Votes too were for sale in some of the small boroughs. Voting was not secret, which encouraged bribery and intimidation. The system made it possible for some great men to become borough-mongers, that is to establish control of a large number of seats. The largest electoral empire of the 18th century was that of the Dukes of Newcastle, who controlled a dozen seats in three counties. A ministry could strengthen its position by gaining the support of some of the great borough patrons. Yet no ministry could depend on placemen and the dependents of borough patrons alone. The county electorates were large and there were a number of open boroughs with large electorates. In these places public opinion could not be ignored. If there was political stability in the 18th century, it was not because every one had been bribed into submission, but because the great divisive issues of the period before 1714, such as religion, the succession and the struggle with France, had diminished in importance and because ministries strove to pursue non-controversial policies. They did not always succeed and when they did not, political instability could recur.

In the 18th century, elections were an expensive business, which is one reason why the Whigs reduced their frequency in 1716. Mr

Thomas Pitt, agent for His Royal Highness the Prince of Wales and Duke of Cornwall, estimated the expenses of the elections in 1747 at Grampound and Tregony, two tiny Cornish boroughs, at £1,200 and £1,050,respectively. 'It must cost,' said this gentleman, writing of a Grampound election, 'damnably dear. The villains have got ahead to that degree and rise in their demands so extravagantly that I have been very near damning them and kicking them to the devil at once. The dirty rascals despise 20 guineas as much as the King's Sergeant does a halfguinea fee.' The Duke of Newcastle spent around £27,000 managing his electoral interests in the election of 1754. Elections were expensive in the big, open constituencies too. Electors expected to be conveyed to the poll and entertained to food and drink. The artist William Hogarth satirized this aspect of electioneering in his famous Election Series of paintings, created around 1754, after a notorious election in Oxfordshire.

Results of the old Election System

Such was the system on which England was governed. In the 19th century, it came to be thought of as immoral. Yet most of the members of both Houses were not mere puppets of the ministers. They did have consciences and if they became persuaded that the ministers were trying to destroy English liberty or were failing to defend the patriotic cause with sufficient vigour, then not all their use of patronage was able to save the ministry. This is a major reason why the political contest in the House of Commons never ceased to be fought. The oratory of politicians who were out of power could weaken confidence in the King's ministers and at times make it impossible for them to carry on. For this reason, it was essential both for the ministers and their opponents to have able spokesmen on their side. Such men needed a secure seat in the Commons which did not need defending at great expense at elections and they could find it in one of two ways. They might have a family seat. The great parliamentary orator, the Elder Pitt sat for the family borough of Old Sarum. That seat was not available for his son, the Younger Pitt, who had to rely on the other way of gaining a safe seat. He was offered the seat of Appleby in Westmorland by its patron Sir James Lowther, who imposed no conditions, hoping, presumably, to bask in reflected glory if Pitt's political career took off. Plainly, the parliamentary system of the 18th century offered opportunities to men of great talent. The main criticism that can be levelled against the system is its limited responsiveness to public opinion, but that usually mattered little, since with the eclipse of the great issues of the Stuart period, popular interest in politics was usually slight. In any case, the system was by no means impervious to popular opinion, should it become aroused.

The Tories did not offer a political system different from that operated by the Whigs; but they were less successful because the Whigs had the patronage of the Crown behind them, and because the Whig leaders were richer. The Whig party machine was in the hands of an oligarchy of rich noblemen – the Pelhams (the Duke of Newcastle was a Pelham), the Russells, the Cavendishes, and others – whose wealth frequently enabled them to outbid the local Tories, though, of course, a substantial minority of Tories was always returned. And though the Whig oligarchy dominated the central government, the local government of the countryside was dominated by the squires, who were often Tories. The squires, as unpaid Justices of the Peace administered the countryside and drew their power from local influence. So the power of the Whig oligarchy at the centre was limited by the power of the squires, many of them Tory, at the circumference.

Tory influences

The Whigs under George I made an important change in the direction of English foreign policy. Louis XIV had died in 1715, and the ministers of the young Louis XV concluded a peaceful alliance with England, for which Stanhope was largely responsible. By the inclusion of Holland in 1717, this agreement became the Triple Alliance, which kept England at peace with France for a quarter of a century. Not until colonial rivalry became acute was the alliance broken.

Stanhope Foreign Minister 1717-21

23

The South
Sea Bubble
1720

It was a financial crisis which brought about Stanhope's fall and paved the way for the rise of Walpole. The gambling spirit was rife in the 18th century, and finance was even less understood by the public than it is to-day. The South Sea Company had been founded by Harley in 1711; after the Peace of Utrecht it received the monopoly of the trade with Spanish America, under the Asiento Treaty. Its trade was never really profitable, but in spite of this fact the company offered to take over from the government the £51 million of National Debt. The scheme was opposed in Parliament by a minority, of whom Walpole was one. But the company gained the confidence of the country, which it did not deserve, and its stock rose to fantastic heights. By June 1720, £100 South Sea Stock reached its highest figure at £1,060. Then came the reaction; a panic as sudden as the former speculating mania set in; by December South Sea Stock had fallen to £135. Thousands of people of all classes were ruined; the South Sea Bubble had burst.

Fall of the
Ministry
1721

Some relief was obtained by distributing the private property of the directors, to the amount of £2,000,000; but there was a universal outcry for revenge. Ministers were involved in the proceedings, and the government fell; one minister, Craggs, committed suicide. Sir Robert Walpole had been lucky enough to be out of office at the time of the Bubble and had opposed it on behalf of the Bank of England. For him, therefore, the crisis was an opportunity. He could not, however, pursue the populist course and attack the fallen ministers, since popularity was only one of the keys to power. The other was royal favour and the King did not want a thorough investigation which could have exposed his close friends and his mistress. Walpole came to be called the Screen because of his role in shielding the court in the affair. His rewards were the posts of Chancellor of the Exchequer and First Lord of the Treasury, which he held from April 1721.

ROBERT WALPOLE (1676-1745)
(1742 portrait by Arthur Pond)

2. Sir Robert Walpole

Sir Robert Walpole came of a long line of Norfolk squires, and was third of a family of nineteen children. He was educated at Eton and King's College, Cambridge, and, after the deaths of his father and two elder brothers, succeeded to the family estates. Walpole had all the vices of the 18th-century country gentleman: his manners were coarse, and he had few intellectual pleasures – none to compare with

Character of Walpole

his chief delight, which was hunting. He had a low opinion of human nature, and took a cynical pleasure in distributing the various bribes, in the shape of titles, places, and pensions, to the members of his party. But in this respect he was no worse than the Whigs who preceded and followed him in office. Walpole was more than a great parliamentary manager; he was a great minister. He loved his work, and he gave himself up to it with all the devotion and quiet persistence of a successful man of business.

Walpole succeeded to power after eighty years of revolutions: old
End of the   men still living could remember the battle of Worcester, the death of
Revolution- Cromwell, the Restoration, the Popish Plot, and the landing of
ary era   William of Orange. Walpole prided himself on giving England twenty years of quiet government. The year 1742, when he fell from power, was the hundredth anniversary of Edgehill, the first battle of the Civil War; he had done much to produce the political stability which still seemed elusive when he came to power. The South Sea Bubble seemed to some a portent of revolution that might have given the Pretender his chance, had he been ready to take advantage of it. The election of 1722 was the most hotly contested of the century. The Whigs won very comfortably, but they were so divided that their
Peace policy victory was no guarantee of stable rule. Despite this unpromising background, Walpole achieved a period of stable rule such as England had not known since the time of James I.

In Walpole's time government was still in fact as well as in form the King's government. The way in which he handled the aftermath of the South Sea Bubble won him the lasting confidence of George I. The difficulty was that so bad were the relations of George and his heir that the favour of the father seemed to guarantee dismissal by the son, once he succeeded in 1727. When Walpole informed the new King that his father had dropped dead on the way to Hanover, George II's reaction was one of joy. He told Walpole to take his directions henceforth from Sir Spencer Compton. Everyone assumed that Compton would take over as Prime Minister. Fortunately for

Walpole, Compton proved a nonentity who could not even write the Commons' address to the new King without Walpole's help. Though advised to curry favour with one of George's mistresses, Walpole realized that the Queen's influence was far greater. As he later said, 'He seized the right sow by the ear.' Queen Caroline's assistance was vital in perpetuating his power in 1727. Yet his ability to do what the King wanted done was even more important. Walpole demonstrated his ability in 1727, when he procured an increase in the Civil List (the part of the revenue set aside for the King's use) from £700,000 to £800,000. Thereafter, Walpole was secure in the King's favour, except for a brief wobble at the time of the crisis over the Excise Bill (see below). After that setback, the King showed his commitment to his minister by dismissing from his court two of Walpole's enemies. By the late 1730s, however, a new threat appeared on the horizon. George's eldest son Frederick was by then in his thirties. As was traditional in his family, he loathed his father and began to gather around him opponents of Walpole. Such opposition was dangerous, because it did not have the taint of disloyalty that other opposition to the King's government could easily acquire.

George II and Queen Caroline

In his twenty years of rule, Walpole did his best to remove the passion from politics. His motto was '*Quieta non movere*', which might be translated as 'Let sleeping dogs lie'. Religious issues had been a perennial source of passion in the years before 1714, as Anglicans had worried about danger to their Church from nonconformists. Traditionally, the Whigs had upheld the rights of nonconformists, a policy continued as late as 1719, when the Schism Act, limiting nonconformist education, and the Occasional Conformity Act, making more difficult nonconformist evasion of the laws preventing them from holding local office in town corporations, were repealed. Once Walpole came to power, however, no more was done for the Whigs' traditional supporters. Walpole and Bishop Gibson of London formed a close alliance. Whiggish low churchmen dominated the bench of bishops. They had no wish to harry nonconformists, who

27

tended to decline in numbers and even to convert to the Anglican Church. The high churchmen, who had wanted to harass nonconformists, were silenced, in that Convocation, the clergy's equivalent of Parliament, no longer met. Religious peace was established in England. Walpole's management of Parliament was correspondingly easier, since his system did not readily work if issues of conscience were often raised.

War could be divisive as well as religion, as Walpole, whose political apprenticeship had coincided with the War of Spanish Succession, well knew. England, he believed, needed rest from war as much as from revolution, and Walpole gave it her. The Secretaries of State (foreign ministers) maintained the alliance with France and kept on good terms with the aged French minister, Cardinal Fleury, who loved peace as much as Sir Robert. Walpole refused to embark on continental wars, and once remarked with pride (during the War of the Polish Succession of 1733-5): 'Fifty thousand men slain this year in Europe, and not one Englishman.'

The Prime Minister and the Cabinet

By tradition, Sir Robert Walpole has become known as the first Prime Minister. He was not the first man to be so called by contemporaries. For example, the term had been applied to the Earl of Stanhope, who had headed the government from 1716 to 1721. What was unusual about Walpole was that he remained in the Commons, thereby setting an important precedent, though not one that was invariably followed afterwards. He most certainly did not have the powers of a modern premier. He was not able to appoint

Powers of the Crown

ministers of his own choice, because ministers were still in every sense the King's ministers. Walpole sometimes had to endure as cabinet colleagues men with whom he was hardly on speaking terms or whose policies ran counter to his own, though he could use his intimacy with the King to attempt to secure their removal. He had initially to put up with Carteret as secretary of state (in charge of foreign affairs), because of the latter's friendship with the King, but after Carteret had damaged his credit with George, Walpole managed to get him removed to Ireland in 1724. The interesting feature of the story is that its outcome was determined by Carteret's standing with the King, not by his standing with Walpole.

By the time of Walpole, the Privy Council, once the centre of government, had become an unwieldy body which rarely met except on grand formal occasions. Its place at the heart of government had been taken by the cabinet, a small body consisting of the most important ministers, who met a few times a week to discuss affairs of state, usually, in practice, foreign affairs. It is not clear whether the King ever attended or not, but the cabinet acquired the habit of meeting without him, largely because the first two Hanoverian Kings were often abroad attending to the interests of Hanover. In Walpole's time, foreign affairs were run by two secretaries of state, one for northern and one for southern Europe. Given the pre-eminence of foreign affairs among the government's concerns, the secretaries could expect to wield great influence within the ministry. Occasionally, their ambitions to control policy led to conflict. From the start of his ministry, Walpole's brother-in-law Lord Townshend had been a member of the government, becoming senior Secretary of State in 1724. Townshend's foreign policy, however, proved expensive and forced Walpole to raise the land tax. In 1730 the two men quarrelled and Townshend resigned. Walpole explained the disagreement thus: 'As long as the firm of the house [was] Townshend and Walpole the utmost harmony prevailed; but it no sooner became Walpole and Townshend than things went wrong.' The quarrel did not simply reflect Walpole's megalomania. Foreign policy inevitably had very serious financial implications, so that there had to be a close liaison between the minister in charge of the finances and the minister in charge of foreign policy. This was especially the case when the finance minister had to extract the money from the House of Commons. In recognizing Walpole as Prime Minister, contemporaries realized that the 18th century English system of government could work only if the First Lord of the Treasury was pre-eminent under the King. There was not yet, however, collective cabinet responsibility, because there was too little to bind the cabinet together. Loyalty to the Prime Minister was bound to be weak when the ministers owed their appointment to someone else, that is the King. Party discipline was fragile too when party principles were rarely at stake and party strife largely in abeyance.

Walpole was not the first minister to attempt the management of Parliament, but he did so in more favourable circumstances than anyone before him. The bigger state apparatus which had come into existence during the wars with France had increased the patronage at the disposal of ministers. Even more important, the leading minister no longer worked in a context of intense party strife which constantly limited his options and made it difficult for men to vote as they had engaged to do. By systematic use of patronage Walpole created the Old Corps of Whigs, who formed an essential element in his majority. Yet on their own they did not constitute a majority. Large numbers of the independent country gentry had also to be won over. Many of them were inclined to vote for the King's ministers, but it was essential to cater for their interests, by, for example, keeping the land tax as low as possible. It was important too effectively to counter critics who might arouse the gentry's suspicions. Walpole was himself an effective speaker. The whole business of managing Parliament was laborious. Walpole's twenty stones of weight did not indicate indolence. He had a marvellous head for figures which served him well as he managed the national finances. He worked assiduously at the creation and retention of his parliamentary majority.

That Walpole could never take his majority for granted was demonstrated by the crisis over his Excise Bill in 1733. Walpole believed that his majority would be more secure if he could win the favour of the country gentry by lowering the land tax from four shillings in the pound to one. To achieve this, he would need to find an alternative source of revenue. This he hoped to do through the Excise Bill, which he introduced in 1733. The Bill contained a

The Excise Bill, 1733

proposal that excisemen should collect the duties on spirits and tobacco in the shops and inns at which these articles were sold, instead of having customs officials collect them at the ports. Walpole expected a gain in revenue, because smuggling would be checked. Walpole's opponents ensured that the proposal roused a tremendous outcry. It was alleged that the new Excise would lead to the employment of numerous officials, which would further increase the ministers' stock of patronage and so threaten English liberty. In addition, the excisemen would employ the hateful method of raiding private houses to collect the tax. Crowds marched about the streets, crying, 'No slavery, no excise!' Walpole's majority in the Commons began to crumble and he decided to give way and abandon the scheme.

In the Excise crisis Walpole's opponents harped on themes calculated to arouse the suspicions of backbench MPs. Walpole's government was said to rest upon a gigantic machinery of corruption which threatened to undermine the British constitution and rot the fabric of society. The opposition called for the elimination of placemen from the Commons. They wanted shorter parliaments, which would mean repealing the Septennial Act. The army was seen as a potential instrument of absolute rule and there were calls for its reduction. Both Whig and Tory backbenchers could be agitated by such fears and Walpole was concerned to stop them combining. Raising the spectre of Jacobitism and claiming that the Tories were covert Jacobites were his favourite means of achieving this aim, but inevitably this weapon became less effective as the menace of the Pretender diminished. Most of the backbench critics of the government had no political ambitions for themselves, but they were usually led by politicians of a different stamp. One of the leaders of opposition was Henry St John, Lord Bolingbroke, once a Tory leader, who returned from exile in 1725. In the opposition newspaper, *The Craftsman*, he lashed out against Walpole in brilliant and vindictive articles; he called Walpole 'the brazen image which the King hath set up'. Bolingbroke had no hope of achieving office, but other

Walpole's colleagues

Bolingbroke and the Opposition

31

opposition leaders certainly did. One such was Lord Carteret, whose attacks on Walpole were designed to make him such a nuisance to the government that it would be compelled to offer him office in order to silence him. A similar strategy was pursued by William Pitt.

William Pitt

Pitt was at this time twenty-seven years of age. He was the grandson of Governor Pitt of Madras, who had amassed a large fortune in India, which he spent in buying estates and pocket boroughs in England. William Pitt was educated at Eton and Trinity College, Oxford. He obtained a commission in a cavalry regiment, and then in 1735 entered Parliament. He sat for the family borough of Old Sarum (near Salisbury) which contained few, if any, inhabitants. He at once joined the opposition to Walpole, and made a great impression by his first speech in Parliament. 'We must muzzle this terrible cornet of horse,' remarked Walpole, and struck his name off the Army List. But it required more than a Walpole to muzzle Pitt; indeed, nothing short of death could silence that amazing oratory, perhaps the most remarkable to which the House of Commons has ever listened. His eloquence was a superb art; no actor ever played upon the feelings of his audience with greater skill than did Pitt. 'The terrible,' said one contemporary, 'was his peculiar power; then the whole House sank before him.' 'His words,' remarked Lord Lyttelton, 'have sometimes frozen my young blood into stagnation, and sometimes made it pace in such a hurry through my veins that I could scarce support it.' His subjects were as magnificent as his methods – 'great subjects, great empires, great characters'. Such was the man who joined the ranks of the opposition to the ageing Walpole.

3. War against the Spaniards, the French, and the Jacobites, 1739-48

The death of his friend Queen Caroline in 1737 made little difference to Walpole's political strength, since he had long been so high in

George II's favour. For other reasons, the quiet period was passing. Walpole detested war, for he remembered the War of Spanish Succession and how deeply it had divided the English ruling classes. He believed that the stability over which he had presided rested on the long peace and the low land tax which it had made possible. Yet war was about to break on Britain.

Under the Asiento Treaty of 1713, the British were allowed to supply Spanish America with slaves, and also to send one ship a year to the Spanish Main for other trade. But the British had for long been infringing this treaty by sending unlicensed trading-ships into West Indian ports. The Spanish authorities were angry, and tried to catch the offenders. The coastguards caught one Captain Jenkins, and – according to his own story – cut off one of his ears. His return to England with this story aroused a storm of indignation; he was brought before the House of Commons and produced his ear in a bottle. The Opposition demanded war with Spain. Walpole tried to settle the matter peaceably, but national feeling was too strong for him. Many people were convinced that an attack on the Spanish Empire would be an easy and profitable business. Walpole was obliged to give way, and declared war against his better judgment. 'They are ringing their bells now,' he remarked, as the bells of London announced the news; 'they will be wringing their hands soon.'

Jenkins' Ear

The War of Jenkins' Ear is chiefly remarkable in being the first of that series of wars against France and Spain which lasted three-quarters of a century. Philip V had, in 1733, signed the Family Compact with his nephew Louis XV, linking the two Bourbon powers together in a defensive alliance. The war which England so lightly declared against Spain in 1739 therefore led to a French war. This, as we shall see in the next chapter, was the signal for the outbreak of a general colonial war.

The Spanish war met with little of the success which its supporters had prophesied. After Admiral Vernon's initial success at Porto Bello, English forces in the Americas met with a succession of disasters.

War with Spain, 1739

33

Anson's Voyage 1740 — Even the gallant exploit of Admiral Anson, who imitated Drake by sailing round the world, attacking Spanish ports on the way, did not affect the issue. Meanwhile, Walpole was blamed for the ill success of the war which he had done all he could to avoid. In 1742 he was

Resignation of Walpole 1742 — defeated in the Commons, and resigned. Among the charges afterwards made against him was that he had called himself Prime Minister, an office which was declared to be unknown to the British Constitution. He retired to the Lords as Earl of Orford, and died three years later.

The new administration was called the 'Broad Bottom' Ministry, because it consisted not only of Walpole's former supporters, but also of some of those who had opposed Walpole in the hope that they would be bought off with the offer of ministerial posts. The Earl of Wilmington was its nominal head, but its most influential members

Carteret — were Henry Pelham and Lord Carteret. Pelham managed Parliament; Carteret was high in the King's favour. It was Carteret, backed by the fiery little King, George II, who plunged England into the war which was now raging on the Continent – the War of the Austrian Succession.

The Emperor Charles VI had no son to succeed him as ruler of the

War of the Austrian Succession — Habsburg dominions in Austria, Hungary, Bohemia, and Belgium. But before he died he obtained a promise – called the Pragmatic Sanction – from the leading European powers that his daughter, Maria Theresa, should be acknowledged as Queen of Hungary and ruler of his other possessions. Charles died in October 1740, and Maria Theresa ascended the Habsburg throne. The new King of Prussia, Frederick II (the Great), who had succeeded his father six months earlier, sent her friendly messages, and even a promise of military help in case of need. Yet less than two months later, without the slightest provocation or excuse, he led 30,000 troops across the Austrian frontier. In a few months he had overrun the province of Silesia, which Maria Theresa was unable to save from his clutches.

In the general European war which followed, France joined Frederick. George II personally headed an army of English and Hanoverians which came to the aid of Maria Theresa. He won the battle of Dettingen in 1743, being the last English King to lead his troops in battle. There was a loud outcry against the war in the country and in Parliament, led by Pitt. England, Pitt said, was being dragged into a war in which she had no concern, in the interests of that 'despicable electorate', Hanover. The clamour was so great that Carteret had to retire. Henry Pelham, head of one of the great Whig families, was now the virtual Prime Minister, a position which he held for eleven years from 1743 to 1754.

Dettingen 1743

Pelham Prime Minister 1743-54

The war in Germany was at first fought by France and England as 'auxiliaries' to the main combatants. But England was also at war with Spain, who was France's ally, and Louis XV formally declared war on Great Britain in 1744. This war lasted four years. There was further fighting in Germany, but the Austrians failed to dislodge Frederick from Silesia. When peace was made at Aix-la-Chapelle in 1748, he kept the province as part of Prussia. The French restored Madras to England in exchange for Louisbourg in Canada, which the British colonists had captured.

Anglo-French War 1744-8

Treaty of Aix-la-Chapelle 1748

In the midst of the French war the Jacobites made one final bid for the throne. The Old Pretender did not come in person to make this attempt, but sent instead his son, Charles Edward, the Young Chevalier – the Bonnie Prince Charlie of Scottish history and song. Prince Charles, unlike his father, was a good leader; the enthusiasm which he inspired among the Highlanders did not die down in one generation. But tragedy waited on the Stuart cause, as so often it had before.

The 'Forty Five'

The Prince landed at Moidart in the West Highlands in August 1745, and many clansmen flocked to his standard. Soon all Scotland was at his feet. The gallant young prince won hearts by his noble bearing and his willingness to share the hardships of his men, for he slept in the heather like a common soldier. In September the bells of

Prestonpans, 1745

Edinburgh rang out to welcome him. Then he routed a small English army under Sir John Cope at Prestonpans and it seemed as though the rebellion was about to succeed.

The Pretender at Derby

Two things, however, were against it; the French, cut off by the British Navy, sent no help, and the English Jacobites did not rise. Nevertheless, Charles Edward invaded England with about 5,500 men. He took Carlisle, and Manchester, and by December he was at Derby. There was a panic in the capital, and a run on the Bank, because there was no army between Derby and London. But King George refused to be disturbed – 'Pooh! Don't talk to me that stuff!' he said, when it was suggested he should leave London. Just before Christmas, however, the prince was forced to turn back, for his Highlanders would go no farther. The prince had attracted no more than 300 English supporters, a number that did not make up for the number of Scots who had deserted. Admittedly, the prince had not been forcefully opposed, but Englishmen no longer had adequate militia training and possessed few firearms, so that attacks on the Prince's army would have been suicidal. All the indications are that the English greatly resented the invasion: they showed what they felt by killing, attacking or jailing any Jacobites who were left sick on the road. The English were well aware too that the Prince enjoyed close relations with their French enemy. The French connection more or less ensured that the Prince would win minimal support in England. As the reality of English hostility sank in with the invaders, the English government was at last getting its act together. The Duke of Cumberland had over 10,000 men a day's march from Derby, while General Wade was hurrying from the north with as many again. Retreat to Scotland seemed the more promising option.

Yet Scotland had been deeply divided by the invasion. Men like the Duke of Argyll and Lord Loudoun were loyal to George II. Even the clans were split. Some of the northern ones, such as the Mackays and Monroes were hostile to the Pretender, while such clans as the Gordons and Mackenzies were divided. Scottish Protestants were rarely enthusiastic about the Catholic Stuarts. It was also the case that the Union with England was beginning to win Scottish friends, especially among the commercial interests. While the Pretender was in England, Jacobite control in much of Scotland had collapsed. On their return, the Highlanders won one more victory at Falkirk in January 1746, but then they retreated to the hills. The Prince was bitterly disappointed, but he went with them. A royalist army was sent north in the spring, under William, Duke of Cumberland, King George's son. With his 9,000 troops and his artillery, he broke the half-starved Highland army of about 5,000 men on Culloden Moor in April 1746; the Prince stayed till all was lost and then fled to the hills. For months he lay in hiding amid the humble Highland folk, who would not give him up for the reward which the government offered for his capture and which would have meant riches to them. Many tales are told of him and of those, like the heroic Flora Macdonald, who shielded him. At last he escaped and landed safely in France. He lived on in poetry and in song, such as the following song written by Baroness Caroline Nairne in the early 19th century, when the Jacobite tradition contributed to a new Scottish nationalism.

Culloden
1746

Will ye no come back again?
Will ye no come back again?
Better lo'ed ye canna be,
Will ye no come back again?
Ye trusted in your Hieland men,
They trusted you, dear Charlie;
They kent your hiding in the glen,
Your deadin' was but barely.
English bribes were a' in vain;
An' e'en tho' puirer we maun be,
Siller canna buy the heart
That beats aye for thine and thee.

But 'Bonnie Prince Charlie' never returned to Scotland; forty years later he died a broken man and an exile.

The royal duke put down the rebellion with that severity which earned him the name of 'Butcher Cumberland'; his red-coats hunted down the fugitives. A young officer called James Wolfe – whom we shall hear of again – told Cumberland to his face that he would not order his men to do the 'butcher's work'. But 'Sweet William' as the English called him – and named a flower after him (which the Scots called 'Stinking Billy') – did his work but too well. Perhaps 120 men were executed.

The subjection of the Highlands followed, made easier by the road
Subjection of the Highlands system which Wade's troops had built. The Disarming Act was intended to make any new rebellion impossible. Its prohibitions included a ban on the wearing of kilts and tartans, while the bagpipes were proscribed as 'instruments of war'. The clan system was dismantled: the chiefs could no longer claim military service from the clansmen and could no longer exercise a jurisdiction separate from that of the royal courts. The chiefs became landlords on the English model – and heartless landlords they proved to be. Some of them turned their old followers out of their smallholdings, and made the glens into sheep-runs; by the time of the War of American Independence (1775-83), thirty thousand Highlanders had left their ancient homes and sought refuge in America.

In spite of these hardships, southern manners gradually made an impression in the Highlands. Perhaps nothing did so much to propitiate Highland sentiment as the wise decision of Pitt, when he came to power, to raise Highland regiments and to allow them to fight in their national costume. Within a dozen years of Culloden, the Highlanders were fighting for King George in America with as much gusto as they had once fought for the Young Chevalier in their native hills. Even more remarkably, the Highlanders were in the 19th century to make a cultural conquest of Scotland. Tartans, kilts and bagpipes became part of the heritage of every Scot, even those whose ancestors had always lived in the Lowlands.

4. Pitt's Rise to Power

Two years before the end of the French war in 1746 Pitt was given a   Pitt in office
minor post under the government. The Whig lords found him too
dangerous as an opponent, and they at last persuaded King George
to give him the post of Paymaster of the Forces. It was some time
before the King gave way, for he bitterly resented Pitt's contemptuous
references to Hanover. In office, Pitt startled England by haughtily
refusing to take the perquisites, amounting to thousands of pounds
a year, which had usually been attached to the office of Paymaster. It
was this, more than anything else, which distinguished Pitt from the
old Whigs and earned him the respect and love of his countrymen.
He became known as the 'Great Commoner', who openly despised
the old corrupt methods of government. But the Whig party machine
continued to operate, since it was indispensable to the smooth
running of politics.

Henry Pelham's ministry (1746-54) is almost bare of events of   Reform of
note, except the 'Forty-Five' Rebellion already described. It was this   the Calendar
ministry which at last agreed to the reform of the calendar,
substituting for the old Julian Calendar (introduced into Europe by
Julius Caesar) the Gregorian (introduced by Pope Gregory XIII in
1582), which for over a century had been in general use on the
Continent. There was eleven days' difference between the two
calendars, and when the change was made, 2nd September was
followed by 14th September 1752. This gave rise to the popular cry:
'Give us back our eleven days!' Another change was that 1st January
became New Year's Day, instead of 25th March as formerly. The
ministry also passed the Gin Act, in the hope of alleviating the
problem of alcoholism, which had become an epidemic in places like
London and which was satirized by Hogarth in his print *Gin Lane*.
The distillers were subjected to heavy penalties for supplying gin to
unlicensed retailers. No more than Walpole could Pelham insist on
all the measures he thought desirable. An Act making it easier for

Jews to become naturalized citizens had to be abandoned because of an outbreak of xenophobia which threatened to lose the government seats in the election of 1754.

In 1754 Henry Pelham died. 'Now I shall have no more peace,' said the King, and he was right. Pelham had been a good party manager, and his place was difficult to fill. He was succeeded as Duke of Prime Minister by his brother, the Duke of Newcastle. Newcastle Newcastle's had been a Secretary of State since 1724; he was in office altogether Ministry for nearly fifty years. One of the richest men in England, and a 1754-6 staunch Hanoverian, he had been made a duke by George I. He devoted his immense fortune to the Whig party funds, and had a passion for 'managing' the House of Commons. His career shows that expert management was not enough to produce stable government. The duke was in the House of Lords, which meant that he had to rely on someone else to conduct the government's business in the Commons. Whoever he chose had to be acceptable to the King. There were two candidates for the role of leader of the Commons: William Pitt, the spell-binding orator who could be scathing in his denunciations of ministers and impassioned in his appeals to patriotism; and Henry Fox (father of the great Whig statesman, Charles James Fox), who lacked Pitt's fluency, but had an instinctive understanding of the House of Commons. Fox was chosen, since George II would not have Pitt. The latter harassed the Government at every turn in his parliamentary speeches, hoping to force the government to buy him off by offering him office. In 1755 Newcastle plucked up courage to dismiss Pitt from his post as Paymaster General, which removed the last restraints on Pitt's attacks on the ministry.

Meanwhile, it became obvious that war was imminent. After the Diplomatic end of the War of the Austrian Succession, Maria Theresa plotted a Revolution in revenge on the King of Prussia. Her agents persuaded the Court of Europe Versailles to change sides; she also made an alliance with Russia. Frederick, realizing that a formidable coalition for the partition of

Prussia was being formed, looked around for allies. He found one in his uncle, King George II, who had fought against him in the last war, but needed an ally able to defend Hanover. The prime mover in this diplomatic revolution was the Austrian minister, Kaunitz; but when it became known that France was about to change sides, England changed too. Colonial rivalry alone made it impossible that she should fight on the French side. The alliance between Great Britain and Prussia was signed in January 1756, that between France and the Empress in the following May. This was Newcastle's greatest triumph; the alliance with the formidable Frederick of Prussia proved to be very valuable to England in the coming conflict.

Treaty of Westminster, 1756

Frederick was aware that the Elector of Saxony had concluded a secret alliance with Austria. He therefore acted with characteristic suddenness; he invaded Saxony and occupied Dresden. Since Saxony lay between his own kingdom and the Austrian dominions, he was thus able to begin the war with a buffer-state between Prussia and her chief enemy. So in 1756 the Seven Years' War began. Fighting had already broken out between the French and British in India and America.

Outbreak of the Seven Years' War 1756

The outbreak of war in Europe, which was followed by an Anglo-French war in three continents, overwhelmed Prime Minister Newcastle. In the Mediterranean Minorca was lost. Newcastle promised to have Byng, the admiral responsible, hanged, but this was not enough to regain the confidence of the Commons, where the government gave an impression of drift and lack of direction and lacked a defender who could reply to Pitt's expected attacks. In November 1756 Newcastle at last resigned, having been continuously in office for thirty-nine years. The King had no alternative but to overcome his objections to the Great Commoner, and a ministry was formed, including Pitt, with the Duke of Devonshire at its head. It lasted only from December 1756 to April 1757, because Pitt found that he could not manage the House of Commons without the help of the Whig party machine – which meant the help of Newcastle. So

The Pitt-Newcastle Ministry 1757-61

a new ministry was formed in June 1757 which included both the duke and Pitt. Newcastle managed the Commons, and left the conduct of the war to his colleague. At last political stability had been restored. The new ministry had an impregnable majority. Newcastle could deliver the support of the cohorts of placemen, while Pitt appealed to the independent country gentry, both Whig and Tory. With his boundless self-confidence and demonic energy, Pitt was able to convey the sense that a man of vision was at the helm. Some of his assertions bordered on megalomania, such as his boast to Lord Devonshire, 'I know that I can save the country, and that no one else can!' Yet he did succeed in arousing enthusiasm for the war, which the peace-loving Walpole, the reserved Pelham, or the timid Newcastle could not have done.

Date Summary: The Whigs
(1714-56)

ENGLAND (POLITICAL)	ENGLAND (SOCIAL AND LITERARY)	EUROPE, AMERICA AND INDIA

THE WHIGS BEFORE WALPOLE (1714-21)

1714-27 George I		
1714-21 First Whig Ministry		1715 Louis XIV *d*.
1715 Jacobite Rebellion		1715-74 Louis XV
1717 Stanhope, chief minister	1719 *Robinson Crusoe*	1717 Triple Alliance (Britain, Holland, France)
1720 South Sea Bubble		

SIR ROBERT WALPOLE (1721-42)

	1723 Sir Christopher Wren *d*.	
		1725 Peter the Great *d*.
	1726 *Gulliver's Travels*	
1727-60 George II		
	1728 *The Beggar's Opera*	
		1732 Georgia founded
1733 Excise Bill	1733 Pope's *Essay on Man* Kay's Shuttle	1733 Family Compact (France and Spain)
1737 Queen Caroline *d*.		
	1739 First Methodist Society	1739 Anglo-Spanish War
		1740 Frederick the Great *acc*. Emperor Charles VI *d*.
1742 Walpole resigns		1740-8 War of Austrian Succession

WALPOLE'S SUCCESSORS (1742-56)

1742-3 'Broad Bottom' Ministry		
1743-54 Henry Pelham's Ministry		
		1744-8 Anglo-French War
		1741-54 Dupleix in India
1745 Jacobite Rebellion		
		1745 Clive in India
1746 ⚔ Culloden		
	1749 *Tom Jones* (Fielding) 1749 The *Patriot King* (Bolingbroke)	1748 Treaty Aix-la-Chapelle
		1751 Siege of Arcot
	1752 Reform of the Calendar	
		1753 Fort Duquesne (Canada)
1754-6 Duke of Newcastle's Ministry	1755 Johnson's *Dictionary* 1756 Macadam born	1755 French defeat Braddock 1756 Treaty of Westminster (England and Prussia) Black Hole of Calcutta

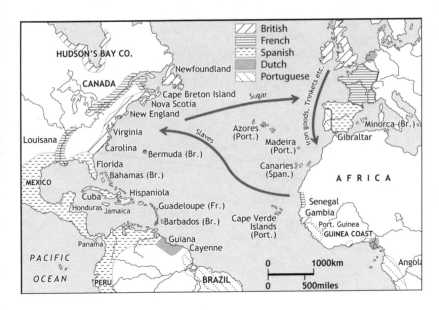

COLONIAL EMPIRES OF THE EUROPEAN POWERS. 18TH CENTURY

II

RIVAL EMPIRES IN THE SEVEN YEARS' WAR, 1756-1763

1. Britain and France

THE five maritime powers of western Europe all possessed colonial empires in the 18th century. Of these five powers, the two smaller and weaker, Portugal and Holland, were the first to drop out of the colonial race; the struggle between the remaining three, Britain, France, and Spain, took place in the 18th century. France and Spain fought together against their common enemy, Britain. They were allies in the War of the Spanish Succession, which ended with the recognition of Louis XIV's grandson Philip as King of Spain. Their alliance was renewed by several Family Compacts, between the French and Spanish branches of the House of Bourbon, of which the first was signed in 1733.

Colonial rivalry of Britain and France

The war of 'Jenkins' Ear' against Spain was, as we have seen, a colonial quarrel, caused by a British infringement of the Treaty of Utrecht. It led, within five years, to a war with France (1744-8), which proved to be but the preliminary round of a great contest which lasted for two generations. Britain's main concern was not with the empire of Spain; its chief rival was France, and the French and British empires were about to engage in a struggle to the death.

The French empire was very similar to Britain's. The French had trading posts, as Britain had, in India, where in the time of Dupleix and Clive the battle for supremacy was fought out. India was a problem in itself; the other main theatre, both of trade and war, was the Atlantic. On the eastern side of that ocean lay the home countries and the West African slave-markets; on the western side, North America and the West Indian sugar islands. In Africa the English had several slave-trading posts, of which Gambia was the chief; the

The French Empire

West Africa

West Indies

45

French held the mouth of the Senegal, and Goree near by. In the West Indies the French held the islands of Guadeloupe and Martinique, and had established a colony on the island of Hispaniola, called Haiti. By the middle of the 18th century Haiti was exporting twice as much sugar as Jamaica; Guadeloupe and Martinique did more trade than the English island of Barbados.

North America
Georgia 1732

In North America the British gained, at the Peace of Utrecht, the French colony of Acadie, renamed Nova Scotia. They now held the whole Atlantic coastline, with the exception of Florida, which belonged to Spain. In 1732 Georgia, the thirteenth and last British colony in America, was founded, just north of Florida, by General James Oglethorpe. The general was a philanthropist who was rightly disgusted at the state of the English prisons; he tried to give a few thousand ex-prisoners the chance to start life afresh in the New World. The foundation of Georgia was resented by the Spanish in Florida, who attacked the new colony, but were driven off.

Louisbourg
Other French Forts

The French were by no means daunted by the losses they had sustained at Utrecht, which gave their rivals Acadie, Newfoundland, and Hudson Bay. Their position was indeed strong, for they held a commanding position in three areas – the Gulf of St Lawrence, the basin of the St Lawrence, and the Mississippi Valley. In the Gulf they held the mainland coast and all the islands, with the exception of Newfoundland. For though they had lost Acadie, they still retained the Île de St Jean, and the Île Royale – later known as Prince Edward Island – and Cape Breton Island. On the latter island they proceeded in 1720, soon after Utrecht, to erect the strongest fortress in North America, Louisbourg, to command the entrance to the Gulf. The French colony of Canada, or New France, embraced the St Lawrence valley and the Great Lakes; and here again they built forts at strategic points, such as Fort Niagara, between Lakes Ontario and Erie. They also built forts such as Ticonderoga on Lake Champlain, which commanded the approach to Canada from the Hudson valley. Lastly, the French held Louisiana, which gave them the command of the Mississippi valley, along which also forts were built at intervals.

It was the design of the French to shut up the British in their coastal colonies and develop the rest of the continent themselves. The Appalachian Mountains, which formed a natural western barrier to the British colonies, seemed designed by nature to forward the French plan. Nevertheless, the British colonists were unwilling to see the whole Mississippi-Ohio basin fall into French hands, to be linked up, at no distant date, with the French northern colony of Canada. Governor Burnet, of New York, built at his own expense Fort Oswego, on Lake Ontario; Virginian traders crossed the Appalachians and reached the Ohio; companies were formed to develop this region. When the French met the Virginian pioneers, they regarded them as interlopers and arrested some of them. To such treatment the British colonists were unlikely to submit.

The British on the Ohio

The war between Britain and France (1744-8), arising out of the War of the Austrian Succession, gave the rival colonists a chance to fly at each others' throats; nor did they cease their strife when the official peace was proclaimed in 1748. During the war the New England colonists captured Louisbourg; but this important conquest had to be given up at the Treaty of Aix-la-Chapelle in exchange for Madras. The French, meanwhile, had been very active in Nova Scotia, where they were continually stirring up their ex-colonists to rebel against British rule. Halifax, a British town, was founded in 1749 to counteract French influence; and then the British Government took the extreme step of deporting several thousand Frenchmen from Nova Scotia to other parts of British North America.

First capture of Louisbourg 1745

Halifax

The threat to British interests was increased by the building in 1753 of Fort Duquesne, on the Ohio, within striking distance of the British colonies. Fort Duquesne completed the chain of French forts from the Gulf of St Lawrence to the Gulf of Mexico. The governor of Virginia, Dinwiddie, recognized the seriousness of the menace, and in 1754 sent out a young colonial officer, named George

Fort Duquesne 1753

Washington, to take Fort Duquesne. But Washington was
outnumbered, and forced to retreat. Next year the home government
dispatched General Braddock to America, to drive the French from
the Ohio. The French, however, with some Indian allies, ambushed
Braddock and his little army in the woods. The British were
marching in column, according to the drill-book; Braddock refused
to take Washington's advice and order his men to scatter to the woods.
The result was that most of them were killed, including the general.
Washington drew off the survivors, and retired to Virginia.

Braddock's
defeat 1755

Such was the position of the rival colonists in North America at
the outbreak of the Seven Years' War in 1756. In some respects the
advantage appeared to lie with the French. Their colonists were
traders and hunters rather than settlers, and they were used to
fighting; the whole French empire in America, with its defensive
forts, was founded on a military basis. Besides this, the French had
many Indians on their side, for they had been far more tactful in their
dealings with these potential allies, since they depended on trading
with them. The English colonists were farmers who advanced by
expropriating the Indians. But, in spite of these facts, it was
impossible that North America should pass into French hands; the
whole number of French settlers was only 80,000; the British
colonists outnumbered them by 25 to 1. It was not likely that, with
such small numbers, the French could permanently prevent their
rivals from expanding across the continent. As for their military
preparations, these were counteracted by the fact that the British held
command of the sea, and so were able to prevent French
reinforcements from being sent to North America.

The rival
colonists
compared

2. The Seven Years' War

(i) *British Defeats: 1756-7*

The seizure of Saxony by Frederick the Great precipitated a
European war. The French realized that this would mean for them

a struggle with Great Britain in all parts of the world – a struggle for which their colonists in America and India were quite prepared. In all the ports of France naval preparations were hurried forward, for much depended on striking a blow at Britain's naval supremacy.

The first blow was struck in the Mediterranean. In April 1756, without a declaration of war, a French fleet sailed from Toulon and landed a force on the island of Minorca. Port Mahon, the capital, was besieged. Admiral Byng, with a small British fleet, was at Gibraltar. He sailed to Minorca to see what he could do, engaged the French fleet in battle, but was unable to effect a landing. He sailed back to Gibraltar to refit his ships, and while he was away Port Mahon fell. There was a howl of popular rage in England when the news arrived; Newcastle was terrified and decided to sacrifice Byng. The admiral was tried by court martial for failing to relieve Port Mahon; he was condemned to death and shot on his own quarter-deck. Of this shameful affair Voltaire caustically wrote in *Candide: 'Dans ce pays-ci* [England] *il est bon de tuer, de temps en temps, un amiral, pour encourager les autres.'* [In England, it's a good thing to kill an admiral from time to time to encourage the others.] On the admiral's tombstone it is written that 'bravery and loyalty were insufficient securities for the life and honour of a naval officer'.

The French take Minorca 1756

Admiral Byng 1757

Meanwhile, the French had sent to Canada the able Marquis de Montcalm as military commander. Montcalm drove the British from Fort Oswego, their solitary station on the Great Lakes, and then prepared to advance from Lake Champlain. But here the British forts held him up, and it was lucky for the colonists in New York that they did. In the same year the English in India suffered the loss of Calcutta, and the outrage of the Black Hole. The only bright spot was that Newcastle resigned in December 1756.

Montcalm in Canada 1756

The Pitt-Devonshire ministry, which lasted during the first four months of 1757, was followed, after a short interval, by the famous Pitt-Newcastle ministry, which presided over a series of remarkable

Pitt in power 1757-61

successes. The tide of disaster did not immediately turn. Cumberland had been sent with an army to Germany, where he was soundly beaten by the French and forced to sign the Convention of Klosterseven, by which he had to evacuate Hanover. In America the army of regulars and colonials made no progress against Montcalm. The situation, as it appeared at the end of 1757, was thus gloomily summed up by Lord Chesterfield: 'We are undone at home and abroad. The French are masters to do what they please in America. We are no longer a nation. I never yet saw so dreadful a prospect.' Chesterfield's remarks perhaps represented the general feeling of depression; Pitt was more sanguine.

Rossbach
Plassey 1757

Even that winter the tide began to turn. Frederick won the greatest of all his victories at Rossbach in Saxony over the French, which ensured that the French would not be freed from anxiety about the situation in Germany. And from India came the amazing news of Clive's victory at Plassey, which gave the vast province of Bengal to the East India Company.

(ii) *The Victorious Years: 1758-60 – Canada*

The Navy

Pitt was inclined to attribute all the successes of 1758-60 to himself. He did maintain his fanatical belief in Britain's imperial destiny during the dark year of 1757 and for a while he united most parliamentarians and most of the public behind the vigorous prosecution of the war both in Europe and in the Americas. Yet he had perforce to leave much to others. As always, the navy was crucial to British success. The Navy Secretary, John Cleveland, and the First Lord of the Admiralty, Anson, had much more to do with British naval strategy and success than Pitt did. They sent squadrons to blockade the French Atlantic ports, and so prevent reinforcements from being sent to America. A similar watch was kept, by the Gibraltar squadron, on the Mediterranean. The naval authorities realized how vital it was to prevent the French fleets joining up, since then they might have challenged English control of the sea. This sound strategy was supplemented, at Pitt's insistence, by raids on the

THE SEVEN YEARS' WAR IN NORTH AMERICA

French coasts, with the aim of distracting the French from dangerous attacks elsewhere. Cherbourg was captured and its forts destroyed in 1758, but many of the raids were not very successful.

Pitt, who had once condemned the employment of British troops in Hanover, did commit himself wholeheartedly to the anti-French cause in Germany. He added a British army to the Hanoverian forces which had been placed under the Duke of Brunswick's command, and so helped to clear the French out of Hanover. Money was poured out to the tune of £670,000 a year to enable Frederick the Great, now hard pressed, to continue the struggle. Thus Pitt kept France busy in Europe, a condition, he realized, of victory elsewhere. 'We shall win Canada,' said Pitt, 'on the banks of the Elbe.'

Germany

While Frederick was defending Prussia against Austrians, Russians, French, and Swedes, Britain launched her offensive against the French colonial empire. This, as far as Britain was concerned, was the main effort of the war, and it depended on her keeping command

West Africa

West Indies

51

of the sea. The French were unable to save their stations in India, where they steadily lost ground. They lost also Senegal and Goree, in West Africa, and with these places fell the whole French slave-trade. Another British expedition was sent to the West Indies, and took Guadeloupe in 1759. Meanwhile, in order to reverse the situation in North America, a great assault on Canada was planned. The bold strategic conception owed much to Pitt, but of course he could not control events from London and the initiative had to be left to the generals on the spot.

Canada
1758-60

The attack on Canada was planned along three lines of advance:

1. A naval and military expedition was to take Louisbourg, the capture of which was an essential preliminary to an advance up the St Lawrence.

2. An advance up the Hudson valley was to seize the forts on Lake Champlain, and then the troops were to go on to the St Lawrence.

3. An attack was to be launched on Fort Duquesne, and then the expedition was to gain control of the Great Lakes.

Second
capture of
Louisbourg
1758

In 1758 the first of these attacks was a brilliant success. A fleet under Admiral Boscawen brought an attacking force to Cape Breton Island: the famous fortress of Louisbourg fell, and so the way was opened to the estuary of the St Lawrence. On land the main advance up Lake Champlain was a failure, for General Abercrombie sustained a bloody repulse before Ticonderoga at the hands of Montcalm. But a detachment of Abercrombie's army advanced up the Mohawk (a tributary of the Hudson) and took Forts Oswego and Frontenac, on Lake Ontario. At the same time Brigadier Forbes, pushing across to the Ohio, found Fort Duquesne abandoned and burnt. Forbes renamed the place Fort Pitt. 'I have used the freedom,' he wrote to Pitt, 'of giving your name to Fort Duquesne, as I hope it was in some measure the being actuated by your spirit that now makes us masters of the place.'

Fort Pitt
(Pittsburg)
1758

Quebec 1759

The next year – 1759, the year of victories – witnessed one of the best-known incidents in British history. A British fleet of 170 ships,

JAMES WOLFE (1727-59)
(Portrait *c*.1767 by J.S.C. Schaak)

under Admiral Charles Saunders, was sent up the St Lawrence, conveying the army of General James Wolfe, the brilliant young commander whom Pitt had picked out from among his seniors. The problem was to reach the French forts (which guarded Quebec) on the Heights of Abraham, towering above the river. The army was disembarked under cover of darkness, and while part of the fleet opened a bombardment to distract the defenders, the Heights of Abraham were scaled. The sailors, who had found a path up the apparently inaccessible cliffs, led the way up, carried the ammunition and small guns, and placed Wolfe and his army on the Heights. This amazing feat was carried out in the dim light of dawn; the French defenders were therefore taken completely by surprise. Both Montcalm and Wolfe were mortally wounded, but Wolfe lived to hear that the French were routed. Thus in September 1759 Quebec fell into the hands of the British.

Fall of
Montreal
1760

The French tried to recapture Quebec during the winter, but failed to do so. After this the end was only a matter of time. The other British lines of advance, from Lake Champlain and Lake Ontario, were now pushed forward; the French were obliged to concentrate all their defences on Montreal. The converging attacks advanced on the town, and it fell in 1760; with it fell the French dominion in North America.

Quiberon
1759

While the British were occupied with the conquest of Canada, the French planned a counter-attack, nothing less than an invasion of England. Their plans were discovered by British intelligence and the fleet destroyed the French ships in Le Havre. During the summer of 1759 the French navy strained every nerve to break the blockade of their ports. The Mediterranean fleet, however, was defeated off Lagos in Portugal. Later, the Brest fleet got out, but in November 1759, Admiral Hawke swept down on the enemy among the rocks and shoals of Quiberon Bay (Brittany). The chief pilot warned the admiral of the danger of the hidden shoals. 'You have done right,' said Hawke, 'to warn me of the danger. Now lay me alongside the enemy.' In a few hours the wreckage of the French fleet justified the daring and resource of the admiral. The danger of a French invasion of England was over.

Death of
George II
1760

The Battle of Quiberon Bay was one of the three great victories which led to 1759 being dubbed 'the year of victories.' The others were the triumph at Quebec and the Battle of Minden in Germany. At Minden the general commanding the British and Hanoverian troops, Prince Ferdinand of Brunswick, defeated the French. So rapid was the succession of victories that Horace Walpole, son of Sir Robert, wrote: 'It is necessary to enquire every morning what victory there is, for fear of missing one.' The year after the victories in October 1760 George II died. He had lived to see the minister whom he had once hated so heartily raise the prestige of Britain to undreamt-of heights. At the old King's death the Great Commoner was at the height of his glory.

(iii) *The Fall of Pitt and the End of the War.*

The capture of Quebec and the victory of Quiberon decided the fate of Canada and of Britain. It only remained to continue the attack on what was left of the French empire. In the West Indies the French islands fell in rapid succession. In India the French fought a losing fight. The decisive battle of Wandewash took place in 1760. Pondicherry fell the next year, and French India shared the fate of French America.

But Choiseul, now the French *premier ministre*, planned yet another counter-stroke. He persuaded the new King of Spain, Charles III, to renew the Family Compact and come into the war. Pitt learnt of what was intended, and he demanded that war should instantly be declared against Spain. Most of the Cabinet, afraid of the combination of France and Spain, and aware that people in Britain were increasingly war-weary, refused to take so bold a step, and appealed to the young King to support them. George III decided against Pitt. The minister at once resigned in October 1761. Fall of Pitt 1761

Pitt's predictions were soon fulfilled; the Family Compact was published, and Britain had to declare war against Spain in 1762. The Spaniards, however, soon regretted their decision, for the Spanish West Indies went the way of the French. Havana, the capital of Cuba, was taken; the Philippines were captured by an expedition sent out from India. War with Spain 1762

Meanwhile, George III was anxious for peace, and the negotiations were entrusted to the Duke of Bedford by his new Prime Minister, the Earl of Bute. The French, after their colonial losses, were no less anxious to come to terms, so they abandoned their ally, the Empress Maria Theresa. This was unfortunate for the Empress, but exceedingly fortunate for Frederick the Great. The last years of the war had been disastrous for Prussia, since the country had been invaded from north, south, and east by Swedes, Austrians, and Russians, and even Berlin was abandoned to the enemy. But the accession of a new Tsar, Peter III, took Russia out of the war. The Peace negotiations

Events in Germany defection of France convinced the Empress that it was useless to continue the struggle. So she had to let her old enemy, Frederick, escape after all. Though he had been nearly beaten, his obstinate valour, the British victories, and a growing war weariness everywhere ensured that he should not be a loser, and he kept Silesia.

The Treaty of Paris of 1763, which ended the Seven Years' War, made the following changes in the colonial position of the Great Powers:

The Treaty of Paris 1763

1. France retired from North America, ceding Canada and Cape Breton Island to Britain, and Louisiana to Spain (as compensation for Spanish losses). She retained only certain fishing rights off Newfoundland, which later caused many quarrels.
2. Britain also acquired from France Senegal, Minorca, and four West Indian islands, but restored Goree, Pondicherry, and the two largest French islands in the West Indies, Martinique and Guadeloupe.
3. Britain acquired Florida from Spain, but restored Cuba and the Philippines.

The Peace was much criticized by Pitt, but though perhaps more could have been taken from Spain, France remained a great power and it is doubtful if more could have been taken from it without prolonging the war. British opinion, except perhaps in London, was by this time desperate to end the war. At the climax of the war, there had been 95,000 troops and 80,000 seamen in British pay. The costs were correspondingly enormous. Whereas the War of Spanish succession had cost on average £5 million a year, the Seven Years' War cost £13.7 million a year. Some even felt that the war had been fought for the sake of Frederick II, whose popularity with British opinion at the time of Minden had since waned. Pitt did not speak for the majority of his countrymen when he complained of the treachery of the government in abandoning the alliance with the Prussian King.

The conflict between the colonial empires of France and Britain thus came to an end with a severe setback for the former. The future of North America, as of India, lay within the British empire. But the enormous triumph of Britain almost at once gave rise to misgivings. Was it too complete? Could Britain hope to keep all she had gained, or prevent France from plotting a war of revenge? There were some, even in 1763, who foresaw the answer to these questions. During the war the government in London had intervened in America as it never had before. If such intervention became a habit, then the colonists in America might begin to resent it and acquire a desire for independence. The French flag had vanished from North America, but with it went the need for the British colonists to rely any longer on the protection and support of the mother country. 'England,' said a French observer, 'will soon repent of having removed the only check that could keep her colonies in awe.' This prediction proved to be correct. The American War of Independence, by which France obtained her revenge for 1763, was the indirect result of the victory which Britain gained in the Seven Years' War.

The British Empire in 1763

3. Clive in India

(i) *The Struggle in the Carnatic.*

The Anglo-French struggle in India took place at the same time as that in other parts of the world. It was considerably affected by the weakness of government in India. This weakness was the result of the break-up of the Mughal Empire after the death in 1707 of the Emperor Aurangzeb, the last of the Mughals who was able to keep his wide dominions together under one rule. His successors retained but a shadow of the former power of the Mughals; soon their authority was limited to a small district round the capital, Delhi.

Death of Arungzeb 1707

Break-up of the Mogul Empire

The viceroys who ruled provinces into which the Empire was divided became, to all intents and purposes, independent sovereigns. But the process of disintegration went further still; for the *nawabs*

57

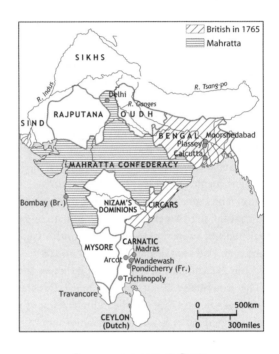

India in the time of Clive

The Mahrattas

(Hindustani for princes) of the smaller provinces asserted *their* independence of their superiors. To add to these disruptive tendencies, the power of the Mahratta Confederacy (a group of Hindu princes, whose armies consisted of bodies of light horsemen) had become a terror to central India, from the Ganges to the Godavari, from the Bay of Bengal to the Arabian Sea. Their trade was war and plunder and they had become a terror to the peasantry. Most of the Muslim rulers were too weak to resist these formidable foes; the whole country, dissolving into anarchy, was ready to succumb to any power which could offer the blessings of peace and protection. No one could have imagined that it was the destiny of a European trading company to unite India under one rule, still less that it would accomplish this task in less than a hundred years.

The French and English East India Companies were for many years solely concerned with questions of trade. The anarchy of India at first alarmed them and then fired their ambitions. The French, like the English, had trading-posts on all the coasts of India; the chief were Mahé on the Malabar coast, Pondicherry and Karikal in the Carnatic, and Chandernagore in Bengal. Pondicherry was the Company's headquarters, and there, in 1741, came Joseph François Dupleix as governor-general. Dupleix had large views on imperial affairs, and he was a fervent patriot; his first thought was to weaken his English rivals. The outbreak of war between Britain and France in 1744 gave him the chance to attack Madras, which fell in 1746 after making but a feeble resistance. The opportune arrival of a French fleet from Mauritius, under Admiral La Bourdonnais, helped to hasten this event. But, to Dupleix's disgust, Madras was returned to the British at the Treaty of Aix-la-Chapelle, as the French government considered it of less value than Louisbourg, for which it was exchanged.

It was in the same year that events in southern India turned the thoughts of Dupleix in another direction. His soldiers, recently employed in the attack on Madras, were now standing idle – but what might not well-trained French soldiers do in India? Dupleix saw that they might do a great deal. He determined to use them by joining in the frequent wars among the native princes. In this way French military aid could be made to turn the scale in native quarrels, and the French Company would become the arbiter of southern India, perhaps of the whole of India. These immense schemes which floated before Dupleix's mind were afterwards written down in his *Memoirs*, in which he strove to justify his policy; they seemed absurd to the directors of the French Company. But the British, in the next generation, turned Dupleix's dreams of European conquest of India into a reality.

The French in India

Dupleix 1741-54

His Indian policy

At first all went as well as Dupleix could wish. The Nawab of the
Carnatic was killed in battle by a usurper called Chunda Sahib, who
gained the victory with the aid of 400 French soldiers. Chunda Sahib
was enthroned as Nawab of the Carnatic in 1749, but he relied on
Dupleix to maintain his position; in fact he was as much a puppet of
the French Company as, later on, the nawabs of Bengal were of the
English. In 1751 another usurper was installed, by the same means,
as Nizam of the Deccan; this was an even greater triumph, since the
Nizam was the most important prince in southern India. The new
Nizam gave Dupleix a high-sounding title and recognized his control
over his vassal, the Nawab of the Carnatic. Dupleix's ambitions
seemed about to be realized.

His failure was due, in a large measure, to the hostility of the
British, and especially to the fighting spirit of Robert Clive. Clive
was a young man who had come out to India in 1743 as a clerk in the
East India Company; but his natural daring and pugnacity could ill
support a sedentary life. He had taken a commission in the army during
the previous war, and now suggested to the governor of Madras a
bold stroke against the ambitious Frenchman. There was only one
town holding out against Chunda Sahib and his French allies, and
that was Trichinopoly, in the south of the province. Here Mohammed
Ali, a son of the late nawab, had taken refuge; the town was being
besieged by the French and the current nawab. Clive volunteered to
lead a British force to Arcot, the capital of the province, and so draw
Chunda Sahib's army away from the siege of Trichinopoly. The plan
succeeded; Clive took Arcot, and defended it for fifty days with a
few hundred men against an army of several thousands. The defence
of Arcot not only had the desired effect of relieving Trichinopoly, but
raised the prestige of the British to a level with that of the French.
From this time the Indians began to doubt the invincibility of Dupleix
and his Frenchmen, which had hitherto been unquestioned.

The next year Major Lawrence, assisted by Clive, forced a French
army to surrender before the walls of Trichinopoly. Matters were

The French
in the
Carnatic

In the
Deccan

Robert Clive

Arcot, 1751

Trichinopoly,
1752

ROBERT CLIVE (1725-74)
(Portrait *c*. 1773 by Sir Nathaniel Dance-Holland)

going badly for Dupleix; he had spent a great deal of money, and yet his schemes were being ruined by English interference. But he still had an army in the Deccan, and did not despair of retrieving his position in the Carnatic. The French Company, however, took a more serious view of the situation, and they determined to recall their governor-general. He was superseded in 1754 and forced to return to France, where his great services were unrewarded and he was left to die in poverty.

Recall of Dupleix 1754

His successor made a formal treaty of peace with the British; but this peace was not of long duration, owing to the outbreak of the Seven Years' War. Clive was engaged in the conquest of Bengal, and in his absence the French made a final effort to drive the British from the Carnatic. They did not succeed. Their new military leader, the Comte de Lally, son of an Irish Jacobite, was a brave soldier but a bad

Lally in the Carnatic

commander; he quarrelled with practically all the French officials in India. He was not as skilful as Dupleix in diplomacy and he recalled the French troops from the Deccan. Relying, as he did, on French military efficiency rather than on intrigues with the Indians, he was hampered by lack of supplies, which could not be brought in so long as England retained command of the sea. In 1758 he was forced to abandon the siege of Madras when an English fleet appeared off the coast. In 1760 Lally encountered the main British army under Sir Eyre Coote at Wandewash, half-way between Pondicherry and Madras. The victory went to the British, and Lally retired to Pondicherry. The British blockaded the town by land and sea, and it had to surrender in 1761. Lally was taken a prisoner to Madras.

Wandewash

Fall of
Pondicherry
1761

These events decided the fate of the French in India. When the Treaty of Paris came to be signed, Pondicherry and their other towns were restored to them, but, on Clive's suggestion, a clause was inserted forbidding the French to keep armed forces in India. Henceforth they had to use their possessions as trading stations only. The field of expansion in India was thus left clear for the English Company. The Comte de Lally was not just ignored like Dupleix. He was accused of having sold Pondicherry to the English, was unjustly convicted of treason, and beheaded (1766).

End of the
French power
in India

(ii) *The Conquest of Bengal.*

Siraj-ud-
Daula

The fertile plain of Bengal, with its teeming population, did not become a scene of European conflict until the outbreak of the Seven Years' War. The British, French, and Dutch stations on the Hooghli – Calcutta, Chandernagore, and Chinsura – lay within thirty miles of each other, but they remained at peace, both with each other and with the native rulers of Bengal. This state of affairs was altered by the action of a new nawab, Siraj-ud-Daula, who succeeded to the throne of Bengal in 1756.

The Black
Hole, 1756

Siraj-ud-Daula decided to attack the British settlement of Calcutta. When he took the town in June 1756, some of the defenders escaped by water, but somewhere between 60 and 150 prisoners were shut up in the infamous 'Black Hole', a small guard-room, 18 feet by 14. Most of the prisoners suffocated to death. The remaining residents took refuge twenty miles down the river. Siraj-ud-Daula retired to his capital.

When the news from Bengal reached Madras, the governor decided to send an expedition to recover Calcutta. A fleet of five ships under Admiral Watson conveyed Colonel Clive with 900 British and 1,500 native troops (sepoys) to Bengal. The fleet sailed up the Hooghli, and Calcutta was retaken. Shortly afterwards the British attacked the French station at Chandernagore by land and water, and the garrison surrendered. *Watson and Clive in Bengal 1757*

The British expedition had now accomplished all and more than it had set out to do. But with Clive inaction was impossible, and events in Bengal invited interference. An important Indian banking family was willing to subsidize a British counter-attack on the nawab. Though British relations with the nawab were outwardly friendly, Clive formed a conspiracy with Mir Jafar, a great noble of the nawab's court, to overthrow Siraj-ud-Daula. At last the nawab, suspecting treachery, decided to attack the British once more. Clive was ready for him at Plassey with an army of 3,200 men, one third British and two thirds Indian; the nawab's army numbered 50,000. Clive waited some time before deciding to attack, since his chances of success depended on the expected treachery of Mir Jafar. Siraj-ud-Daula, however, brought about his own ruin by ordering a retreat; Clive fell on the demoralized Bengalis, and confusion spread through their ranks. Plassey was not a battle; it was a panic-stricken rout. The British lost 20 men, the Bengalis perhaps 500. Mir Jafar's contingent took no part in the action. *Plassey 1757*

After the rout of Siraj-ud-Daula's army the English entered Murshidabad, the Bengali capital, and installed Mir Jafar as nawab. Siraj-ud-Daula was killed by Mir Jafar's son. The new nawab had promised to pay £1,000,000 to the Company in compensation for *Mir Jafar, Nawab of Bengal* their losses at Calcutta, and considerably more than that sum in gratuities to Clive and other Englishmen. It was found, however, that the Bengal treasury did not contain the requisite sum; Mir Jafar was therefore obliged to make the payments by annual instalments. The British completed their triumph by capturing Chinsura, the Dutch station on the Hooghli. Clive returned to England in 1760, and was awarded a peerage.

Bengal 1760-5

He was away from India for five years, and during his absence the Company's officials worked their will in Bengal. Their conduct left much to be desired; they regarded Bengal as a place to make their fortunes, regardless of the welfare of the inhabitants. In fact, the welfare of the people was no business of theirs: they had power without responsibility – always a dangerous combination. The nawab was forced to make laws favouring British traders at the expense of his own subjects. Finally the British deposed him, and set up his son-in-law, Mir Kasim, in his stead.

Mir Kasim was treated in the same way as his predecessor, and was soon driven into revolt against his masters. Warren Hastings, a member of the British Council in Bengal, warned his fellow members that they were making themselves 'lords and oppressors' of Bengal, but his warning went unheeded. The Council deposed Mir Kasim, who had proved too independent for its liking, and set up Mir Jafar again. Mir Kasim fled to Oudh, where he joined forces with the nawab of that province, and with the Mughal emperor. These allies attempted to drive the English from Bengal, but in 1764 were heavily defeated by the Company's forces at the battle of Buxar, the most complete victory yet won by an English army in the East.

Battle of Buxar, 1764

Shortly after this Clive was requested by the East India Company to return to Bengal. His mission was to effect a major change in British dealings with India. Until this point, the British had been in India as traders, with no responsibility to the Indians and with no aims other than those of making the Company profitable and amassing wealth for themselves as individuals. By 1765, however, the

Clive's last visit to India 1765-7

British were acquiring political power, which presented ample opportunities for extortion from the local populace. Clive now took advantage of the victory of Buxar to conclude the Treaty of Allahabad, by which the Great Mughal granted the *diwani* (that is, the right of collecting and administering the revenue) for the provinces of Bengal, Bihar, and Orissa to the British. This meant that the East India company had ceased to be simply a trading company, but had acquired governmental powers and with them the obligation to rule with due attention to the interests of the people under their sway. Unfortunately, neither Clive nor the Company Directors in London drew this conclusion. They chose what they called a dual system. The Company took the surplus profit of the administration, but left responsibility for just government to the nawab and his unscrupulous servants. Inevitably, the result was not justice, but oppression. To the Company's officials Clive forbade private trading and the taking of presents, and their salaries were raised to make up for the losses which these new regulations entailed. Yet the Company's employees found ways round the regulations and a trickle of wealthy *nabobs*, as those who enriched themselves in India were called, continued to retire to England. Clive had not guaranteed the purity of the East India Company.

Clive met with much opposition in his dealings with the Company's officials and in his efforts to introduce a new and more honest standard. His own dealings with Mir Jafar in 1757 (before Plassey) were not unnaturally brought up against him, but that did not deter him from pursuing what he now thought to be the right course. But he made many enemies, who followed him to England when he retired two years later.

It was partly through the machination of these men that Clive, on his return, was attacked in Parliament. He was accused before a Parliamentary Committee of having received bribes from Mir Jafar during his first governorship of Bengal. He defended himself with his usual spirit, and contended that he had received no more than his

(margin note) Treaty of Allahabad 1765

(margin note) Clive before Parliament 1772

right, and, further, that he might have helped himself to much more had he so chosen. He described the gold, silver, and jewels which he had seen in the treasury of the nawab's gorgeous palace at Murshidabad. 'By God, Mr. Chairman,' he exclaimed, 'at this moment I stand astonished at my own moderation!' This line of argument was scarcely convincing; the Committee came to the conclusion that Clive had been guilty of receiving sums of money from native rulers. But lest this verdict should appear to reflect too harshly on the honour of one who was thought to have served Britain well and whom Pitt had once described as a *heaven-sent general*, the Committee added the famous rider: 'Robert, Lord Clive, did at the same time render great and meritorious services to his country.'

Two years later Clive committed suicide. His health had long been poor, and was not improved by the knowledge that many of his countrymen regarded him as a tyrant. He belongs to the buccaneering stage in the development of the British Indian empire. He was an adventurer in circumstances where individual initiative, daring and courage could achieve great feats, such as the overthrow of a major Indian ruler, or the thwarting of the ambitions of a great European power. His career was characterized by ruthlessness and greed, but perhaps only a man largely unfettered by moral principle could have achieved what he accomplished. Clive's tragedy was that he lived into a time when in India the day of the adventurer was passing. Adventurers were no longer necessary, but instead embarrassing. The contrast between the values he hoped to champion after 1765 and those which had made him a great hero in the 1750s was stark. It gave his enemies a golden opportunity to attack him.

Death of
Clive, 1774

III

GEORGE III AND THE LOSS OF AMERICA

I. The Political Instability of the 1760s

WHEN George III succeeded his grandfather as King, the Whig oligarchy had been ruling England for nearly fifty years. It was the fixed intention of the young King to break the power of this oligarchy, and to substitute for it a non-party patriotic government. Impatient for power, George's father, Frederick Prince of Wales, who died in 1751, had been bitterly critical of his father, George II. The future George III accepted his father's criticism of the corruption of politics and supposed that it was his duty to cleanse the political system. In his private letters, he expressed contempt for his grandfather: 'The conduct of this old K.[King] makes me ashamed of being his grandson.' George II, he imagined, had allowed himself to become the puppet of Whig grandees like the Duke of Newcastle. In contrast, as George III, he would break the hold of such people on politics and institute a government which would reach out to all his subjects, including the Tories. It suited some critics at the time and later Whigs to claim that George planned to act unconstitutionally by reviving the powers of the Stuart monarchs. This interpretation was wholly false. George accepted the results of the Revolution of 1688. He was to prove a champion of the supremacy of Parliament. His plans involved making use of his powers to dismiss and appoint ministers, but no one denied that he possessed such powers and previous Hanoverian monarchs had made full use of them.

There was much in the character of George III to attract the loyalty of his subjects. He had been brought up as an English gentleman, and in tastes and manners he looked the part. English was his native tongue, and he was in all respects a striking contrast to his two German predecessors. His love of England and his devotion

George III 1760-1820

Revival of the Tories

Character of George III

His Virtues

KING GEORGE III (1738-1820), REIGNED 1760-1820
(Portrait *c*. 1761 by the studio of Allan Ramsay)

to what he conceived to be her interests were genuine. 'Born and educated in this country,' he said in his first Speech from the Throne, 'I glory in the name of Britain.' Such sentiments naturally evoked feelings of affection, and these feelings were strengthened by the virtues of the young King. George III was free from the vices for which his grandfather and great-grandfather and his own sons were notorious; his private life was without scandal. He was a model son, a devoted husband, and an indulgent father. His tastes were those of a simple country gentleman, and his subjects admired him for them. 'Farmer George' he was affectionately nicknamed.

George III had a very strong sense of his duty as King, but he suffered from a strong sense of inferiority and felt unequal to the task of reforming politics. Since he had come of age in 1756, George's mentor had been Lord Bute, a Scottish aristocrat and friend of his mother. It was unfortunate that Bute's understanding of politics was very limited and yet George looked upon him as a pupil might look on an admired schoolmaster. He soon discovered his idol's feet of clay.

His Defects

Both Bute and George III imagined that the chief problem in politics was the entrenchment in power of a large body of corrupt Whigs. By 1760, however, the Whigs lacked cohesion. They stood for the principles of 1689 and the dynastic change of 1714, but these things no longer marked them off from anyone else once Jacobitism was dead. Under the first two Georges loyalty to the throne meant being a Whig, but George III welcomed Tory country gentlemen to court and in the counties Whig monopolies of patronage and local office were opened up. Lacking distinctive ideas, the Whigs fractured into quarrelling groups of men tied together by bonds of family, friendship and patronage. Henry Pelham had succeeded in gaining a stable majority from 1746 to 1754 by means of his talents at compromise and conciliation, but there was nothing stable about the association of Pitt and Newcastle which had carried Britain through the Seven Years' War. Theirs was purely a marriage of convenience

The King's Friends

which lasted only so long as all issues were suspended other than that of how to win the war. Pitt was an impossible colleague, who would tolerate no criticism of himself, but who interfered constantly in Newcastle's domain. The breakdown of the partnership in 1761 was eminently predictable.

What was required in 1761 was a restoration of political stability. The qualities needed were those of Pelham, a genius for compromise and conciliation. The prejudices which George III had imbibed could only make things more difficult. Thus the King was delighted to see the back of Newcastle, who resigned in 1762. George little appreciated that the duke's control of Whig politics had been a potent force for stability. Bute took over as Prime Minister in May 1762. With the full backing of a popular young King, he stood a good chance of creating a stable parliamentary majority. Yet in April 1763 he resigned. A contemporary described him as 'the greatest political coward I ever knew'. Bute did have to endure criticism of unusual virulence, much of it from the gutter press. Despite the highly proper tone of the court, he was accused of illicit relations with the King's mother. He was said to be plotting an Eleven Years' Tyranny like that of Charles I. His Scottish origins occasioned an outbreak of rabid Scotophobia. The chances of respectable, let alone parliamentary opinion responding to these attacks were negligible, but Bute wholly lacked the robustness of a Walpole and decided to leave his royal pupil in the lurch. For the next few years, rumours abounded that Bute was still the King's real confidant and they weakened the ministries that followed by suggesting that royal support might be withdrawn.

The political instability of the 1760s was not all the fault of Bute or George III. The leading personalities among whom the King had to choose were deeply flawed in one way or another. George Grenville, who became Prime Minister after Bute's resignation, had many valuable qualities. His obsession with thrift and economy went down well with the country gentlemen in the House. He exuded solid

Fall of Newcastle 1762

Bute's Ministry 1762-3

competence. Unfortunately, his relationship with the King went from bad to worse. George found him pedantic and tedious and his habit of lecturing and hectoring the monarch made him intolerable. Grenville was obsessed with the matter of Bute's supposed influence, an influence that was in reality in sharp decline. When Grenville tried to force the King to deprive Bute's brother of his post, the King turned back to Newcastle's allies rather than put up with Grenville any longer. George declared: 'I would sooner meet Mr Grenville at the point of my sword than let him into my cabinet.'

Grenville's ministry is famous for the passage of the Stamp act and the response to it in America. At the time, however, it was the Wilkes case which contributed more to the turbulence of politics. John Wilkes, the outspoken editor of *The North Briton*, was soon to be the hero of London. No. 45 of his paper contained a reference to the King's Speech on the recent peace treaty. The paper said that the King had given 'the sanction of his sacred name to the most odious measures and to the most unjustifiable public declarations from a throne ever renowned for truth, honour and unsullied virtue'. George III considered that this was an accusation of personal dishonesty; he insisted that the author or authors should be prosecuted for seditious libel. Accordingly a general warrant (i.e. one mentioning no names) was issued against the 'authors, printers and publishers' of *The North Briton*; under this Wilkes and forty-eight other persons were arrested. Wilkes claimed that, as a Member of Parliament, he could not be arrested for libel; and he also challenged the legality of general warrants. Lord Chief Justice Pratt upheld the former plea, and Wilkes was released.

Wilkes claimed to stand for the liberty of the subject against a ministerial plot, and he was partially vindicated when Lord Chief Justice Camden ruled general warrants illegal. The House of Commons, however, disliked his posturing. By a considerable majority the House declared that Parliamentary privilege did not extend to libel, ordered No. 45 of *The North Briton* to be burnt by

Grenville Ministry 1763-5

Wilkes, No. 45, *The North Briton*

the common hangman, and later expelled Wilkes from the House. He was wounded in a duel, and fled to France, not waiting to face the main charge of libel. He was outlawed by the Court of King's Bench when he failed to answer the charge on 1st November 1764. He was, however, to be heard of again.

Wilkes expelled from the House 1764

In July 1765 Grenville was succeeded by Lord Rockingham, an ally of Newcastle, who also became a member of the government. Most of the ministerial team had so little experience of affairs of state that the King described them as 'an administration of boys'. Conscious of this weakness, Rockingham attempted to bring Pitt into the administration, but Pitt had no intention of working with Newcastle's friends again and the attempts to bring him in merely advertised the ministry's weakness. In the end, it was the King who turned to Pitt.

Rocking-ham's Ministry 1765-6

Great things were expected of Pitt, who was now created Earl of Chatham and became head of a 'non-party' ministry. Unfortunately, however, the great man's health gave way. He suffered terribly from gout, and experienced some sort of nervous collapse. He shut himself up in his house, and refused to communicate with his colleagues, half of whom spent their time quarrelling with the other half. After two years of confusion Chatham resigned and the Duke of Grafton became the nominal head of the ministry. Grafton was a young man presiding over bickering colleagues, whose position was fatally undermined by Chatham, who recovered sufficiently by 1770 to denounce all the main policies of the ministry, including its handling of another Wilkes affair.

Ministry of Chatham 1766-8 and Grafton 1768-70

In 1768 Wilkes returned to England and stood as a candidate for Parliament. He was chosen by the electors of Middlesex, but Parliament declared him incapable of sitting. He stood again for Middlesex, and was again returned. The House ordered a third election; Wilkes was opposed by a certain Colonel Luttrell, whom he defeated by a four to one majority. The House, now clearly going beyond its rights, declared that Colonel Luttrell was the member for Middlesex. This decision produced riots in London, and Wilkes was

The Middlesex Elections 1768-9

the hero of the hour. There is no doubting his popularity in London and Middlesex and a petitioning movement on Wilkes' behalf collected sixty thousand signatures from the country. On the other hand, the Commons were resolutely unimpressed. Meanwhile the ministry was attacked in the anonymous *Letters of Junius*, which contained violent attacks on Grafton and his colleagues. The authorship of these Letters has never been discovered.

Letters of Junius 1769-72

It was during this unhappy state of public affairs that the genius of Edmund Burke produced an important piece of political writing. Burke was an Irishman who had become secretary to Lord Rockingham. Though he never held high office he was the most influential political thinker in Britain in the 18th century. His *Thoughts on the Cause of the Present Discontents* was written in 1769, and published the following year. It contained a careful analysis of the political situation. Burke was a loyal Whig, who viewed with dismay the decline of his party since the accession of George III. He examined Chatham's experiment in 'non-party' rule and the other unstable combinations of politicians which had governed Britain in the 1760s and he pronounced them wanting. To achieve results in politics men had to combine in a party and skills in managing a group of supporters were essential for a successful political leader. Burke's defence of party came at a time when most men disapproved of party and favoured a patriotic government recruited from all sources. What Burke did not appreciate was that party bonds were unlikely to be strong unless his Whigs were opposed by another party.

Edmund Burke

It was not Burke's Whigs who were about to end the incoherence of British politics. In 1767 George III had introduced Lord North into the Cabinet as Chancellor of the Exchequer. When in 1770 George accepted Grafton's resignation, North became Prime Minister. There followed at last a lengthy period of political stability. This was partly because North was personally acceptable to George III, just as Walpole had been acceptable to the first two Georges. Like previous successful Prime Ministers, North made good use of crown

Rule of George III and Lord North 1770-82

patronage to build support for his ministry, but his majority was not simply bought. He was 'Lord' North only by courtesy, as the eldest son of a peer, and he was an effective debater in the Commons. His speeches were based on a mastery of his brief, they were convincingly argued and they were always good humoured. He had been well trained in the financial departments of state and commanded respect whenever he spoke on financial matters, the ones that mattered most to many backbenchers. The reassuring stability which North provided was welcome to most MPs, especially after the agitation associated with Wilkes. The bases of his power were very similar to those on which the pre-eminence of Walpole and Pelham had rested. In contrast to them, however, North's ministry sometimes attracted the label 'Tory'. This was not how he thought of himself – he accepted the Revolution of 1688 as completely as anyone – but the group round Burke and Rockingham were beginning to appropriate the 'Whig' brand for itself and to designate opponents as Tories.

2. The Quarrel with America

Attitude of the American Colonists to Britain

In the mid-18th century, most inhabitants of the mainland British American colonies seem to have been content to be part of the British empire. They were proud of their heritage of British freedom, handed down, they believed, from the far past and triumphantly reasserted against the Stuarts. The sign and guarantee of their freedom was the existence in each colony of a representative assembly, elected by the property-holders, which, in the American context, meant most men. Theoretically, these assemblies were subordinate to royal governors, but in practice the governors had to act as the assemblies wanted, since otherwise they would be starved of funds. British authority was accepted because it was rarely exercised and also because the largely Protestant Americans needed protection against the Catholic power of France. It was clear to royal governors, who knew how assertive colonial assemblies could be, that British control was fragile. Lord

Cornbury, governor of New York in Anne's reign, had said of the colonists: 'If once they can see they can clothe themselves without the help of England, they – who are already not very fond of submitting to government – would soon think of putting into execution designs they have long harboured in their breasts.' The design which Cornbury foresaw, though, was a design for the independence of an individual colony, not a design for an independent United States. The colonies seemed far too quarrelsome for that to be possible.

The British American colonies were included within the economic system of the old colonial empire. In common with all European powers who held overseas possessions, Britain treated her colonial market as a monopoly. The colonial system had been established in Stuart times, when Charles II's Navigation Act of 1660 had been passed. The colonists had to import manufactured goods – e.g. woollen and hardware articles – from Britain, and not from other countries. Since British goods were usually cheaper than others, this was no hardship, but perhaps it mattered more that there were restrictions on American manufactures for the benefit of British ones. On the other hand, the coffee, sugar, rice, and tobacco consumed in Britain could be bought only in the British colonial market, a rule which conferred a big advantage on the colonies which produced them. The colonies which fitted least well into the system were the northern ones of New England, few of whose products were required in Britain. To acquire the means to pay for their imports from Britain, they had developed a trade in molasses with the French West Indian sugar islands. From the molasses they distilled rum, which could be traded with the native Americans for furs or with Africa for slaves. The British West Indies found themselves undercut by the French in the New England market and to help them, the London government had imposed a heavy duty on French molasses. The New Englanders evaded it by bribing the customs officers. In general, the old colonial system was accepted, because wherever it hurt important interests in

The Mercantile Empire

the American colonies, it was not enforced. It was acceptable too because the colonies were undoubtedly prospering. The population was roughly doubling every thirty years. Luxury as well as essential goods were being imported from England. The northern colonies had built up an impressive mercantile marine.

Effects of the Conquest of Canada 1763

George Grenville Stamp Act 1765

The overthrow of the French power in Canada was a turning point in the history of America. It was prophesied at the time that, now all fear of the French was removed, the American colonists would break away from Britain; they would bring to an end a state of dependence which was no longer necessary. Yet if the British government had been content to leave the colonies pretty much alone, as it had before the Seven Years' War, a conflict with the colonies might have been indefinitely postponed. To George Grenville, Prime Minister from 1763 to 1765, however, carrying on as before did not seem a viable policy. The empire which Britain had gained needed defending, against the native Americans beyond the Appalachian Mountains and against French and Spanish desire for revenge. Grenville reckoned that the necessary troops would cost about £200,000 per annum. It seemed unreasonable to expect Britain to foot the whole bill. Britain's national debt had increased to £140 millions, incurring interest charges of four or five millions annually. British taxes had already been increased: for example, an unpopular cider tax had been imposed. Grenville therefore proposed that the lightly taxed Americans should meet part of the bill. He began by tightening up the old commercial system in 1764. Hitherto, its function had been to regulate trade; now Grenville used it to produce revenue. In the case of molasses, Grenville reduced the duty, but he took steps to enforce it by making efforts to put down colonial smuggling. In 1765, he went further and imposed a stamp duty on legal documents, intended to raise £60,000 a year.

Opposition to the Stamp Act

There was nothing at all unreasonable in Grenville's proposal; the tax was light, and it was proposed to spend the revenue derived from it, not in England, but on the defence of America. Nevertheless, the tax aroused a storm of opposition in America, and, in fact, could not be collected, since those appointed as collectors were intimidated into resigning. The colonists denied the right of the British Parliament, sitting at Westminster, to impose taxes. They claimed that if the British were allowed to levy any tax without consent, their future demands could not be limited and no American's property would be safe. They raised the cry: 'No taxation without representation'; but, in fact, they did not really wish to be represented in the Westminster Parliament, nor, in 18th-century travelling conditions, would such a thing have been practicable for a country 3,000 miles away. The main effect of the proposed taxation was to create a united opposition in America; delegates from nine of the thirteen colonies met at New York in 1765 to protest against the Stamp Act.

Scarcely any one in Britain was prepared for this opposition, and to Grenville himself it came as a surprise. He resigned next year, owing to differences with the King, and Lord Rockingham succeeded him. Rockingham's policy was largely influenced by Burke, who sympathized with the colonists. Pitt also spoke against the Stamp Act, and the government decided to repeal it. At the same time, however, a Declaratory Act was passed, saying that Great Britain had the right to pass laws binding the colonists in all cases. Rockingham seemed to have found a way of defusing the crisis without giving up the principle of Parliamentary sovereignty, to which opinion in Britain was much attached. The crisis was over, but neither side in the dispute now trusted the other. The Americans suspected the British of designs against their liberty. Many of the British believed that American insubordination would only increase if Britain continued to appease them.

Repeal of the Stamp Act, 1766

Next year, 1767, when the so-called Chatham Ministry was in power, the Chancellor of the Exchequer, Charles Townshend, decided to take advantage of the distinction which some Americans had made between duties imposed to regulate trade and 'internal' duties like

American Import Duties Act 1767

those imposed by the Stamp Act. He acted to increase the revenue by levying a tax on tea, and on certain manufactured articles (chiefly glass and paper) entering American ports. As was entirely predictable, this Act met with the same reception in America as Grenville's measures. There were riots in many colonial towns, especially in Boston, the capital of Massachusetts, which from now on took the lead in opposing the British government. Four thousand British troops were quartered in Boston – equal to nearly a quarter of the number of the civil population. The inhabitants provoked an incident with the soldiers in 1770: this was the Boston Massacre, in which five people were killed. At home, Parliament passed resolutions condemning the disloyalty shown in Massachusetts, and an address was sent to the King thanking him for the measures he had taken to safeguard Britain's interests.

British statesmen were by no means united in their views. Burke
Attitude of warned the Government that it was proceeding on a perilous course,
British and Chatham spoke against the policy of taxing the colonies. 'I
statesmen rejoice,' he said, 'that America has resisted.' Yet Burke and Chatham spoke for few of those who counted in British politics. Most MPs were angry at the growing insubordination of the Americans and had no sympathy with their rejection of Parliament's authority. The autonomy or independence at which the American leaders seemed to be aiming was regarded in Britain as certain to be fatal to the imperial commercial system. That system was regarded as the main foundation of British economic and political might. In short, it was necessary to reduce the Americans to obedience if Britain's status as a great power was to be preserved. In 1768 Grafton succeeded Chatham as nominal head of the ministry, and North had succeeded Townshend as Chancellor of the Exchequer. Grafton was in favour of abolishing all the recent taxes, but after a debate the Cabinet decided in March 1770 to retain that on tea as a symbol of Parliament's power to tax and legislate. Thus the whole question remained unsettled.

BOSTON TEA PARTY, 1773
(from a 19th-century lithograph)

In the same year North succeeded Grafton as Prime Minister. In 1773 North introduced a new Tea Act. Hitherto the East India Company had been compelled to sell its wares by public auction in London; merchants, English and American, had then had the handling of the tea. The new Act allowed the Company to send its tea direct to America and sell it there, and so crush the private dealers. The fact that the Act (by granting the Company a remission of British duties) would halve the price of tea to American consumers was not sufficient to outweigh the hatred of American merchants for the Company's monopoly or the self-styled patriots' determination to pay no taxes without consent. Hostile demonstrations, were held; and in Boston Harbour a party of men disguised as American Indians boarded the East India Company's ships and threw the chests of tea into the sea. The news of this 'Boston Tea Party' was received with rage in England. Though the attack was on private property, not directly on the British government, the 'Tea Party' was perceived as the last straw. The colonists

George III
and Lord
North, 1770

Tea Act 1773

Boston Tea
Party, 1773

were apparently intent on defying imperial authority and had to be brought to obedience if the empire were to survive.

The Government at once adopted strong measures. In 1774 the port of Boston was declared closed until compensation was paid, and a Massachusetts Government Act was passed, which strengthened the governor and weakened the assembly. Town meetings were severely restricted. The colonists interpreted these measures as clear proof that the British government was aiming to subject them to despotic rule. In resisting, they would be doing no more than the English Parliament had done when it resisted Charles I. By an unfortunate coincidence, the British government also legislated in 1774 for its Canadian territory. The Quebec Act extended the boundary of Canada to the Ohio, which looked like an attempt to limit American expansion and granted to the French Canadians the free exercise of their Roman Catholic religion, which offended anti-Catholic prejudices in New England. Most seriously of all, the Act replaced the elected with a nominated assembly, because an experiment with the former among the French population had not worked. The American colonists concluded that the same fate was in store for them. Affronted by the Acts passed by the British government, the first American Congress, representing all the thirteen colonies except Georgia, met at Philadelphia. The delegates declared for a general stoppage of trade with Britain until grievances should be redressed. At the same time they forwarded a protest to the British government and demanded the repeal of the recent Acts.

Next year the first blood was shed. General Gage, in command of the British troops in Boston, sent out some men to prevent the colonists collecting military stores. There was some firing between the British regulars and the colonial militia at Lexington and Concord. After this the British did not venture out of Boston, for the whole of Massachusetts was in revolt.

Meanwhile a second American Congress was held, and a petition, known as the Olive Branch Petition, was sent to King George,

Margin notes:

Acts against Massach-usetts 1774

Quebec Act, 1774

First American Congress 1774

Lexington 1775

Second American Congress 1775

containing an offer to return to the position of 1763, but denying the legislative power of the British Parliament. The King and the Cabinet, however, were bent on enforcing the recent Acts. They were not alone. Even Burke, who opposed the Acts, admitted: 'the popular current...at present sets strongly against America'. On the American side, preparations for war were already far advanced. The same Congress which sent the Olive Branch Petition appointed Colonel Washington, who had seen service in the Seven Years' War, as General and Commander-in-Chief of the American Army. George Washington was a Virginian planter, a man of quiet tastes and averse from publicity. But he was also a man of inflexible will, one who was incapable of turning his back on a task to which he had devoted himself. His acceptance of the command did much to rally Virginia and the southern colonies to the side of New England, where the centre of the revolt lay. The appointment of General Washington was to prove a significant contribution to eventual victory for the colonists.

George Washington

3. The War of American Independence

The British army which was sent out to reconquer the rebellious colonies was under the command of Sir William Howe, a soldier of no particular ability. Howe took up his quarters at Boston, bringing 10,000 reinforcements to the troops already there. Soon after his arrival the first main engagement of the war took place. The town of Boston was built on a peninsula, connected with the mainland by a narrow isthmus called Boston Neck. But the Neck and the town itself were dominated by the Charlestown Hills and Dorchester Heights. The Americans seized a position near Bunker Hill. Howe drove them from this position but they retired in good order.

General Howe Bunker Hill 1775

Meanwhile the Americans tried to invade Canada, and sent a force up the Hudson and Lake Champlain route. This army arrived at Quebec, and delivered an attack, which, however, was beaten off

Invasion of Canada 1775

by Sir Guy Carleton, the energetic Governor of Canada. The failure of this expedition decided the fate of Canada.

Washington, during the latter part of 1775, had taken command of the American army before Boston. Howe permitted him to occupy Dorchester Heights which, like Bunker Hill, overlooked the town, which the Americans proceeded to bombard. After this Howe was compelled to evacuate Boston, which he did, bringing off his troops by sea to Halifax in Nova Scotia, in March 1776.

Evacuation of Boston 1776

In the same year the third American Congress met at Philadelphia and drew up the famous Declaration of Independence on 4th July 1776. The Declaration summed up the case for independence in the following words:

The Third American Congress

Declaration of Independence 4 July, 1776

'We hold these truths to be self-evident: – "That all men are created equal; that they are endowed by their Creator with certain unalienable rights; that among these are life, liberty, and the pursuit of happiness. That to secure these rights, governments are Instituted among men, deriving their just powers from the consent of the governed; that, whenever any form of government becomes destructive of these ends, it is the right of the people to alter or to abolish it, and to institute new government, laying its foundations on such principles . . . as to them shall seem most likely to effect their safety and happiness".'

Finally, it was resolved:

'that these United colonies are, and of right ought to be, Free and Independent States; that they are absolved from all allegiance to the British Crown, and that all political connection between them and the State of Great Britain is, and ought to be, totally dissolved.'

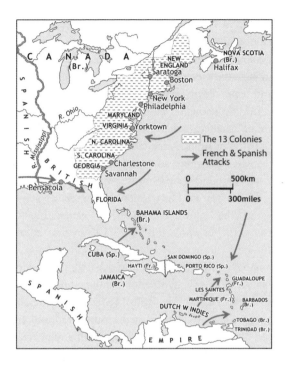

CANADA (Br.)

NOVA SCOTIA (Br.)

NEW ENGLAND

Halifax

Saratoga

Boston

New York

Philadelphia

MARYLAND

VIRGINIA Yorktown

N. CAROLINA

S. CAROLINA

GEORGIA Charlestone

Savannah

Pensacola

FLORIDA

BAHAMA ISLANDS (Br.)

CUBA (Sp.)

SAN DOMINGO (Sp.)

HAYTI (Fr.)

PORTO RICO (Sp.)

JAMAICA (Br.)

GUADALOUPE (Fr.)

LES SAINTES

MARTINIQUE (Fr.)

BARBADOS (Br.)

DUTCH W INDIES

TOBAGO (Br.)

TRINIDAD (Br.)

SPANISH EMPIRE

R. Ohio

R. Mississippi

BRITISH

The 13 Colonies

French & Spanish Attacks

0   500km

0   300miles

WAR OF AMERICAN INDEPENDENCE AND THE MARITIME WAR

The scene of the war, meanwhile, had shifted to the middle colonies. Howe landed on Long Island, and drove Washington's army from its defensive position there, after which the British occupied New York, which they held for the rest of the war. Howe could have taken Philadelphia, but he failed to seize his chance, and gave Washington time to recover. The British hope was to complete their control of the middle colonies and thereby sunder the northern and southern centres of resistance and achieve a stranglehold on colonial lines of trade and communication.

New York taken, 1776

Accordingly, in 1777 it was decided to send an army southward
Burgoyne's from Canada, under General Burgoyne, to seize Albany in central
army New York colony and join forces with Howe. It was not realized that
it was essential to the success of this plan that a detachment of Howe's
army should come northwards from New York to meet Burgoyne.
Instead of effecting a junction with Burgoyne, Howe employed all his
men in fighting a campaign in the south of the middle colonies. There
he won the battle of Brandywine Creek and captured Philadelphia.
Meanwhile, when Burgoyne advanced down the Hudson valley, he
found himself surrounded by a hostile population, and by a rapidly
Burgoyne's increasing American army. His position, without reinforcements, was
surrender at hopeless, and the reinforcements never came. He therefore
Saratoga surrendered with his whole force of 3,500 men at Saratoga, 17
1777 October 1777.

Two months later Washington settled down for the winter at Valley
Washington Forge, Pennsylvania, with an army of less than 4,000 men; Howe's
at Valley forces were at least 10,000. The British general was quite unaware of
Forge, the desperate straits to which the Americans were reduced, but which
1777-8 we can read of in Washington's dispatches. His men were almost
destitute of supplies: 'few men,' he wrote, 'have more than one shirt,
many only the moiety [half] of one, and some none at all'. A large
proportion of the men were barefoot, so that 'their marches might be
traced by the blood from their feet'. There was never enough to eat;
the men, ill clothed and half starving, had to endure the fierce cold of
December in this appalling condition. Half the army melted away –
from sickness or desertion. But the remainder held on, faithful to their
general, who never gave up hope in the darkest hour. It says much for
the character and perseverance of Washington that he was able to
maintain an army in the field under these conditions. He was saved by
the caution of the British general, which must have seemed justified
by what had happened to Burgoyne. Throughout the war, British
generals were hampered by difficulties of communication and supply
in the wide spaces of America and by their ignorance of the enemy's

whereabouts. Their best hope was to force the enemy into a pitched battle, which they were likely to win with their trained soldiers, but this they never succeeded in doing.

Saratoga had not been a disastrous military defeat, but its consequences were very serious. The news of Saratoga was received in Europe at Christmas 1777. It at once decided the French government to take up the cause of the colonists, and to form an alliance with them. From 1778, therefore, Britain and France were at war. The effect of this was decisive, because the war in the American colonies became a sideshow, since there were more important interests to be defended. The French navy opened an attack on the West Indies, which had to be defended at the same time as the French hampered British communications with the mainland of America and threatened an invasion of Britain itself. The actual fighting force sent by France to America arrived in 1780 and made its mark only near the end of the war; but the French naval action made it impossible for Britain to concentrate on reconquering the colonies. As if the Royal Navy was not stretched enough, there was also the menace of American privateers who attacked British ships. One adventurous captain, Paul Jones, even landed on the coast of Scotland in 1778, and then captured two British ships off Scarborough. When William Pitt, Earl of Chatham, died in 1778, the empire, which in his ministry had been raised to the first place in the world, had been brought to the verge of disruption, and France, which he had humbled, was about to take its revenge.

France declares war, 1778

Paul Jones

Death of Chatham 1778

Certainly, the government's expectation that the war would be short was dashed. It was obvious too that it would be very expensive. Taxes on both rich and poor had to be raised. British merchants, who had found the first years of war profitable in view of heavy government spending on war materials, were alarmed at the prospect of war with all the other naval powers. There was still a great deal of support for the war, but this was by no means as unanimous as in past wars against France. The Americans were mostly Protestants;

they spoke about liberty in a way that resonated with many Englishmen; and they were cousins, which helps to account for the lukewarmness of East Anglia about the war, since the ancestors of many New Englanders had come from there.

In 1779 Spain joined France, and the two powers attacked Britain in the Mediterranean, where Gibraltar and Minorca were besieged. The French also sent a fleet to attack Britain in India, and in 1780 Holland joined the ranks of Britain's foes. Britain, therefore, had to fight a maritime war against the other naval powers of Europe, to defend Gibraltar, the West Indies, and India, and at the same time to carry on the war against the colonists. In this war, it was Britain that was over-stretched, whereas in previous wars it had been France which had been forced to fight on land and sea. In these circumstances it is scarcely surprising that the thirteen colonies were lost. Disputes also arose with other European powers over the question of the rights of neutrals. Neutral powers claimed that they had a right to trade with belligerents and that neutral ships could carry any goods save certain 'contraband of war', specified by treaty. The British Navy searched ships for contraband and sometimes went farther and tried to interfere with peaceful trade, and so extend blockade law beyond its natural limits. Russia, Sweden, Denmark, and other states bound themselves together in an Armed Neutrality, threatening to declare war if their rights as neutrals were not respected.

In America, Howe was superseded by Sir Henry Clinton, who decided to extend the war into the southern colonies. Charleston, the capital of South Carolina, was captured, and Lord Cornwallis, who was in charge of the campaigns, won several battles in North and South Carolina in 1780. In spite of these successes, however, Cornwallis lacked the manpower to hold the southern colonies. Next year he advanced to Yorktown, in Virginia, with 7,000 men. Washington was now joined by a French army under General de Rochambeau, and these allies laid siege to Yorktown. At the same

The Maritime War 1778-83

The Armed Neutrality

War in the Southern Colonies

time, a French fleet, under Admiral de Grasse, entered Chesapeake Bay, and blockaded Yorktown from the sea. Cornwallis, thus cut off from help by water, was besieged on land by a Franco-American army which outnumbered his by more than 2 to 1. His position was hopeless, and in October 1781 he surrendered.

Surrender of Yorktown, 1781

4. The End of the Old Empire

The long tale of disaster from America was received month by month by a despondent British nation, unused to defeat in its wars. The King and his government became very unpopular. The competence of the political elite was seriously called into question. A petitioning movement protesting against the inefficiency and corruption of the government began in Yorkshire and spread to other parts of the country. In 1780 the Commons carried a motion that the 'influence of the Crown has increased, is increasing, and ought to be diminished'. It was at the beginning of the same year that London was for four days at the mercy of a wild anti-Catholic mob, led by a crack-brained fanatic called Lord George Gordon. The Gordon Riots were caused by the introduction of a Bill in Parliament, removing some of the laws against the Roman Catholics. Wild scenes were enacted; shops, factories, and breweries were broken into or destroyed – the last with baleful effect on the mob – while Catholic chapels were burnt to the ground. The riots were at last quelled by the personal intervention of the King, who took the responsibility of ordering the military to charge on the mob. These scenes revealed the undercurrent of savagery which lay beneath the surface of 18th-century London, then unprotected by a proper police force. The riots may have helped to discredit popular protest, but disunity over their objectives probably did more to ensure the failure of the critics of the system of government.

The Gordon Riots, 1780

The fall of Yorktown ended the war in America; even the King
began to see that further hostilities against the colonists would be
useless. Lord North insisted on resigning in 1782. It was a bitter
moment for the King, and for a short time he talked of abdicating his
crown and retiring to Hanover. There was nothing to do but call in the
former opponents of North, whose avowed purpose it was to end the
war and recognize the independence of America. George III, therefore,
reluctantly consented to Lord Rockingham's forming a ministry.

Resignation of North 1782

Meanwhile, the war against France and Spain was continued, and
some welcome victories saved what remained of the British empire.
Though Minorca fell in 1782, the French and Spaniards failed to
take Gibraltar, which was brilliantly defended by its commander, Sir
George Eliott. Equally cheering was the great victory ('Battle of the
Saints') won by Admiral Rodney over the French off the islands of
Les Saintes, near Dominica, in the West Indies, which restored
British naval power in the Atlantic. In the following year it fell to a
new ministry, that of Shelburne, to make a general peace.

Rodney's naval victory 1782

During the short Rockingham Ministry (February-July 1782)
Burke's Economic Reform Bill was passed. It aimed to reduce
government patronage and therefore the number of government
placemen in the Commons. The measure proved ineffective. Charles
James Fox, the most eloquent of Rockingham's ministers, wished to
go further and abolish the rotten boroughs, but he could not carry his
party with him; his violent opposition to the King's personal influence
also earned him the hatred of George III. When Rockingham died
in July 1782, therefore, George gave the premiership, not to Fox, but
to Lord Shelburne. Fox and Burke thereupon resigned from the
Cabinet. Shelburne, who held office for a year, was regarded by the
King as the lesser of two evils, the greater being Fox. The new
Premier was a man of exceptional ability, but he did not inspire
confidence; his enemies nicknamed him the 'Jesuit of Berkeley
Square'. The chief work of his ministry was to make a general peace
with all Britain's enemies.

Rockingham Ministry 1782

Shelburne Ministry 1782-3

By the First Treaty of Versailles, the war was brought to an end on the following terms:

Treaty of Versailles 1783

1. Great Britain acknowledged the independence of the United States of America. Britain secured a promise that Congress should recommend to the various states the restoration of property confiscated from the Loyalists. But this 'recommendation' was ignored by the States, and the Loyalists were vindictively persecuted by the Americans. Many of them – about 100,000 – sought new homes in Canada and Nova Scotia. In this way, the loss of America secured Canada for the British empire. Previously, it had been inhabited mostly by Frenchmen, but they were from then on a minority.

2. The boundary between Canada and the U.S.A. was fixed at its present line, and not (as in 1774) at the line of the Ohio. The boundary west of the Great Lakes was left for future determination.

3. France received back her West African settlement of Senegal, and acquired the islands of Tobago and St Lucia in the West Indies.

4. Spain received Florida and Minorca, which she had lost in 1763 and 1713 respectively.

The year 1783 thus marked the point at which the British and the Americans came to the parting of the ways. For the former colonies, now the United States, independent development was just beginning. Great difficulties lay ahead of the infant American nation. That America survived, and became a great power, was due in the first instance to the guiding hand of George Washington, and his friend Alexander Hamilton. In 1787 a Convention met to draw up the Constitution of the United States; Washington was chosen as the first President. He first took office in 1789, the year in which the French Revolution burst upon Europe. While this storm was raging in the Old World, Washington and his advisers had the hard task of trying to weld thirteen different and differing states into a nation.

End of the Mercantile Empire

The U.S.A.

NORTH AMERICA IN 1763

New era
in British
history
begins

There were those who predicted that defeated Britain would become an insignificant island: such was the prophecy of Horace Walpole, son of the Prime minister. Yet for Britain, the loss of the colonies did not prove to be the disaster that had been widely anticipated. The political separation of Britain and its former colonies did not alter economic realities. Britain continued to be the best source of the manufactures which the Americans required: by 1800 a quarter of British exports went to the old colonies. Though they were no longer compelled to sell their raw materials to Britain, the

NORTH AMERICA IN 1783

country remained the biggest market for many of their products, especially for cotton. It appeared that Britain did not need the old colonial system which it had fought to maintain. Nor was Britain's expansionist vigour checked. Thwarted in one area of the globe, the British turned to others even more distant in the south Pacific. Shaken by disasters in America, the political elite was about to prove itself resilient enough to survive a temporary crisis of confidence and to lead the country to greater triumphs than it had yet experienced.

Date Summary: War and Empire (1756-83)

SEVEN YEARS' WAR (1756-63)

BRITAIN	AMERICA AND INDIA	EUROPE
1756 Newcastle resigns	1756 Montcalm in Canada	1756 French take Minorca
1756-7 Devonshire Ministry		
1757 Execution of Admiral Byng		
1757-61 PITT–NEWCASTLE MINISTRY	1757 ⚔ Plassey, CONQUEST OF BENGAL	1757 ⚔ Rossbach
	1758 Louisbourg and Fort Duquesne	
	1759 FALL OF QUEBEC	1759 ⚔ Quiberon
1760 George II *d.*	1760 Fall of Montreal	1760 Russians enter Berlin
1760-1820 George III	⚔ Wandewash	Rousseau's *Contrat Social*
	1761 Fall of Pondicherry	
1761 Pitt resigns		1762 England at war with Spain
1762 Newcastle resigns		1762-96 Catherine the Great (Russia)
1762-3 Bute Ministry	1763 TREATY OF PARIS ends Seven Years' War	

THE QUARREL WITH AMERICA (1763-75)

BRITAIN	AMERICA AND INDIA	EUROPE
1763-5 Grenville Ministry		
1764 Wilkes' Case	1764 ⚔ Buxar	
Hargreaves' Spinning Jenny		
1765-6 Rockingham Ministry	1765 Treaty of Allahabad	
	1765 STAMP ACT	
1766 *The Vicar of Wakefield*	1765-7 Clive in India (3rd visit)	
1766-8 Chatham Ministry	1766 Repeal of Stamp Act	
	1767 American Import Duties Act	
1768-70 Grafton Ministry	1768-79 Cook's Pacific Voyages	
1768-9 Middlesex Election (Wilkes)		
1768 *Royal Academy*		
1769 Burke's *Present Discontents*		
Watt's Steam Engine		
Garrick's Shakespeare Festival		
1770 Wordsworth born	1770 BOTANY BAY	
1770-82 North Ministry	1773 Boston 'Tea Party'	1772 First Partition of Poland
	North's Regulating Act (India)	
	1774 Quebec Act	1774-92 Louis XVI

AMERICAN WAR OF INDEPENDENCE (1775-83)

BRITAIN	AMERICA AND INDIA	EUROPE
	1774-85 WARREN HASTINGS	
	1775 ⚔ Bunker Hill	
1776 Gibbon's *Decline and Fall*	1776 DECLARATION OF INDEPENDENCE	
Adam Smith's *Wealth of Nations*	1777 Saratoga	
1778 Chatham *d.*	1778-83 Maritime War	1778 Voltaire *d.*
1780 Gordon Riots		1780 Empress Maria Theresa *d.*
Irish Commercial laws repealed	1781 Surrender of Yorktown	
1782 North resigns	1782 'Battle of the Saints' (Rodney)	

IV

THE AGE OF WESLEY AND DR JOHNSON

1. The Writers

ENGLAND in the 18th century was a land of strange contrasts; and if we look at it through the eyes of the men whose names stand at the head of this chapter we shall see two very different worlds. Paradoxically enough, Johnson, who was uncouth in manners and appearance, moved in a highly cultivated society; Wesley, who was a man of far greater polish than Johnson, passed most of his long life in scenes of squalor and human suffering. Let us glance first at Dr Johnson's England.

The reigns of Anne and the first three Georges, which fill the 18th century, were notable for a remarkable growth in both the power and the volume of the printed word. At the death of George I there were three daily and five weekly newspapers in London, and by the middle of the century every important provincial town had its local newspaper. *The Gentleman's Magazine*, for long a most popular weekly publication, first appeared in 1731. 'The people of Great Britain,' said a writer in 1738, 'are governed by a power that never was heard of as a supreme authority in any age or country before. It is the government of the Press. The sentiments of these scribblers have more weight with the multitude than the opinion of the best politician in the kingdom.'

The Power of the Press

This, it must be remembered, was written years before the art of reading was a universal accomplishment.

The reading public, however, was growing. The great writers of Queen Anne's day – Addison, Swift, and Defoe – still flourished in the reign of her successor and their works achieved immense popularity. Defoe's *Robinson Crusoe*, which appeared in 1719, is one of the most widely read works of fiction in the English language. Few

Robinson Crusoe and Gulliver's Travels

SAMUEL JOHNSON (1709-84)
(1775 portrait by Joshua Reynolds)

writers have excelled Defoe in power of realistic description – for example in the account of the discovery of the footprint in the sand, or in Crusoe's first meeting with Man Friday. Swift's *Gulliver's Travels*, like *Crusoe*, is a tale of adventure; and, though it was intended as a satire on English society, it may be read with pleasure as a good story.

The 18th century saw also the birth of the English novel. *Pamela*, which was published in 1740, was written by Samuel Richardson, a middle-aged printer, and took the form of letters supposed to be written by a servant-girl. The success of *Pamela* led to the publication of *Clarissa Harlowe*, by the same author, in eight solid volumes. Another novelist whose work is still read today was Laurence Sterne, a clergyman, who described life in Yorkshire in *Tristram Shandy*, published from 1760 onwards. Nearly twenty years earlier, Henry Fielding, a barrister, had written *Joseph Andrews*, a novel which was shortly followed by his masterpiece, *Tom Jones*. In *Tom Jones* the life of the 18th century is vividly evoked; his Squire Western is an amusing caricature – the full-blooded, foul-mouthed country squire, who passed his days in hunting and his nights in drinking. For a more sober picture of country life we can turn to Oliver Goldsmith's *Vicar of Wakefield*, which appeared twenty years later. Goldsmith's story is written with a desire to improve the mind; but it has neither the fire nor the artistic merit of *Tom Jones*. Goldsmith was also the author of a famous comedy, *She Stoops to Conquer.* A later playwright, whose works (e.g. *The School for Scandal*) are still performed, was Richard Sheridan, who portrayed the doings of polite society, with its interminable chatter and its preoccupation with trifles.

The English Novel

Tom Jones

The Vicar of Wakefield

Goldsmith and Sheridan

In the 18th century the civilization of ancient Greece and Rome was very much admired and ancient models had a powerful influence on many of the arts. The earlier 18th century is often called the Augustan age, implying a similarity with the culture of the age of Augustus in ancient Rome. This classical influence is reflected in the poetry of the age, especially in the writings of Alexander Pope (1688-1744, Pope was the arbiter of English taste for many years. His translation of Homer was widely read and his *Essay on Man* contains some of the best-known epigrams in the English language, such as 'Hope springs eternal in the human breast' or 'the proper study of mankind is man'. Pope wrote in the heroic couplet, a regular, formal metre which exactly suited his style. He valued wit highly, and like other writers of his age he frequently wrote parodies and satires. In his day, his work defined what poetry was. 'If Pope be not a poet,'

Pope
Gray and
Burns

said Dr Johnson, 'where is poetry to be found?' The remainder of the century – until the French Revolution – was much dominated by Pope's influence. Thomas Gray (1716-71) is famous largely for a single poem, his *Elegy in a Country Churchyard*. It owed much to his reading in the classics, but also shows an appreciaton of the picturesque which characterized the later 18th century.

Gibbon

The second half of the century produced the greatest historian who has ever written in the English language. Edward Gibbon (1737-94) was born at Putney of well-to-do parents; his comments on his parentage (in his *Autobiography*) are highly characteristic of the man and of the age: 'My lot might have been that of a slave, a savage or a peasant; nor can I reflect without pleasure on the bounty of Nature, which cast my birth in a free and civilized country, in an age of science and philosophy, in a family of honourable rank, and decently endowed with the gifts of fortune.' He was a precocious boy,

Gibbon at
Oxford

and his prodigious learning was the result of his own exertions. The fourteen months which he spent at Magdalen College, Oxford (aged 15), he described as 'the most idle and unprofitable of my whole life'. He gave a devastating, though perhaps exaggerated, account of the life of the Magdalen dons – 'decent easy men, who supinely enjoyed the gifts of the founder; their days were filled by a series of uniform employments; the chapel and the hall, the coffee-house and the common room; till they retired, weary and well satisfied, to a long slumber. From the toil of reading, or thinking, or writing, they had absolved their conscience.' Gibbon's own life was the opposite of all this. He was a born scholar, and read widely in Greek, Latin, French, and English authors. Though some have quarrelled with his prejudices, no one has ever questioned the soundness of his learning,

*The Decline
and Fall of the
Roman
Empire*

which, considering the vast scale of his work, was stupendous. His great book, *The Decline and Fall of the Roman Empire* (published in 1776) covers thirteen centuries of European history, from the Age of the Antonines (c. AD 150) to the fall of Constantinople in 1453. Gibbon was one of the greatest masters of the English language. His incomparable style must be studied to be appreciated; his grand prose seems to march on from page to page, from chapter to chapter, like the conquering armies of the Romans he so much admired.

Another famous product of the age was Samuel Johnson (1709-84). Johnson had not the advantage, which Gibbon notes with so much satisfaction, of being born of wealthy parents. His father was a struggling Lichfield bookseller, and though Samuel was sent to Pembroke College, Oxford, he had to leave without taking a degree; his father died in poverty shortly afterwards. Johnson, after teaching at a private school, went to London to seek his fortune, and scraped a living as a journalist. Among other employments, he wrote the account of the Parliamentary debates for the *Gentleman's Magazine*. When he was nearly forty, he was commissioned to write a Dictionary, the publication of which brought him fame.

In his later middle age and old age, Johnson was the centre of an admiring literary circle in London. His immense learning, his scathing wit, and his downright judgments on every subject under the sun, made him the best-known character in town. His extraordinary personality still lives in the pages of Boswell's *Life of Johnson*. This biography contains not only the most minute account of the sayings and doings of one man ever written, but also gives a faithful picture of that 18th century London society in which the Doctor lived. Boswell was consumed with a passion for noting down the sayings of the great; his enormous industry has made the figure of Dr Johnson one of the most familiar in our literature. The brilliant pen-picture which Macaulay painted of the Doctor was derived from a reading of Boswell. Everything about Johnson, wrote Macaulay in the 19th century, is familiar to us –

'his coat, his wig, his figure, his face, his St Vitus' Dance, his rolling walk, his blinking eye, the outward signs which too clearly marked his approbation of his dinner ... his inextinguishable thirst for tea, his trick of touching the posts as he walked, his

Dr Samuel Johnson (1709-84)

Boswell's Life of Johnson

Description of Dr Johnson

mysterious practice of treasuring up scraps of orange peel, his morning slumbers, his midnight disputations, his gruntings, his puffings, his vehemence, his insolence, his fits of tempestuous rage.'

No man was so hardy as to dispute with the Doctor when he was roused – or woe betide him! One Sir Adam Ferguson ventured to express the opinion that in English politics it was important to preserve a balance against the Crown. The Doctor, who was a strong Tory, settled the matter at once. 'Sir,' he said, 'I perceive you are a vile Whig. Why all this childish jealousy of the power of the Crown? The Crown has not power enough!'

2. The Arts and the World of Fashion

The Country Gentleman

Fielding, in *Tom Jones*, drew a picture of the coarse-minded country squire, which has often been taken as typical of the 18th century. But the hunting squire, who was drunk every night of the week, was after all but an amusing stereotype. The personal papers of hundreds of gentry families show that most were literate, educated and civilized. A good many country gentlemen passed their time in cultured pursuits, and spent their money collecting books, pictures, and furniture. The wealthiest members of the landed class engaged in conspicuous consumption on a grand scale. They were the people who built the country mansions of Georgian England, laid out parks and gardens, had pictures painted and ordered fine furnishings. This is the age, not only of Dr Johnson, but of Robert Adam, Capability Brown, Thomas Gainsborough, Josiah Wedgwood, and Thomas Chippendale.

Architecture

Sir Christopher Wren died in 1723; Renaissance architecture, which he had done so much to popularize, was the favourite style in England for another hundred years. The most influential architects of the early 18th century were Sir John Vanbrugh, who designed

Blenheim Palace as a residence for the Duke of Marlborough; and Nicholas Hawksmoor, who built the quadrangle of Queen's College, Oxford, one of the chief ornaments of the famous High Street. Their showy and imaginative adaptations of classical architecture were superseded in the 1720s by a more restrained and austere style based on the work of the 16th century Venetian architect Palladio. A good example of this style is Holkham Hall in Norfolk, designed by William Kent. By the 1760s and 1770s the Adam brothers were the most fashionable architects and interior designers. They drew on a much wider range of sources for their interpretation of classical architecture and rejected rigid rules, seeking always to put their personal stamp on buildings. Their output was prodigious. Two of the grandest examples are Syon House and Osterley Park, both to the west of London. The 18th century was not simply a great age of the country house. It was also an era of town planning. Bath is perhaps the best example. John Wood senior set about the building of the city on Palladian lines in the period 1729-36, when he completed Queen Square. He and his son, also called John Wood, went on to design the public buildings, the Circus and the Royal Crescent.

The Adam Brothers

Bath

Gardening

The 18th century was a great age for gardening, and during it many of England's beautiful parks were laid out; thousands of acres, too, of new forests were planted. In gardening, we may distinguish two main periods. In the first, the formal garden, which was much in favour under William III (and so is often called the Dutch garden), took pride of place. Trees were carved into fantastic shapes, masses of yew or box were tidily clipped and arranged in symmetrical patterns, and the flower-beds were laid out in geometrical designs. This formal style, however, gave way to a novel type of landscape gardening. Now sculptured hedges and neat walks were discarded. Nature was all the rage, and instead of contrasting an ordered garden with raw nature, the landscape-gardener aimed to let the garden shade imperceptibly into its natural surroundings. Defoe, describing

The Dutch Garden

Landscape Gardening

in his *Tour through the Whole Island of Great Britain* of 1724-7 the garden of a great house he saw in Essex, wrote: 'The Walks and Wilderness go to such Distance, and in such a Manner, up to the Hill, that the Sight is lost in the Woods adjoining, and it looks all like one continued planted Garden, as far as the Eye can reach.' The 'English garden' originated early in the century, when William Kent created the first ones and Charles Bridgeman invented the ha-ha, which allowed the garden boundary to disappear and the landscape beyond to be an extension of the garden. Capability Brown transformed enormous numbers of parks in the third quarter of the century, when the serpentine lake became an essential feature. Pope had written: 'All garden is landscape-painting. Just like a landscape hung up.' Perhaps the best illustration of this idea is the park at Stourhead in Wiltshire, where the landscaped grounds, with artfully placed temples, look like a picture by Claude Lorrain.

Furniture Inside the houses, the taste of the owners was equally in evidence. This was the period of the great furniture-makers, Chippendale, Hepplewhite, and Sheraton (1751-1806). Chippendale, who worked largely in mahogany (a wood imported from the Spanish West Indies), relied on the natural beauty of the wood; Sheraton inlaid the mahogany with satinwood, tulip wood, and even brass. The carving of the chairs, tables, and cabinets turned out by these great masters of their art was always of the most careful workmanship.

Pottery Another art which flourished in 18th-century England was
Wedgwood pottery making. The potteries at Derby, Worcester, and Chelsea were
(1730-95) all founded about this time, while in Staffordshire Josiah Wedgwood, greatest of all English potters, set up his famous foundry. His most typical pottery was decorated with designs in white, standing out against a plain background, usually blue. Much of his output was aimed at a sophisticated audience: as a result, decorative details and figurative motifs were often classical in inspiration.

Painting Like the English Renaissance in architecture, the classical school of English painting developed much later than its counterpart on the

MARRIAGE *À LA MODE*
In the third of Hogarth's famous series of pictures the husband visits a disreputable doctor to demand a refund for the mercury pills he has been sold to cure his syphilis. Beside him a young prostitute dabs at an open sore on her mouth, an early sign of the disease.

continent. The most famous portraits in Stuart times were painted by men from the Low Countries, such as Van Dyck and Sir Peter Lely. But in the 18th century a school of native English painters arose, of whom Hogarth was the forerunner. Hogarth painted, or rather caricatured, the life of the common people whom he saw around him, as in his 'Gin Lane,' in which he portrayed the ravages of the craze among the poor for drinking gin. His pictures often formed a series, intended to point a moral, as in 'Rake's Progress', the story of a wealthy young man who devotes his life to fashionable vices

Hogarth (1697-1764)

and sinks into ruin, and 'Marriage *à la Mode*', which tells of the disastrous outcome of a loveless marriage entered into for financial and social reasons. Hogarth had hoped for the foundation of an English school of painting and his hopes were fulfilled with the success of a series of portrait painters, such as Reynolds, Gainsborough, and Romney. To assist the progress of English art, the Royal Academy was founded in 1768 and Sir Joshua Reynolds became its first President. In the 18th century painters made their livings primarily by painting portraits, but Gainsborough also painted landscapes, often for his own amusement.

The 18th century was not a great period for native musical composers. Much the most famous composer working in England during this era was George Frederick Handel, who made Britain his home for nearly half a century. He came to England in 1710, and helped to introduce the Italian opera into London. He won the favour of the new King by composing his *Water Music* for a royal procession along the Thames. After this, he dominated the English opera scene, but his popularity was entirely eclipsed by the immense success of *The Beggar's Opera* of 1728, with lyrics by John Gay. Eventually, Handel turned from opera to choral work. His most famous work in this medium is an oratorio. Handel's *Messiah* (first performed in Dublin in 1742) is probably still the best-known choral work in the British Isles.

The English stage underwent considerable changes in the 18th century. In the first place, it was now patronized by polite society and no longer regarded as fit only for the amusement of vulgar and immoral persons. The artificial comedies of Goldsmith and Sheridan filled the London theatres. Perhaps the most significant development of the century was the revival of Shakespeare. In the preceding century it had been the fashion to rewrite Shakespeare's plays and present them under other names; thus, the *Merchant of Venice* became the *Jew of Venice*, and the *Merry Wives* was rewritten as the *Comical Gallant*. In the 18th century there was a reaction against this custom;

Marginal notes (left column): Reynolds; Music; Handel; Gay; The Stage; Revival of Shakespeare in 1740 *As You Like It* was produced in London for the first time for forty years; next year the *Merchant of Venice* was performed in its original form for the first time for a century. The Shakespearian revival was linked to English patriotism: there was a felt need for a heroic figure in the history of English literature. In 1765 Dr Johnson published his *Shakespeare*, defending Shakespeare's dramatic technique, which had been criticized by foreigners such as Voltaire. Above all, it was the great actor David Garrick who restored Shakespeare to the centre of the English stage. His performance as Richard III convinced spectators that they had seen the greatest English actor in a great English drama. It was Garrick who instituted the Shakespearian Festival at Stratford-on-Avon in 1769 and set going the modern Shakespeare industry. Later in the century Sarah Siddons, a beautiful and accomplished actress, made her contribution: her most famous part was Lady Macbeth.

Garrick (1717-79)

No one living in the 18th century supposed that his contemporaries were all high-minded consumers of the arts. Moralists found much in their society that was reprehensible. There were plenty of clubs in London where men could lose a fortune gambling. By 1770 record losses were recorded, as much as £15,000 in an evening. Cricket and horse-racing throve partly because people bet on the results. The fashion for duelling was another aristocratic vice which moralists frequently criticized. It was considered vital to vindicate one's personal honour, if necessary by means of a duel and juries would rarely convict of murder even the most notorious duellist. Absurd and extravagant fashions attracted some wealthy young men, labelled 'macaronis'. The original macaronis were enthusiasts for Italian culture who wished to offend the stuffy insularity of their fathers' generation. The term came to be applied to anyone guilty of foolish excess, such as delicate hair-dos which suggested affectation and effeminacy.

Gambling

Perhaps it is easiest to imagine 18th century polite society at Bath, where so much of the architectural context survives. We might

Bath

imagine the town under the long reign of Beau Nash, king of Fashion, who ruled supreme in the Pump Room and the Assembly Rooms. There a rigid etiquette governed the entire proceedings; there fortunes were won and lost, heiresses wooed, marriages made and unmade. The tune of the stately gavotte fills the ball-room; the white-wigged dancers move sedately to their places; the candles shine on the lovely dresses, the gay silks and satins of men and women. It is all very beautiful, very dignified and very artificial. Nothing was ever allowed to disturb the tranquillity of this world of wigs and powdered faces, of dancing and music and good wine. Such is how we imagine 18th century Bath, but outside the Pump Room and the Assembly Rooms were the 35,000 inhabitants of the town, most of them plebeians. Even in Bath, it was hard to ignore those who were not part of polite society.

3. The Methodist Revival

The history of the Methodist Revival, in the reigns of George II and George III, reveals a startling contrast with the picture of England outlined in the preceding pages. When John Wesley visited the west of England, he did not go, like most well-to-do persons, to the Pump Rooms at Bath; he went to preach to the colliers of Kingswood, near Bristol, and to the tinners of the Cornish mines.

Wesley's approach to religion was not unique in his era. An evangelical movement within the Church had already begun. This movement aimed to promote a 'vital' religion, appealing to the emotions and firmly based on the New Testament. Men such as Henry Venn, Vicar of Huddersfield, acquired a reputation for preaching to great multitudes, and Samuel Walker of Truro took the lead in a Cornish awakening. The most obvious difference between these men and Wesley was that they worked within the parish-based organization of the church of England, whereas he assumed no responsibility for a parish and was able therefore to work on the

JOHN WESLEY (1703-91)
(1789 portrait by George Romney)

national scale and eventually set up a national organization.

John Wesley (1703-91) was the second surviving son of the Reverend Samuel Wesley, Vicar of Epworth in Lincolnshire. He was educated at Charterhouse and at Oxford, where he was ordained, and became a Fellow of Lincoln College. While at Oxford, he began the habit of early rising, which he kept up till extreme old age; Wesley's day began at four in the morning. He and his brother Charles, who was at Oxford with him, were regular attendants at a

John Wesley
(1703-91)

Wesley at
Oxford

certain religious society in the University. It was this society which received the college nickname of Methodist – a name which Wesley afterwards adopted for his own societies. He was later to define a Methodist as 'one that lives according to the method laid down in the Bible'. In 1735 John Wesley accepted General Oglethorpe's invitation to lead a mission to his newly founded colony of Georgia. The visit was not a success, for Wesley quarrelled with many of the colonists and returned to England a disappointed man.

Wesley's
Conversion
1738

On his arrival in England (1737) he settled in London, where he again came under the influence of the religious societies. It was now that he embraced the doctrine of 'Justification by Faith', and he believed that no man's life or actions were of any value unless he had a lively sense that all his sins had been forgiven by Christ. About this time the first Methodist societies were formed in London. The members used to hold long meetings, sometimes lasting all night, and performed orgies of religious devotion, scarcely surpassed in the times of mediaeval monastic revival.

Origin of the
Methodist
Movement

In conjunction with his brother Charles, and another remarkable man named George Whitefield, Wesley now began a missionary crusade in England and Wales, which was destined to transform the life of the nation. The founders of the movement not only preached all over the country themselves, but sent out field-preachers, often laymen, on a similar mission. Both Wesley and Whitefield preached in the open air – for the doors of the churches were closed to them – to enormous congregations, sometimes numbering 30,000 or 40,000 people. Wesley himself always remained a member of the Church of England; but, by the end of his life, his movement had assumed such large proportions, and was conducted on lines so dissimilar from the Established Church, that a separation was inevitable.

George
Whitefield
His
Preaching

Two things contributed largely to the success of both Wesley and Whitefield: their extraordinary energy, and their remarkable powers as preachers. In the latter respect, George Whitefield surpassed Wesley; he was perhaps the most astonishing preacher who had been heard in Europe since the days of the first Friars. The effect of his sermons was amazing; he often caused a large proportion of his congregation to burst out weeping; some even fell to the ground in an agony of remorse. He himself rarely preached without being affected by tears. To these semi-hypnotic powers he added all the arts of a great actor. On one occasion, he likened the state of an unconverted sinner to that of an old blind man, tottering towards the edge of a precipice. So realistic was the description, that when the preacher came to the point where the old man falls over the edge of the cliff, Lord Chesterfield, who was listening, called out in alarm, 'Good God! He is gone!'

Though Wesley was not Whitefield's equal as a preacher, yet his sermons were attended by thousands of persons a year, and were often accompanied by the same exhibitions of religious fervour as those of Whitefield. In the course of his missionary journeys Wesley travelled thousands of miles a year on horseback, and kept up this remarkable record for nearly half a century, till he was well over eighty. His main centres were London and Bristol. He made one long journey to the west of England nearly every year, and at least one to the north; two of his chief centres were Newcastle-on-Tyne and St Ives in Cornwall. Besides these long journeys, lasting several months, he made several shorter ones – e.g. from London to Bristol and back – in the course of every year. Wesley's influence was spread not only by his preaching,

Wesley's Journeys

[1] Two consecutive years may be taken as examples: 1744: (Jan.) London, Bristol. (Mar.-Apr.) Cornwall, Somerset, S. Wales. (May-June) Bristol, Staffs., Epworth, Yorkshire, Newcastle, Durham, Lancs., Cheshire, London. (July) Bristol. (Aug.) Oxford, Bristol, London. (Nov.) Bath, Bristol. 1745: (Jan.) Bristol. (Feb.-Apr.) Notts., Durham, Newcastle, Yorks, Derbyshire, Wednesbury, Oxford, London. (June-Aug.) Bristol, Cornwall, S. Wales. (Sept.-Nov.) Newcastle, Sheffield, Leeds, Epworth, Newcastle, Yorks, Cheshire, Birmingham, London. (See Wesley's *Journal.*)

but also by his writing and publishing, which were on a large scale.[1]

Attitude of the Clergy

The reception given to the early Methodists by the clergy of the Established Church was often an extremely hostile one. They were outraged that any man, particularly any clergyman, should presume

Their dislike of 'Enthusiasm'

to employ the method of field-preaching, send out lay preachers and attract the poor and ignorant to hear sermons preached in the style of St Francis or Peter the Hermit. The English clergy were, on the whole, a quiet body of men, fond of their libraries and their gardens; but they confined their preaching activities to one weekly sermon. Worthy men though they were in many ways, many of the clergy were devoid of religious zeal, and they hated nothing so much as the 'enthusiasm' (i.e. fanaticism) of the Methodists. Wesley's mission was, like that of the first disciples, to preach the Gospel of Christ to every creature. He acted, over large districts of England and Wales, as if the people were neglected by those whose duty it was to instruct them and the clergy did not enjoy the implied reproach to their ministry. Methodist preachers also had to eke out a living on the pennies that their followers could afford and this too seemed to imply a criticism of the often well-to-do parish clergy whose income came from the compulsory levy of the tithe. It is not surprising that the clergy often raged at his success and sometimes let loose hostile mobs

Mob Violence

upon him.

Charles Wesley

The mobs did not always need encouragement to attack the Methodists. Their attacks on popular pleasures were often resented. The two Wesleys and their followers had to face the most violent persecution during the first few years of their ministry. At Wednesbury and Darlaston, in Staffordshire, terrible scenes were witnessed. At Darlaston the mob broke into a Methodist's house and carried away all his goods; 'not satisfied with this, they sought for him and his wife, swearing they would knock their brains out. Their little children meanwhile wandered up and down, no one daring to relieve or take them in, lest they should hazard their own lives.' At Birmingham the houses of all the Methodists were attacked. 'They first broke all their windows, suffering neither glass, lead nor frames to remain therein. Then they made their way in; and all the tables, chairs, chests of drawers . . . they dashed in pieces . . . What they could not well break, as feather beds, they cut in pieces, and strewed about the room.' At St Ives, in Cornwall, Charles Wesley had just begun to preach, when a mob broke into the meeting-house. They broke up everything, windows, shutters, benches, poor-box – all but the stone walls. At Towednack, near by, 'they assaulted us [says Charles Wesley] with sticks and stones and endeavoured to pull me down. I bade them strike me and spare the people. Many lifted up their hands and weapons, but were not permitted to touch me. My time is not yet come.'

Courage of the Wesleys

The courage with which the Wesleys faced these ordeals, however, eventually won them the respect of their enemies. And when it was established that the Methodists were neither political agitators, nor Papists, nor agents of the Pretender (the worst riots were in 1745), they were suffered to go in peace. After 1745 the persecution died down, and the new movement grew in strength from year to year.

Condition of the Poor

It is time to consider the condition of English society which the work of the Wesleys revealed. It is not too much to say that large sections of the people were living in conditions of hardship, such danger and discomfort, and even of such absolute bestiality as cannot now be easily conceived. The Cornish tinners, for example, among whom Wesley preached for fifty years, worked underground, 'with hardly any room to turn their bodies, wet to the skin . . . by the glimmering of a small candle, whose scattered rays will barely penetrate the thick darkness of the place'.[2] A doctor who worked among these miners saw his patient conveyed to a hut 'full of naked children . . . destitute of all conveniences, and almost of all necessities. The whole, indeed, is a scene of such complicated wretchedness and

[2] Clarke, *Tour through South England*, 1791.
[3] Pryce, *Mineralogia Cornubiensis*, 1778.

distress as words have no power to describe.'[3]

Civilizing influence of Methodism

The moral condition of such people was as deplorable as their physical state. Drunkenness was common in every village. Brutal sports, such as cock-fighting and bear-baiting, were usual, and 'games' of football, played in the village streets, were bloody encounters between half-savage men, who kicked and hacked at one another like wild beasts. Boxing matches between women attracted large crowds. This, too, was the heyday of smuggling, and of the even more pernicious practice of 'wrecking', which was especially prevalent on our western shores. Poor sailors wrecked on the English coast, and seeking help, found 'the Rocks themselves not more merciless than the People who range about them for Prey'. The wreckers used to murder the sailors, break up the ships, and carry away what goods they could.

It is not easy to evaluate the results of the Methodist movement. When Wesley died in 1791, there were 57,000 members of the Wesleyan connection, but the expansion of the movement was still accelerating and many were influenced who never became members. It seems fair to say that Wesley and his preachers brought much of the mass of the people, formerly abandoned by polite society to their own barbarous habits, into contact with a more Christian and respectable way of life. Wesley forbade his followers to engage in the drunken or fighting orgies then common among the poorer classes; and the leaven which the Methodists thus introduced acted in time upon the whole community. 'These indefatigable men,' wrote a Church of England clergyman about the Methodists, 'have perseveringly taught, gradually reclaimed, and at length completely reformed, a large body of men, who, without their exertions, would still have been immersed in the deepest spiritual darkness, and the grossest moral turpitude.'[4]

The Evangelical Movement

The moral reformation which Wesley effected in England during

---

[4] Warner's *Tour*, 1800.

his lifetime did not cease at his death. The Evangelical Movement in the Church of England made headway at the same time. Many followers of John Wesley (like Wesley himself) could not bear to break with the Established Church, and remained within it. Many evangelicals were never followers of Wesley. One of the most significant results, both of Methodism and of the wider Evangelical movement, was the growth of a more humane spirit in English life, which led in time to the abolition of the Slave Trade, to Prison Reform, and to the ending of the crueler forms of 'amusement' in Britain.

Defects of Methodism

There is, however, another side to the picture. There was something harsh and uncompromising about John Wesley, as can be seen from his instructions to the school which he founded at Kingswood, Bristol. 'We have no play-day (he says), the school being taught every day in the year but Sunday, neither do we allow any time for play on any day; he that plays when he is a child will play when he is a man.' Again, Wesley set his face, not only against drunkenness and street-fighting, but against the most innocent amusements and recreations. He was thus in part responsible for the transformation of the Merry – too merry – England of the 18th century which he knew into the joyless England of the Victorian Sunday.

Wesley's School

V

THE CHANGE TO INDUSTRIAL ENGLAND

1. The Land and the Enclosures

Farming to
1700

ENGLAND in 1700 was still chiefly a land of villages; there were no big towns except London, which had well over half a million inhabitants, and agriculture was the occupation of the vast majority of the people. A large proportion of the arable land in England was still farmed on the old open-field system, which had endured from Saxon or earlier times. There were areas which had either never had open fields or had abandoned them and much of the land was there cut up into individual farms in the modern manner. But, in the midland counties, England presented what would be to us an unfamiliar picture: large open fields, without hedges or fences, surrounding each village. These open fields were divided among the villagers as they had been from time immemorial; the 'custom' of the village had decided the size and position of the 'strips' which each man owned. Since the fields were 'open,' individual peasants were tied into communal patterns of cultivation.

The Open-
Field System

Industry in
1700

Next in importance to agriculture came spinning and cloth-making, and that, too, was carried on in the country, where the people made home-spun woollen cloth in their own cottages. Defoe, writing his *Tour of Great Britain* in 1725, thus describes the wool industry under this system, as he saw it in Yorkshire:

'Though we met few people without doors, yet within we saw the houses full of lusty fellows, some at the dye-vat, some at the loom, others dressing the cloths; the women and children carding or spinning; all employed from the youngest to the oldest; scarce anything above four years old, but its hands were sufficient for its own support. Not a beggar to be seen nor an

idle person, except here and there in an almshouse built for
those that are ancient, and past working.'

Such, in brief, was rural England of 300 years ago. Two tremendous changes, both of which took place during the second half of the 18th century, altered this old England beyond all recognition. These two changes were the enclosure of the common fields and the coming of power-driven machinery. The former process destroyed the age-long system of strip-farming; the latter gradually destroyed the 'domestic' or household system, as applied to the cloth industry, as well as minor village industries, and substituted for these the factory system which still dominates British industry.

Two great changes

The enclosures of the 18th century were accompanied by a revolution in the methods of farming as they had been practised for centuries. Pioneers of scientific farming saw that the old methods were wasteful and inefficient and set about devising improvements. Among the pioneers was Jethro Tull, an Oxfordshire farmer, who in 1700 invented a machine for sowing seed, which took the place of the human sower, scattering seed from a basket. Tull's machine was called a drill, and he described it in these words: 'It makes the channels, sows the seeds into them, and covers them at the same time, with great exactness and precision.' Another agricultural improver was Lord Townshend, who retired from politics in 1730, and then till his death in 1738 devoted himself to farming on his Norfolk estate. 'Turnip' Townshend, as he was called, practised a rotation of crops, still known as the Norfolk or four-course system. Under the old system, the farmer had to allow one-third of his land to lie fallow each year, since the soil would not bear corn crops more than two years running. Townshend maintained that, by planting root crops (turnips and mangolds) and clover, all the land could always be kept under cultivation; and further that the planting of the turnips and clover had beneficial effects on the soil. Townshend's rotation of crops was: turnips; barley or oats; clover; wheat. This system not only had the

The Agricultural Revolution

Jethro Tull's Drill 1701

'Turnip' Townshend

New Rotation of Crops

effect of improving the land but provided winter food for cattle, which meant fresh meat throughout the winter. In fact, Townshend's practices were hardly new in Norfolk, which had long been a centre of progressive agriculture thanks to influences from nearby Holland. Townshend's main achievement was to publicize what he and his neighbours were doing. Another Norfolk man who did much to improve farming on his estates (from about 1776) was Coke of Holkham, but he too built upon half a century or more of careful estate management.

Sheep and Cattle

Robert Bakewell

Another sort of change was improvement in the breeding of sheep, cattle and horses. One of the best known men to apply himself to this subject was Robert Bakewell (1725-95) of Dishley in Leicestershire, whose first experiments were made with the longhorn breed of cattle. The shorthorns bred by Charles Colling of Ketton in County Durham, however, proved to be more successful as beef cattle. Bakewell also turned his attention to sheep, concentrating on producing meat rather than wool. Thanks to the experiments of Bakewell and many others, the average weight of sheep sold at Smithfield market almost tripled during the 18th century. Bakewell also turned his attention to breeding horses better capable of supplying traction for agricultural tasks. Horses began to replace oxen for jobs like ploughing in the midlands and south of England.

Arthur Young

Perhaps as important as the new techniques themselves was the great interest in agricultural improvement that developed in 18th century England. In 1768-71 Arthur Young published his accounts of a series of *Tours* round England. There he described and enthused over the agricultural advances which he had noted on his travels. Later he helped to found a board of agriculture which collected information and published reports, so helping to ensure that the new farming practices became widely known and adopted.

The traditional open field organization of agriculture was not readily compatible with the introduction of agricultural improvements. It was easier to experiment with crops if they were not grown in scattered strips and with animals if they did not mingle with the beasts of others on the common pasture. If the land were to be split up into consolidated, individually owned farms, farmers would have much more flexibility to farm as they wished. This process is known as enclosure and it had been proceeding for centuries. It could be brought about by mutual consent, but in the 18th century it was often carried out by means of a special Act of Parliament. This method enabled an obstinate minority of villagers to be coerced, though Parliament usually insisted that at least four-fifths of the property-owners affected should assent. Perhaps the main motive for using Acts of Parliament, though, was that everyone involved ended up with a watertight legal title to their land. Between 1702 and 1750, a few dozen such Acts were passed; between 1750 and 1810, close on 4,000. The process of parliamentary enclosure was expensive, but it was profitable: the rent of enclosed land was double that of unenclosed land. In George III's reign, there were two hectic periods of enclosure: the 1760s and 1770s and the war years 1792-1815. The enclosures of the 1760s and 70s were connected with the relatively high prices of agricultural products at a time when population was beginning to increase rapidly and the low interest rates, which together made investment in agriculture profitable. After 1793 food prices soared, partly because importation in wartime was often difficult, and there was a final spate of Acts of enclosure. In 1803 came the General Enclosure Act, which rendered the process of enclosure easier. Roughly, twenty per cent of the total acreage of England and Wales was affected by the Enclosure Acts. By 1815 only a very small proportion of the land was left unenclosed.

The need for Enclosure

Enclosure Acts

Enclosures were of two kinds: (*a*) enclosure of the common or waste, which was reclaimed for the plough, and (*b*) enclosure of the open (the fenceless) fields, by redistributing the land, i.e. splitting it up into modern farms, divided by hedges. The effects of enclosure, particularly in its second sense, were controversial at the time and have remained so. It does appear that the enclosure commissioners

Distress caused by Enclosure

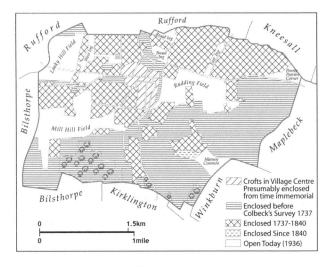

ENCLOSURES
The progress of Enclosure in England. The parish of Eakring, Nottinghamshire.

were scrupulously fair and that small owners of land were not
squeezed out by the expenses of enclosure, since their numbers seem
to have been maintained. Perhaps other developments were more
harmful to rural communities. Landowners tended to create larger
and therefore fewer farms to lease out to tenants on their estates, so
that the latter could enjoy economies of scale and pay higher rents.
There may therefore have been fewer opportunities for villagers to
become prosperous tenant farmers. There was certainly a trend for
farmers no longer to have their labourers living with them in their
family home. The farm workers became mere wage labourers whose
labour might be required only at busy times of the year and who
would suffer from seasonal unemployment. At the same time the
enclosure of the commons deprived such people of the right to graze
animals on the waste and to collect fuel. But we must not paint too

black a picture. The improved farming methods must often have increased the demand for labour. Marling and liming the soil, cultivating winter forage crops such as turnips, intensive hedging and ditching all required more workers, particularly at times of year when there had been little work in the past.

Yet contemporaries were certain that all was not well with English rural society. In 1770 Oliver Goldsmith published his poem *The Deserted Village*, in which he revisits the (fictional) village of Auburn and laments its decay. Once 'every rood of ground maintained its man', but money and progress have become more important than human values. He warns of the future.

'The Deserted Village'

Ill fares the land, to hast'ning ills a prey,
Where wealth accumulates and men decay;
Princes and lords may flourish, or may fade –
A breath can make them, as a breath has made –
But a bold peasantry, their country's pride
When once destroy'd can never be supplied.

The popularity of the poem showed that it struck a chord with the people of the time. Goldsmith's model for Auburn might have been Nuneham Courtenay, where the village was demolished and rebuilt out of sight of Earl Harcourt's house, so that, like Goldsmith's man of wealth and pride, he might have:

Space for his lake, his park's extended bounds
Space for his horses, equipage and hounds.

What was recalled as a sense of community between landowners and villagers seemed to have been replaced by separation and indifference. Landowners were too often absentees who preferred the selfish luxury of life in London, Bath or Brighton to paternalistic care of their tenantry. No doubt, the critics of 18th century landowners

WATT'S STEAM
ENGINE (1769)
Although steam engines
had already been in use for
many years, it was not
until James Watt improved
the design that they
became efficient enough to
be used in industry.

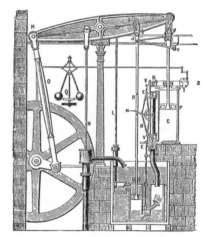

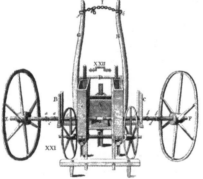

TULL'S SEED
DRILL (1701)
Jethro Tull's seed
planting drill improved
farming practices and
helped to usher in the
agricultural revolution.

HARGREAVES' SPINNING
JENNY (1764)
The spinning Jenny
drastically reduced the
amount of work required to
produce yarn, allowing yarn
production to keep up with
increased demand from
weavers whose productivity
had increased as a result of
John Kay's invention of the
flying shuttle in 1733.

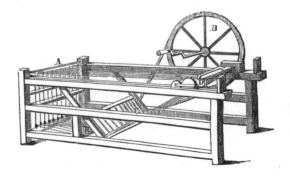

tended to exaggerate the virtues of their predecessors and to be over-influenced by notorious examples from their own time, but it seems impossible to dismiss their complaints altogether.

Writers like Goldsmith seem to have supposed that the countryside was becoming depopulated. This was certainly not the case. The main problem, especially in the countryside of southern England, was that the number of people was increasing much faster than the capacity of agriculture to supply them with jobs. As a result, there was a growing problem of unemployment and underemployment. In some areas, chiefly in the north, industrial employment had begun to increase and there the village poor began to migrate to the towns, where wages were higher. As they left, wages in the villages ceased to fall. In much of the south this did not happen, because the growing industrial areas were a long way off. Wages in town and country stayed low, because of the large reserves of labour. In short, the increase of population had a bigger impact on the countryside than the changes in agricultural techniques and organization.

2. The Coming of Machines

In the 18th century a change developed in the method and scale of industry more far-reaching in its effects than all the wars and politics of the period, for the coming of machinery meant that an entirely new phase was opening in the history of human occupations.

The
Industrial
'Revolution'

The England over which 'Farmer George' began to reign in 1760 was still, as we have seen, chiefly a land of farmers; and such small industries as were carried on also provided employment in the country. But, by the time George III died, this was irrevocably changed; the nation of farmers and village craftsmen had become also a nation of mechanics and factory 'hands'. For it was in Britain that the new machines had their first home; it was a few Britons who invented or applied them. The name 'Industrial Revolution' is usually given to this stupendous change; but it should be remembered that this change in industry was gradual, that it cannot be dated from any particular year, and that since the 18th century it has been spreading from Britain to all the countries of the world. The age of steam has been followed by the age of petrol and electricity; and we cannot tell what new scientific devices will, in as short a space of time, transform the lives of our descendants.

In this section we shall consider only the first phase of this Industrial 'Revolution'. The first inventions were applied to the old woollen industry, and to the new manufacture of cotton, which sprang up in south Lancashire. It was in 1733 that John Kay, a clockmaker of Bury, Lancashire, invented his 'flying shuttle', a mechanical device which enabled a single weaver to make cloth of a width which had required two men. Kay's invention met with opposition and suffered at first from mechanical difficulties, but came widely into use after 1760.

Kay's Shuttle 1733

Improved with Kay's shuttle, looms wove the cloth so fast that the spinners (still working on the old-fashioned spindle) could not keep pace with the demand for more cotton. Then in 1764 James Hargreaves invented the multiple spinning 'jenny', which made it possible for one spinner to work at first eight, and later a hundred, spindles. The 'jenny' was small, cheap to construct and did not require strength to operate. It fitted well into the domestic system of industry.

Hargreaves

Richard Arkwright was a barber and wig-maker of Preston in Lancashire. With the help of others, he developed the spinning frame by 1768. It produced a strong, if coarse, twist as opposed to the softer product of the jenny. The most important fact about Arkwright's machine was that it was too large to fit into a cottage and required more strength than human muscles could supply. The solution to these problems, as Arkwright at once realized, was to place a number of machines in a purpose-built construction and to find a natural source of power with which to run them. Hence Arkwright built a

Arkwright, Crompton

factory at Cromford in Derbyshire. The place is on the river Derwent and water power was used to turn a huge water wheel which in turn drove the spinning machinery. It is interesting that of all the inventors connected with the cotton industry only Arkwright made a fortune and was knighted. What made the difference was not his powers as an inventor, but his abilities as a businessman. A few years later Samuel Crompton, a Bolton man, developed the 'spinning mule', so called because it combined features of the frame and the jenny. It produced a finer thread than the frame and was much used to make muslins, which previously had been imported from the east. The effect of these inventions was to make cotton yarn vastly cheaper: in 1807 the price was one sixth of what it had been in 1786. As a result, many more people in Britain and outside it were able to purchase British cotton goods.

It was not till 1785 that one of Watt's steam engines (which we shall consider presently) was first used in a cotton mill, and even after that the number of water-powered factories continued to increase, partly because the vibration was less. As the output of spun yarn increased, more and more handloom weavers were required to weave it all. In 1784 Edmund Cartwright, a clergyman, invented a power loom, but its progress was very slow. Gradually, improvements were made, but by 1813 there were still only 2,400 power-looms in the country. Thereafter, their spread was rapid: by 1833, there were about 100,000 of them.

Once the cotton industry was freed from dependence on water power, which forced its location near swift flowing rivers, it became concentrated in Lancashire, especially round Manchester. There the cotton trade grew at an astonishing rate; and till the First World War Lancashire was destined to be the main supplier of machine-made cotton goods to the world. The figures for cotton imports give a useful measure of the growth of the industry: 8,000 tons were imported in 1760, 25,000 in 1800 and 300,000 in 1861. A combination of circumstances made the prosperity of Lancashire.

Lancashire Cotton Trade

The damp climate suited the cotton thread; Liverpool and the Mersey were convenient for importing raw cotton from America and exporting cotton goods to the whole world. There was an abundant supply of cheap labour, from Ireland as well as Lancashire itself. An old-established woollen industry was the stem from which the cotton industry developed. Finally, the south Lancashire coalfield was ready for use when steam power came to drive the wheels of the industry. The new inventions were also applied to the woollen industry, which did not, however, grow at so rapid a rate as the cotton. Woollen stuffs were not suitable for export to the tropics, one of the main markets for cottons; the old-established woollen trade was hampered by ancient government regulations, whereas the new cotton industry was not; and sheep could not be produced so quickly or in such large quantities as cotton plants.

Iron

There were also great developments in the coal and iron industries. The manufacture of iron had been carried on in England from early times. Iron is extracted from the ironstone (or iron ore) by heating the latter until the metal is separated from it. The heating agent used for centuries in this process had been wood charcoal; hence the first English ironworks were in Sussex, in the great Forest of Weald. But timber became scarce and production fell. Then came

Coke

the discovery that it was possible to turn coal into coke, and use it instead of charcoal in the smelting process.

Abraham Darby

The first man to use coke in furnaces was Abraham Darby (the elder), at Coalbrookdale in Shropshire (1709). His son, of the same name, improved on his father's methods, and by the middle of the century coke was used in all the various heating processes by which iron is refined and made fit for use. It was, however, not till after 1760 that knowledge of the Darbys' discoveries spread widely, to iron-producing centres in the midlands and south Yorkshire, for example. Even then the quality of the iron was not sufficient for many purposes and it took the technical improvements pioneered by Henry Cort in the 1780s finally to free the iron industry from dependence on wood. When it was free, the increase in the production of iron was startling; England in 1737 produced between 12,000 and 15,000 tons of iron; in 1806 over 250,000 tons. This revolution in the iron industry further encouraged the development of the coalfields – in which Britain was found to be singularly rich – in the Black Country, south Wales, south Yorkshire, south Lancashire, on Tyneside and Clydeside.

British Coalfields

Steam engines had for some time been used for pumping water out of coal mines. It was in 1776 that John Wilkinson, iron-master, first used the steam-engine for 'blowing' in blast furnaces; and soon steam power entirely took the place of water power in all the processes of the iron industry, and also eventually in the cotton industry. In fact the steam engine came to supply the motive power for all the industries which transformed England.

Steam power

The inventor of a practical and economical steam engine was James Watt, an instrument-maker of Glasgow. Watt was a cross-grained, melancholy man, who suffered from headaches; his workmen, when he had any, suffered from his bad temper. There had been steam engines before Watt's, but they were not very effective, because no one had thought of making what is called the 'separate condenser'. The secret of the steam engine is said to have occurred to Watt in 1765; he patented his invention four years later. But he had to wait some years longer, owing to lack of money, before he could make any use of his discovery. Then in 1775 he had the luck to be taken into partnership by an enterprising business man, Matthew Boulton, whose works were at Soho, near Birmingham. The partnership of Boulton and Watt was successful because Watt's inventive powers were sound, and his deficiencies as a business man – which were considerable – were more than made up by the capable Boulton. In addition, Boulton employed skilled craftsmen capable of making the valves and other delicate parts of the engine. From the day when 'Iron-mad' Wilkinson (1728-1808) tried one of Watt's engines in his blast furnace at Bilston (Staffs.), and found it satisfactory, all

James Watt

His Steam engine 1769

Boulton and Watt

went well. The original partners of the firm of Boulton and Watt continued in business for another quarter of a century, and made a large fortune. By 1800 the steam engine was being used in coal-mines, in iron furnaces, and in the textile industries.

3. Roads and Canals

The new industries powered by the machines could not have flourished under the old conditions of transport, which had endured for generations in England. But the coming of machinery coincided with improvements in the transport of goods; the production of coal, iron, and other heavy materials necessitated the making, first of canals (in the 18th century) and then of railways (in the 19th century). At the same time as the canals were made, the roads were improved.

Old English Roads

Packhorses

The great roads which the Romans built in this country were magnificent feats of early engineering; but fourteen centuries of neglect had considerably reduced their original excellence. During all that time no worthy successors of the Roman roads were built: pack-horses, using rough tracks, carried light goods and the mails; heavy traffic usually got stuck in the mud. Teams of pack-horses carried the wool down the Yorkshire dales to the Humber; even coal was so carried from Merthyr to Cardiff, until the making of a road down the Taff Vale in 1767. Heavy goods could be transported over long distances only by water. Coals had for centuries come from Newcastle to London by sea.

Turnpikes

Slow and unpleasant conditions of travel remained with little alteration till the middle of the 18th century. A beginning was indeed made earlier, in Charles II's time, with the institution of turnpike trusts, by which local authorities were empowered to erect toll gates, and repair the roads with the proceeds of the toll. But village activity did not go much beyond filling up an occasional pit in the highway; it was not till the 18th century that turnpike trusts

THE IMPROVEMENT OF ROAD TRANSPORT
The Hyde Park corner Turnpike in 1798. A waggon from the country, drawn
by six horses, is on the left, and a coach-and-four on the right.

THE AGE OF CANAL BUILDING
The Bridgewater Canal at Barton Bridge, where it is carried across the river Irwell.

were organized on a larger scale, and a real step forward in road-making was taken. The mid-century saw a turnpike mania, which by 1770 had created a dense network of roads built with improved materials and regularly maintained. The comfort and speed of ordinary travel were transformed. The age of the flying coach dawned. In 1754 one flying coach advertised its speed in the following terms: 'However incredible it may appear, this coach will actually (barring accidents) arrive in London in four days and a half after leaving Manchester.'

The 'Flying Coach' 1754

The 18th century produced three great road engineers: Metcalfe, Telford, and Macadam. Metcalfe (1717-1810), known as Blind Jack of Knaresborough, had lost his sight through smallpox at the age of six, yet he knew the wild moors of Yorkshire by heart. He designed many of the chief roads in Lancashire, Yorkshire, and Cheshire. Thomas Telford (1757-1834), a Scottish shepherd's son, built the Holyhead Road, and he excited the wonder of his contemporaries by constructing the iron suspension-bridge over the Menai Straits (opened 1826), at 1,000 feet the longest suspension bridge in the country.

Metcalfe Telford

It was John Loudon Macadam (1756-1836) who invented an entirely new process of road-making around 1810. It consisted in using small stones, which could be easily crushed (more easily after the invention of the steamroller) to form a hard yet fairly smooth surface;[1] 'no stone,' Macadam said, 'should be larger than the road-mender could put in his mouth'. Macadam's invention has been an immense boon to travellers, from the stagecoach users in 'good King George's golden days' to the modern motorist. It transformed travelling conditions; and in 1824 (the year before the first railway) the Manchester to London coach did the journey in twenty-four

Macadam Roads 1810

Coaching Days

---

[1] When tar-spraying was invented in the present century, the Macadam roads were given a new name – Tarmac.

hours. The days of the stagecoach in all its glory were, however, not long, for by the next generation railways had come to divert the main traffic into another channel. The coaching inns had to wait for the motor car before they saw a revival of their prosperity.

The improved roads were still unsuitable for long distance transport of bulk goods, because the sole means of traction was still the horse. Yet the industrializing economy was assisted by the improvement of the road system. The old postal service dependent upon post-boys riding in all weathers was replaced after 1784 by one using mail-coaches and gradually the price of sending letters dropped. It became easier to place orders for goods and to remit money to pay for them. Commercial travellers were better able to tour the country.

More essential to industrial development was the creation of the canal network. In the late 17th and early 18th century much had been done to improve river navigation by dredging and widening and as a result the navigable mileage of inland waterways had increased by more than fifty per cent. The canal age began at the end of George II's reign. The English canals were built chiefly for the transport of coal. The Duke of Bridgewater, who was a large colliery owner, employed James Brindley (1716-72), a brilliant engineer but an illiterate man, to build a canal between his coal mine at Worsley and Manchester. Bridgewater encountered much opposition in Parliament; as Brindley wrote: 'The Toores mad had agane ye Duk.'[2] But, when the canal opened in 1761, the cost of carrying goods between the two towns fell from 12s. to 6s. a ton. Encouraged by Bridgewater's success, canal companies immediately sprang up all over England. The Grand Trunk Canal linked Manchester and Hull with Birmingham and Bristol. Telford, the road engineer, built a number of canals in England and Wales; in his native country he

Canals

James Brindley

The Bridgewater Canal, 1761

---

[2] 'The Tories made head against the Duke.'

built the famous Caledonian Canal. Workmen employed in canal-making were known as 'navigators', from which we get the familiar word 'navvy'.

The Canal Age

The interval between the opening of the Bridgewater Canal in 1761 and the opening of the Stockton and Darlington Railway (the first railway) in 1825, was one of sixty-four years. During this period, which may be taken as the first phase of the Industrial Revolution, canals were the principal means of transport for coal, iron, and the products of the new industries, for they offered slow, but cheap carriage of bulk goods. The benefits were felt by country-dwellers as well as industry. Cheap carriage of fertilizers helped to make many agricultural areas productive. Cheap coal helped warm cottages where wood had become scarce and slate carried by canal roofed them. After the advent of the railway, the canal, like its contemporary the stagecoach, was overshadowed by the latest application of Watt's invention – the steam locomotive.

4. The New Towns

The Population of England and Wales

The change from the old to the new England coincided with a remarkable increase in the population. The number of people living in England and Wales at the accession of George III in 1760 was about 7 millions. In the sixty years of George III's reign, the population of England and Wales nearly doubled; it was 12 millions in 1821.[3] This increase was continued during the 19th century; the population was more than trebled during the hundred years 1821-1921, being 40 millions in the latter year. All the reasons for these remarkable increases are not clear, but it seems probable that the rise

---

[3] In 1801 the first Census was taken; the Census has been taken at ten-year intervals since then except in 1941. Estimates of population before 1801 are, of course, not very accurate.

in population in the later 18th century helped to bring about the industrial changes by providing labour for the new industries and consumers for their products. Industrialization then made possible further population growth by providing jobs for greater numbers of people. It is likely too that the new urban workers married earlier and had larger families than had been customary under the old conditions of rural life, since they did not have to wait to inherit land from their fathers before they could marry.

This new urban population grew up in the industrial districts, which were themselves the products of the new industries. East Anglia and the Cotswolds, earlier centres of the wool trade, lacked coalfields, and soon became pleasant old-world backwaters. Norwich, which for centuries had been the third largest town in England, after London and Bristol, had sunk to the tenth place by 1801. In 1700 only Norwich and Bristol had over 20,000 inhabitants, but by 1801 such places as Birmingham, Glasgow, Manchester, Liverpool and Leeds had all grown to be huge, sprawling cities of over 50,000 people, far bigger than anything the old Britain had known (except London). All the cities mentioned were close to coalfields and became ideal locations for factories once the latter shifted from water power to steam power. The cities drew in population mainly from their own rural hinterlands and only to a small extent from the south of England. *The New Towns*

This new industrial Britain first came into existence during that remarkable half-century in which Britain lost the thirteen American colonies and helped to defeat Napoleon. The statesmen who governed Britain during that time had small conception of the fact that a revolution in the way of life of mankind was taking place before their eyes. Still less did they at first believe that it was their duty to regulate the change, or to mitigate its evils. The result was much suffering for their own generation and difficult problems for their successors. The problems passed on from that period were, broadly speaking, two: the slums and the relations between capital and labour. *Attitude of Statesmen to the Industrial Revolution* *Two Problems*

Most Populous Areas

Newcastle

COAL

York

WEST RIDING
CLOTH TRADE

Leeds

Liverpool

Manchester

Chester

Nottingham

Shrewsbury

Norwich

Coventry

EAST ANGLIAN
CLOTH TRADE

Kidderminster

Cambridge

Worcester

Gloucester

IRON

Oxford

Bristol

London

WEST COUNTRY
CLOTH TRADE

Taunton

Portsmouth

IRON

Dover

Exeter

CORNISH
TIN MINES

Plymouth

Falmouth

0   100km

0   100miles

ENGLAND BEFORE
THE INDUSTRIAL
REVOLUTION, 1730

The towns of the Industrial Revolution, it has been said, were 'barracks for cheap labour, not homes for citizens'. Their first radical defect was that they were planless; large cities were allowed to grow up haphazard and uncontrolled. Secondly, in the first and vital stage of the Industrial Revolution, there were no sanitation laws; consequently the jerry-builder could work his will. Houses for the workers had to be built as quickly and cheaply as possible. So built they were, sometimes back to back, sometimes without sanitation, lacking light, lacking air, often lacking decency, and always in long, dreary rows of brick and slate. The slum, it should be noted, was no new thing; slums had existed since the Middle Ages and slums existed in the 19th century in towns untouched by industrialization, such as Windsor. It was the vast scale of this jerry-building that was new.

The New Industrial Towns

Lack of Plan and Sanitation

MAP OF
INDUSTRIAL
BRITAIN, 1930

One problem resulting from housing vast populations in this
manner was the physical threat to their health. This was most
obviously true when epidemics struck, especially outbreaks of
cholera, which occurred every few years in the 19th century as a result
of poor sanitation. Endemic in these areas were diseases such as
typhus and tuberculosis which contributed to the high death rate. In
the early 19th century a labourer in rural Rutland could expect to live
to the age of 38, but a labourer in Manchester lived on average till he
was 17. A second problem was the geographical separation of classes
in the growing towns. Merchants and manufacturers tended to move
away from the noise and smoke of the factories into detached villas
with gardens on the edge of the growing cities. The middle class
flight to the suburbs was noted in Manchester as early as 1795 and

by 1842 it could be said: 'There is no town in the world where the distance between the rich and the poor is so great, or the barrier between them so difficult to be crossed.' No doubt, there would have been a gulf between the classes even had they lived together, but physical segregation made the gulf wider still. Contemporaries were convinced that the growth of the industrial towns had also produced crime and prostitution on a huge scale. The problem of crime reflected in part the failure before the 1830s to develop means of policing appropriate to the new industrial towns.

It is perhaps curious that many people were complacent about the industrial society that was coming into being. Macaulay, who lived in the first half of the 19th century, is typical of his generation in praising the advance in Man's command over Nature; but he was blind to the fact that the chief sufferer in the process was his fellow man. 'Nowhere,' he writes, 'are manufactures carried to such perfection (as in England). Nowhere does man exercise such a dominion over matter.' Again, Wilberforce, in the House of Commons in 1806, described the industrial districts of Scotland and south Wales as places which 'Nature seemed to have doomed to perpetual sterility', but which were now 'covered by the fruits of human industry, and gladdened by the face of man'. Yet complacency was far from universal. From the time when the population of the industrial towns started growing explosively, that is to say from the 1820s, there was no lack of commentators to lament the consequences. William Cobbett published his *Rural Rides* in 1830: he lost no opportunity to lash out at the malign influence of the growing towns. The school inspector Joseph Fletcher, writing in 1847, criticized industrialism for 'its smoke, its dirt, its bustle, its deformation of the face of nature, and the independent rudeness of its millions'. The towns, he claimed, were 'purely places in which to work and make money, not to be at rest and enjoy it'.

5. Laissez-faire

The industrial revolution of the late 18th and early 19th century also bequeathed to later periods problems concerning the relations of capital and labour, between employers and their employees. In the era when the Industrial Revolution began, the dominant idea governing these relations was *laissez-faire*.

Machinery was introduced into industry and steam power was used to drive it, because manufacturers expected to sell large quantities of the products which they would be able to manufacture more cheaply. It is therefore not surprising that the age of mechanical invention and steam power coincided with a huge expansion of British trade. The fall of the old mercantile empire when the American colonies became independent did not involve any loss of trade, even with America. The population of the United States (three millions in 1776) grew rapidly, and for another fifty years the Americans were an agricultural, not a manufacturing people. Trade with America grew apace; Britain imported American cotton, and exported to the States its manufactured goods. In 1782 America sent us 5,400 tons of raw cotton; by 1810 this figure had risen to 59,000 tons. It was the same with India, which came under British political control about the turn of the century; India was one of the best markets for Lancashire cotton goods. Britain captured the trade of the world, in the west as well as in the east. The goods with which Britain supplied far-off cities of India, the growing towns of America, the sugar-isles of the Caribbean Sea, and the nations of the Continent of Europe, were all made in Lancashire, Yorkshire, or the midland towns of England.

The merchants who made their fortune by this world trade had a part in setting going the Industrial Revolution, and they also greatly profited from it. The new machines were invented in Britain, and the country was rich in supplies of coal and iron, the essential materials of the new industries. So it came about that Britain was at least half a century ahead of the rest of Europe in applying machinery to the

Growth of British Trade

The Markets of the World

Britain's lead in Industry

processes of manufacture. The lead which she thus acquired she did not lose for a century: she did not begin seriously to feel foreign competition till the 1870s. Further, the wealth of British merchants and the skill of British workmen, during the first phase of the Industrial Revolution, enabled the country to carry on the long war against France from 1793 to 1815. The weapons which beat Napoleon were made in Birmingham.

Laissez-faire

Opposition to State Interference

The men who made the 'business world' of modern industry claimed the right to manage their affairs in their own way. A phrase was coined by some French economists of the period to describe this attitude: *Laissez-faire!* 'Leave things alone' – 'Let us alone' – was the cry of the businessmen. It meant that they were to be given a completely free hand, and that the state was to abandon its ancient claim to regulate trade; the state, in fact, was not to interfere in business. In the past business had always been, to some extent, regulated. The old Guild System of the Middle Ages had regulated trade down to the minutest detail; in Tudor and Stuart times there had been Acts of Parliament regulating the hours of labour and the rates of wages. Again, the Navigation Acts had regulated the ships in which various goods might be carried to and from Britain.

Adam Smith

The Wealth of Nations

Free Trade

To sweep away all these regulations was the aim of the champions of *Laissez-faire*: it was accomplished during the first half of the 19th century. But long before that opinion had veered round to their side. The man who perhaps more than any one else was responsible for this was Adam Smith, who, like James Watt, came from Glasgow. His *Wealth of Nations*, published in 1776, heralded a new era in British commerce, just as the Declaration of Independence, in the same year, proclaimed the fall of the old mercantile empire. Adam Smith was the prophet of free trade. He held that all government interference is harmful to trade; let the merchants alone (*laissez-faire*), he argued, and they will make Britain a rich country. The regulations of the old colonial system had been, according to Smith, entirely useless and the way in which trade with the former colonies continued to flourish once the system had collapsed seemed to prove him right. He made a convert of the new Prime Minister, William Pitt, who reduced many trade restrictions, and prepared the way for the free trade of the next century.

Besides desiring free trade with foreign nations, the masters of the new industries were anxious to have complete freedom in dealing with their own workpeople. To this end they wished to abolish all the laws which had, from olden times, regulated industry. They succeeded in doing this before the end of the Napoleonic Wars. The Elizabethan Act authorizing magistrates to fix wages had long been a dead letter and was repealed in 1813; the next year the section of the Elizabethan Statute of Artificers which enforced apprenticeship, also for long ignored, was repealed. Even before this the masters claimed, and exercised in practice, freedom from state control. The state, they argued, must let masters and men alone to fix up between them a 'free bargain'. Statesmen agreed to let them alone; but they overlooked the fact that the bargain between the masters and men was anything but free. Masters can afford to wait, but men must sell their labour in the available market or starve.

Abolition of Regulation of Industry

The results of these conditions of employment were twofold. First, the men did not always get a fair deal; secondly, a spirit of antagonism was created. This sometimes led to bitterness between the employees and the employers. But it must be remembered that there had been hardships enough before (as well as during) these industrial changes. Both masters and men were trained in a hard school, and many of the new captains of industry were themselves ex-employees risen from the ranks.

Beginning of Class war

The sufferings of the workpeople during the first phase of the Industrial Revolution were undoubtedly great. The workers had of necessity to live near the factories, in the new towns built to house them. They were also compelled to suffer the iron discipline of the factory itself. Their work was regulated by the clock or factory hooter, no longer, as under the domestic system of production, by their own

The early Factory System

decision. They worked in the employer's premises and could therefore be subjected to many of his rules. For example, in a factory at Tydersley, near Manchester, workers were fined a shilling for opening the window, being dirty at their work, washing themselves or whistling. In a later chapter we shall note some of the evils that were brought to light during the agitation for factory reform. It is sufficient to note here that men, women, and small children were made to work for 12, 14, or even 16 hours a day, tending dangerous machines, breathing foul air, ill paid, under-nourished, lacking the ordinary comforts of life, lacking sleep. 'Whilst the engine runs the people must work – men, women, and children are yoked together with iron and steam. The animal machine . . . is chained fast to the iron machine, which knows no suffering and no weariness.' Workers, in short, completely lost control of their working lives.

Yet the picture of the factory workers' misery can be overdrawn. After all, workers had originally to be attracted to the new factories and it was primarily the prospect of economic gain which drew them. Wages seem certainly to have increased before the outbreak of the French wars, which created difficulties by increasing the price of food. No doubt, there was something of a conflict between employers and employees, in that the former had to minimize wages and maximize profits not necessarily to live in luxury, but to find the capital to plough back into the business. If there is a painless way to industrialize, very few countries managed to find it. The legacy of problems with industrial relations certainly existed, but perhaps it was unavoidable.

VI

BRITAIN AND THE FRENCH REVOLUTION

1. Pitt's Peace Ministry

AT the time of the negotiation of the Treaty of Versailles in 1783, England was governed by a ministry under Lord Shelburne. From this ministry, the able Whig politician, Charles James Fox, was excluded. Fox was one of the most remarkable men in the history of English politics. A fast liver and an inveterate gambler, he was notorious as one of the boon companions of George, Prince of Wales, afterwards the Prince Regent (and later still King George IV). Yet Fox had serious interests. It was one of the contradictions of his character that he enjoyed an all-night debate in the Commons as much as he enjoyed an all-night gambling orgy. He was no heartless rake – like his royal companion – with no feelings beyond the gratification of his own pleasures; he was a kindly man, and he had a real love of English liberty. Like most of the Whigs, he sympathized with the American Revolution; and later on he was foremost among prominent Englishmen in sympathizing with the French Revolution, though doing so cost him both loss of prestige and loss of friends. His conduct then proved that the man of fashion had convictions and principles which he valued above popularity or the friendship of princes.

In 1783 Shelburne's ministry, which had never had an assured majority in the Commons and was riven by differences over the peace with America, collapsed in the face of attack from a new political combination, an alliance of Fox and Lord North. George III was naturally angry at the 'desertion' of North, but for the moment he could do nothing. Fox and North together commanded a large majority in the House of Commons, and the King was obliged to appoint a new ministry, in which these allies were both made

Charles James Fox

The Fox-North Ministry

April-December 1783

Secretaries of State. But the King had not long to wait for his revenge. Fox prepared an India Bill – meant as a necessary improvement on the Regulating Act passed by North ten years before – which passed the House of Commons. The Bill provided for the supervision of the East India Company by a Commission composed of Fox's nominees removable only by an address from Parliament. Such appointments were usually made by the Crown; so this looked like an attack on royal power. It also looked like an attempt on Fox's part to gain control of wealth and patronage on a scale that might enable him to buy a permanent majority in Parliament. The House of Lords, strongly influenced by the King, threw it out. The King, with unseemly haste, at once sent a message to Fox and North that he had dispensed with their services. So fell the Fox-North Coalition, after eight months of power.

William Pitt, Prime Minister 1783-1801

Importance of his Premiership

The King's choice now fell on young William Pitt, aged 24, who had been Chancellor of the Exchequer under Shelburne. Pitt was appointed Prime Minister in December 1783, a position which he held for the next seventeen years. George III called an early general election the next spring in the hope of strengthening Pitt's position. The electorate was persuaded to see the issue in terms of a corrupt aristocratic conspiracy against a principled monarch. In the caricatures Pitt was 'Master Billy' or the 'infant Hercules', while Fox was depicted as Guy Fawkes, Satan or Cromwell. Especially in the more open constituencies, Pitt's victory was overwhelming; the supporters of North and of Fox lost seat after seat, and the young Premier then commanded the confidence of King, Lords, and Commons. This election showed that, even before the great Reform Bill, the people of Britain could express their will when they felt deeply enough on a subject. Called in to save the King from Fox and North, William Pitt proved to be something more than a stop-gap. 'A kingdom trusted to a schoolboy's care,' laughed his enemies; but the 'schoolboy' proved the master of them all. He also proved to be no puppet of the King. Particularly when the only alternative appeared to be Fox, George III came to rely entirely on Pitt, whose position was as supreme as Walpole's had been. The decline of the King's mental powers also favoured the ascendancy of the Prime Minister. Yet the King was never a cipher. The total ascendancy of Pitt once the Whigs split over their attitude to the French Revolution paradoxically restored the King's freedom of manoeuvre, because he was able to find an alternative leader of the cause he favoured. In 1801 it was the King who precipitated Pitt's resignation and appointed a new Prime Minister in the person of Henry Addington.

Born in the year of victories, 1759, the second son of the Great Commoner, the younger Pitt had been trained from earliest youth to a political career. His serious boyhood, his precocious learning, and his own and his father's ambition, all combined to deprive Pitt of his youth. For Pitt was never young, never knew a life free from care; and when at last, prematurely aged at 46, he sank under the tremendous burden of the Napoleonic War, he had scarcely reached middle age. Though he could unbend in private, among a few intimate friends, his manner to colleagues and political foes alike was one of haughty reserve. In the House of Commons, in an age of great debaters, Pitt was always impressive, though he was not his father's equal as an orator. Like his father, he was absolutely indifferent to money. He scorned titles and rewards for himself, though he lavished them – with feelings not unmixed with contempt – on others. His private life was singularly free from the vices of the time, with the exception of that of heavy drinking. Pitt, like most men of that generation, drank far more than was good for his health, particularly of port; and this habit, combined with the toil of his work, helped to undermine his constitution.

Pitt's first ministry lasted seventeen years, the first ten of which (1783-93) were years of peace. One of his most successful measures, the India Act of 1784, was passed in his first year of office; it settled the government of India till the Mutiny. In 1785 the Premier made an attempt at Parliamentary reform, asking leave to introduce a Bill

Character of William Pitt

India Act 1784

to dis-franchise some of the rotten boroughs, the owners of which were to be compensated. But a majority of the Commons (whom he had left free to vote as they liked) were hostile to the measure and he immediately dropped it. In the same year Pitt also tried to bring about a commercial union between England and Ireland. This was also opposed in Parliament, and again the Premier dropped the proposal. Thus two serious questions, Parliamentary reform and relations with Ireland, each of which nearly caused a revolution later on, exposed the limits of Pitt's power. His followers did not offer unconditional support.

Proposed Reform Bill Ireland

It was in the realm of finance that Pitt was most happy. He held the post of Chancellor of the Exchequer himself. The financial position of the government in 1783 was not good. The revenue was declining and it was hard to raise loans. A collapse of confidence and national bankruptcy were not impossible. One priority was to raise revenue. That meant attacking the smugglers, who smuggled as much as one fifth of all imports. He extended the right of search of suspect cargoes, but relied heavily on making smuggling less profitable by reducing duties on such articles as tea, wines, spirits and tobacco. Despite the reduced duties, revenue from them went up because smuggling declined. Pitt imposed a variety of taxes, on windows, servants, gloves, hats, and hair-powder, items selected because they were luxuries and would fall on the rich. By 1790 revenue had increased by 47 per cent and there was a surplus of £1.7 million.

Pitt's Budgets

When Pitt assumed office, the government was burdened by debts, many of which were short-term and very costly to service. Pitt's restoration of confidence in the long term stability of the country enabled him to persuade government creditors to buy government stock at 5 per cent. Looking to the future,in 1786, Pitt established the Sinking Fund, setting aside £1,000,000 a year – to accumulate at compound interest – to pay off the National Debt. He hoped by this means to pay off the Debt in twenty-eight years, little expecting that

The Sinking Fund

most of these years would be spent in piling up a further enormous debt because of a great continental war. The importance of Pitt's financial measures can best be appreciated by comparing his achievements with the contemporary failures of French governments. In France, governments did not restore the finances to surplus or successfully manage the debt and the result was national bankruptcy and political revolution.

Pitt also arranged a Commercial Treaty with France (1786). The duty on French wines was lowered, so that claret could compete in the English market with the products of Portugal; at the same time the French lowered the duty on English cotton, woollen, and steel goods. In answer to the ridiculous argument that it was wrong to make such a treaty with our 'hereditary foe', Pitt nobly declared that to say that one nation must always remain the enemy of another was weak and childish. Thus, with the co-operation of the French ministers, the first step was taken towards the realization of Adam Smith's ideal of free trade.

Commercial Treaty with France 1786

In the winter of 1788 political affairs were thrown into confusion by the illness of the King. George suffered from porphyria, a recurrent, hereditary metabolic disorder, given its name because the urine of the sufferer turns purple. It was the accompanying mental disorder that mattered politically, because it rendered the King incapable of carrying out his constitutional duties. Fox and the Whigs proposed that the royal powers should be exercised in full by the Prince of Wales, since they knew that the Prince would at once dismiss Pitt and install them in power. This project was defeated by the long arguments over the Government's Regency Bill of 1789, by which the prince was to rule as Regent, but with strictly limited powers. Even so, Pitt's government would have been in grave danger had the King not recovered before the Bill came into operation.

Regency Bill, 1789

The most important crisis in foreign affairs faced by Pitt in the 1780s concerned the United Provinces (Holland), where French influence had increased alarmingly, thanks to a patriot movement which looked to France for support against the Stadholder (governor) William V. Pitt saw it as essential to prevent Holland from falling under French control and subsidized anti-patriot forces. In the end, the crisis was resolved when the King of Prussia intervened with an army in favour of his sister, the Stadholder's wife, and France backed off. The crisis had ended Britain's long isolation and had marked the humiliation of the French monarchy, which never recovered from the setback.

Nootka
Sound, 1790

Pitt scored a more trivial success against Spain. The Spaniards in America had advanced up the Pacific coast from California; in 1789 they ejected some English settlers from Nootka Sound, in Vancouver. Pitt insisted that the English were the first comers, and that the island was an English possession. The Spaniards gave way in 1790, and the future of what became British Columbia was assured.

Russia

Partitions of
Poland

Pitt was less successful in his relations with Russia. The Empress Catherine the Great was busy seizing territory along the Black Sea from Turkey. When Pitt protested in 1791 against the seizure of Ochakov, Catherine took no notice, and it was obvious that British diplomacy was powerless in the east of Europe. Shortly afterwards Catherine proceeded, with the aid of the King of Prussia, to despoil her defenceless neighbour, Poland, which soon ceased to exist as an independent country (by the Second and Third Partitions of Poland, 1793 and 1795). By that time the outbreak of the Revolution in France had directed the attention of statesmen elsewhere.

Achievements
of Pitt

To sum up Pitt's peacetime achievements; he was, first and foremost, a Premier whose capacity for work and detailed mastery of his brief on almost every occasion made him indispensable to the King and enabled him to dominate Parliament. He was therefore able to provide the country with stable and efficient government over the lengthy period of seventeen years. The divisions and disillusionment of North's final years were in the far past when Britain had to meet the challenge of revolutionary France. Second, Pitt was an extremely able Chancellor of the Exchequer, and put the national finances on a sound footing. Third, he was responsible for measures settling the government of India and of Canada, both of which have deservedly been praised.

For Pitt, unlike his antagonist Charles James Fox, politics was the art of the possible. He was often intellectually convinced of the case for important reforms, such as parliamentary reform or free trade with Ireland, but as Prime Minister he believed that he had duties to the monarch who had appointed him and to the majority of MPs from the country gentry who sustained him in power. He could not therefore forge ahead insisting on measures which they rejected. His first duty was to provide stable government, but indulging his personal convictions was likely to prove destabilizing. The strength of Pitt's convictions on some issues is hard to doubt. This is true above all of his detestation of the slave trade, on which he spoke in the Commons on 2nd April 1792. Even Fox had to admit that the speech was 'one of the most extraordinary displays of eloquence' he had ever heard. Yet Pitt accepted that abolition could not be forced through Parliament. The only course consistent with continuing to provide stable government was the unheroic one of waiting for the consensus to shift.

His limitations

2. The Humanitarian Movement

One of the most significant changes in English life during the 18th century was the growth of the humanitarian movement. This movement was not just a matter of individuals doing good to their fellow men, but of attempts to mobilize public opinion on behalf of humane causes. Often the leaders of such movements were inspired by religious motives. Religious societies like the Quakers and the Methodists were influential; so was the wider evangelical movement. The two most important agitations, begun by humane men from no motive of self-seeking, were those conducted against the ill-treatment of prisoners, and against slavery.

Humanitarian movements

The apostle of prison reforms was John Howard, a Dissenter, who spent the greater part of his life in examining the state of prisons in England and in Europe. In England he found that an iniquitous system prevailed, by which gaolers, who were paid no salary, were allowed to charge the prisoners for board and rent. Since many prisoners could not afford to pay this debt to the gaoler, they remained in prison after their sentence had expired until it was discharged; many poor wretches had been there for years. Another evil was the filthy and insanitary state of the prisons which were breeding grounds for fatal fevers. The vileness of the prison air was such that Howard declared, after visiting the prison dungeons, that he was unable to travel in a closed carriage, as his clothes were impregnated with the stench. Prisoners were often kept in irons and otherwise ill-treated: frequently they lost their reason. Prisoners of different ages and sexes were herded together. Such things had been going on for centuries; it is to the credit of the men of the late 18th century that the public conscience was at last aroused. John Howard published his *State of the Prisons* during the American War; he was thanked by Parliament for the revelations which he had made, and some of the worst evils were dealt with by legislation in 1784. Howard also made several journeys on the continent, and visited the prisons of the chief European countries. Elizabeth Fry (1780-1845), a Quaker, was a later prison reformer, and she did much to improve the conditions among women prisoners.

John Howard (1726-90)

State of the Prisons

Elizabeth Fry (1780-1845)

Perhaps the most impressive achievement of the 18th century was the movement for the abolition of the slave trade. Africa had formed a slave-market for Europe since Roman times. After the Romans, the Arabs continued to raid Africa for slaves, and when the first Christian traders – the Portuguese – appeared off the West-African coast in the 15th century, they also engaged in the same cruel trade. In the next century the Spaniards and Portuguese began the Atlantic slave trade, and their example was followed by the English, led by John Hawkins. This slave trade, between Africa and the West

The Slave Trade

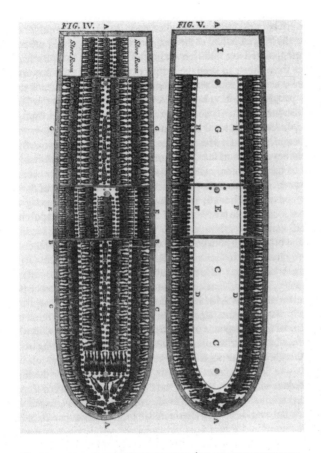

DIAGRAM OF A SLAVE SHIP FROM THE ATLANTIC SLAVE TRADE.
From an Abstract of Evidence delivered before a select committee of the
House of Commons in 1790 and 1791.

Indies or the Southern States of America, had been in progress
above two hundred years when Pitt came to power, and Britain had
the greatest share of it. It was in 1787 that twelve men – of whom
nine were Quakers – met together to form a Committee for the

William Wilberforce (1759-1833)

Suppression of the Slave Trade. The two most prominent members of this committee were Thomas Clarkson and William Wilberforce. Wilberforce, who was a well-known evangelical member of

Parliament and a friend of Pitt, tried, for many years unsuccessfully, to persuade Parliament to abolish the slave trade. But it was the efforts of Clarkson and others in arousing the public conscience to the diabolical nature of the trade that ensured the eventual success of the movement. One of the worst cruelties of the whole business, apart from the actual capture of the slaves, was the way in which the negroes were crowded together in the slave-ships, which plied their trade across the Atlantic. The horrors of the 'middle passage', as it was called, cannot be described: suffice it to say that the 'Black Hole' of Calcutta was worse only in degree than the holds of the British slave-ships. It was usual for 45 per cent of the slaves to die on the voyage to America; it was not uncommon for as many as 80 per cent to perish.

The Anti-Slavery Campaign (1788-1833)

The 'Middle Passage'

The slave trade was first discussed in Parliament in 1788, and in the same year a Bill was passed to check the cruelties of the 'middle passage'. But Wilberforce had to wait another nineteen years before Parliament abolished the Slave Trade; and it was a generation after that before the slaves in the British Empire were set at liberty in 1833.

3. The French Revolution

The 18th century has sometimes been called the Age of the Enlightened Absolutism. There were certainly plenty of absolute monarchs in Europe, and some of them, like the Emperor Joseph II, were enlightened men. No continental country had anything to compare with the parliamentary rule under a constitutional King, which had flourished in Great Britain since 1689. The Tsars of Russia, the Habsburg rulers of Austria, and the Kings of Prussia were all monarchs whose rule was subject to no constitutional checks in their own dominions; and the example of these great sovereigns was imitated by the princes of every petty German and Italian court. France was the original home of absolutism. The grand structure of the French monarchy, raised by Cardinal Richelieu and Louis XIV

European Despotisms

The French Monarchy

in the seventeenth century, was the most imposing in Europe. The Estates-General (which had in the Middle Ages corresponded roughly with the English Parliament) had not met since 1614. Yet the monarchy was not as powerful as it looked and its efforts to modernize the French state in the course of the 18th century had mostly been defeated by vested interests.

There were great social inequalities in France. The nobles had indeed lost all political power; but they had retained, from mediaeval times, the social privileges attaching to their rank. They were exempt from the payment of the heavier taxes which pressed so hardly on their inferiors; and they were lords of their own villages, where the peasant was forced to pay various dues. The French nobility were debarred by custom from certain kinds of economic activity and from marrying with the lower orders; and so there was a great gulf fixed between them and the rest of the population. The lot of the peasants was extremely hard. The demands of the government, the Church and the seigneurs were heavy, and the rising population reduced the average size of peasant plots and increased the number of landless people in the countryside. A bad harvest was liable to reduce large numbers in rural France below subsistence level.

The French Nobility

It was not, however, the miseries of the peasants which directly produced the French Revolution; nor, indeed, were the hardships they endured as bad as those endured by peasants in eastern Europe. The ferment of ideas, which affected the Revolution, arose among the nobles and the middle class, or bourgeoisie, which included tradesmen, lawyers, doctors, and all the thinking and reading section of the community. The influence of the great French writers of the period on this class was considerable. Voltaire, who spent the latter part of his life in exile in Switzerland, attacked injustice wherever he saw it. He had himself suffered under the system of *lettres de cachet*, whereby the French government was enabled to imprison any man for an indefinite period without trial, and without cause shown. Voltaire cried out against the barbarous laws, relics of the Middle Ages, by

The Peasants and the Bourgeoisie

Voltaire (1694-1778)

which, in France, men were sent to a cruel death, or to lifelong imprisonment, for small offences. In particular, Voltaire attacked the Catholic Church for persecuting men in the name of religion. His writings helped to awaken a public conscience in France.

Writers like Voltaire and Jean-Jacques Rousseau may have helped to make traditional monarchy resting on divine right seem out of date and to create notions of national sovereignty, but, probably, their influence has been exaggerated. The prestige of the French political system declined chiefly for other reasons than intellectual attacks upon some of its features. Foremost among these was the declining international success of the monarchy. Under Louis XIV (1643-1715) France had been easily the greatest European power, but the Seven Years' War (1756-63) had seen France humiliated overseas by Britain and in Europe by Prussia. In addition, Louis XV (1715-74) had acquired an unsavoury reputation as hopelessly decadent and wallowing in luxury and immorality, while the upright and well-meaning Louis XVI (1774-92) was married to *l'Autrichienne* (the Austrian woman), Marie Antoinette, who had the misfortune to be a Habsburg, born into the dynasty which had so often been France's enemy. In the years before the Revolution the gutter press was full of tales of her (alleged) immorality and extravagance.

It was financial difficulties which brought the old French monarchy to its ruin. The effort of the American War (1778-83) had indeed fulfilled its object in defeating Britain; but the expense of the war crippled the French government. Louis XVI (1774-92), a well-meaning young man, gave his confidence to several finance ministers in turn, but none was able to make the French state solvent. The peasants were already taxed to the limit of endurance; to impose a drastic tax on all landed property might have solved the difficulty, but the King did not feel able to take such a drastic step on his own authority. Finally, in May 1789, Louis summoned the Estates-General, which had not met for 175 years.

Rousseau

Financial troubles

Meeting of the Estates-General May 1789

The Estates-General, which met at Versailles, was divided into three 'estates': clergy, nobles, and the *Tiers État* (the Third Estate i.e. everyone other than nobles and clergy). It voted by estates, not by the number of individual votes: and the *Tiers État* saw that they would always be outvoted by the other two. After some quarrelling with the other estates, the *Tiers État* insisted on the formation of a National Assembly, where clergy, nobles and members of the Third Estate would all vote as individuals, and swore that it would not separate until it had drawn up a new constitution for France. Louis XVI consented to this arrangement, and so the National Assembly set to work. But very soon King Louis, spurred on by his spirited Queen, Marie Antoinette, seemed about to attempt to overawe the Assembly by a display of military force. The Paris mob then interfered for the first, but not for the last, time in the Revolution. The French Revolution would not have been possible had a great constitutional crisis not coincided with great unrest in Paris. The root cause of the trouble in the capital was the high price of bread, which made it easy for political agitators to whip up the mob. There was a riot on 14th July 1789 during which the old state prison, the Bastille, was destroyed. Later in this memorable year, the mob forcibly escorted the King, Queen, and members of the royal family from Versailles to Paris, where they took up their abode in the Tuileries Palace.

Fall of the Bastille July 1789

The work of the Constituent Assembly, as the National Assembly was now called, went on uninterruptedly after the summer of 1789. The constitution-makers derived their ideas partly from the example of England, partly from the successful revolution which had just taken place in America, where some Frenchmen had served in the French army during the American War and partly from general theories of national sovereignty. Modelling their conduct on that of the Americans, the French drew up in August 1789 a declaration, called the Declaration of the Rights of Man and of the Citizen. Some of the clauses of this famous document laid down that men are born free and equal in rights; that sovereignty resides in the people; that

Work of the Constituent Assembly

Declaration of the Rights of Man, 1789

law is the expression of the general will; and that no man should be molested for his opinions, provided his conduct does not injure the community. A few days after the issue of this Declaration, an enthusiastic Assembly declared that the remains of feudalism, such as manorial dues paid to the nobles, should be abolished throughout France; and many nobles voluntarily gave up their privileges.

The new Constitution replaced the absolute monarchy by a limited monarchy: the King could delay the action of the laws in certain cases, but he could not override them. There was to be one Assembly elected by the people, who were also to elect their own officials, including the civil servants, judges, and even the bishops and clergy. Louis XVI tried to escape from a humiliating position – as he considered it – by flight from the country. He was detected near the frontier at Varennes, and brought back to Paris a prisoner in June 1791. The French Constitution of 1790

The meeting of the Legislative Assembly – as the Assembly elected under the new Constitution was called – took place in September 1791. At first it seemed that the Constitution would work, and that the Revolution was over. But it was not so. The King was horrified at the laws which reduced the priests throughout France to the level of servants of the state; no good Catholic could agree with such an arrangement. In some country districts a revolt, religious in character, began; with this the King was in sympathy. Another cause of friction was the action of certain of the nobility, who had fled across the frontier to Germany, and who were intriguing with the German princes against the new French government. The Assembly now decided to confiscate the property of these emigrés, as they were called. The King disapproved; his own brothers were among the emigrés. But he soon resolved that he must himself rely on foreign help, if the ancient monarchy of France was ever to be restored. Legislative Assembly 1791-2
The Clergy
The Emigrés

Meanwhile, the emigrés were doing their best to persuade the German governments to act against France. In August 1791, Austria and Prussia issued a Declaration, from Pillnitz, warning War with Austria and Prussia 1792 the revolutionaries to do no harm to the King. But, when Louis XVI agreed to the new Constitution, they declared themselves satisfied. It is untrue to say that France was attacked by the military monarchies of Europe; France went to war in order to consolidate the Revolution. The Girondins – the party in power – declared war on 20 April 1792; and Austria and Prussia launched a half-hearted attack.

Revolution of 10 Aug. 1792

The advance of the German armies under the Duke of Brunswick, and the suspicion that the King was intriguing with the enemy, produced a violent revolution in Paris, which involved the fall of the monarchy. The Revolution of 10 August 1792 was engineered by the extremist party, known as the Jacobins. The Tuileries was stormed and taken, and the King's Swiss guards massacred. Louis XVI surrendered, and the monarchy was formally abolished. A month later a new assembly, called the Convention (1792-5), was elected. At the same time, Republican armies were raised all over France to defend the country and the Revolution. It was then that

September Massacres

the September Massacres, which horrified Europe, took place in Paris. Thousands of royalists, priests, and nobles were dragged out of prison and done to death in the streets. The massacre was caused by a fear that the prisoners might escape, and that it was not safe to leave them behind while the army marched away to defend the frontier.

Valmy 1792

A tremendous enthusiasm inspired the French soldiers as they marched, singing the new revolutionary song, the *Marseillaise*, to defend the Republic. The republican watchwords were 'Liberty, Equality, and Fraternity'; and for these ideals the soldiers of the Revolution were ready to die. The history of the world was changed by the battle of Valmy in September 1792, when Brunswick's army retreated before the ragged and ill-disciplined but enthusiastic soldiers of the Republic. Henceforth, nothing could stop the French; they defeated the well-drilled soldiers of the absolute monarchs time and time again, against all military calculation.

In Paris, enthusiasm for the Revolution increased after Valmy; the Convention passed a resolution saying that France would help all nations struggling to be free. The King was brought to trial and executed as a traitor to his country in January 1793. 'We fling down, as a gage of battle,' said Danton, 'the head of a king.' The Jacobins knew now that they must win or die. Soon the more moderate men were excluded from power; a Reign of Terror began, under the auspices of the cruel but efficient Committee of Public Safety.

To understand the events of the Reign of Terror, we must first appreciate the fact that France was now fighting for its life against a Europe fearful of revolution and bent on its destruction. The alliance of Britain (from 1793), Austria, Prussia, and Spain was a formidable one; the French were attacked on all their frontiers. It was in these circumstances that the Committee of Public Safety under Robespierre ruled with a ruthlessness seldom paralleled. Royalist prisoners were first put to death; then, as the inner circle of the revolutionary leaders narrowed, all those who disagreed with the extremists were guillotined. The Catholic-Royalist rebellions in Brittany, La Vendée, and Lyon were crushed with fearful barbarities; the waters of the Rhone and the Loire ran red with the blood of the enemies of the Republic. Within two years – by 1795 – these methods had succeeded; opposition to the Revolution in France itself was stamped out. And, by that time, the Jacobin armies had thrown back France's foreign enemies.

As the danger was removed, Robespierre was overthrown and guillotined and the Terror died away; and among the things drowned in its blood was the idealism of the early revolutionaries. Those who survived in positions of power were self-seeking intriguers. The Committee of Public Safety was abolished, and the Convention gave way to a new Government called the Directory (five Directors and two Assemblies) which ruled France for five years (1795-9). It was during these years that the military genius of Napoleon Bonaparte was first demonstrated to the world.

Execution of Louis XVI 1793

The Reign of Terror 1793-4

The Directory 1795-9

4. Burke, Fox, and Pitt

Fox and the
French
Revolution

IN England the first news of the French Revolution was received by all classes with feelings of delight. When Fox heard of the fall of the Bastille, he said: 'How much the greatest event it is in the history of the world, and how much the best!' The ancient absolutism of the Bourbons, so long Britain's most dangerous enemy, was at last brought low. A parliamentary experiment was to be tried in France, and the labours of the National Assembly were followed sympathetically.

Burke's
*Reflections on
the Revolution
in France*
1790

Its
limitations

The publication of Burke's *Reflections on the Revolution in France* in 1790 struck a different note. The Revolution of 1688, he believed, had been glorious because it was rooted in previous English history and because in many ways it had changed so little. By contrast, the French revolutionaries were attempting a complete break with the past and it would prove disastrous. Burke warned his readers that power in France would certainly pass into more and more violent hands as the Revolution proceeded, and that the probable outcome would be a military tyranny. The correctness of these prophecies – which were fulfilled in the Reign of Terror and the advent of Napoleon – was certainly remarkable. Preoccupied with the dangers of revolutionary experiment, however, Burke entirely failed to appreciate the enthusiasm with which many people might greet the slogans of the French revolutionaries: *Liberté, Egalité, Fraternité*.

Burke's book, which had a profound effect in England, showed the reaction of the governing classes to the growing anarchy in France. To him, and to them, the English constitution, set up by the 'Glorious Revolution' of 1688, was the last word in perfection; beyond that he could not see. England had been ruled for a hundred years by her aristocracy; that the aristocracy should ever share its power with the common people was, in 1789, a strange and unsettling idea. It was the fear that the example of the Jacobins might be followed in England that attracted the governing classes to Burke's

EXECUTION OF LOUIS XVI, 21 January 1793

view. The Revolution was dangerous, said Burke, because it included attacks on property; the upholders of the rights of property must rally in their own defence. These views naturally gained ground after the September Massacres of 1792 and the execution of Louis XVI in 1793 had shown the correctness of Burke's opinion of the course of the Revolution.

A reply to Burke was forthcoming when Tom Paine issued his *Rights of Man* in 1791. Paine, an English Quaker's son who had lived in America, was a strong supporter of the American and French Revolutions. His pamphlet – which sold in tens of thousands – insisted that the people had the right to alter any existing government at their pleasure. These democratic views found many supporters in England; it was only when in 1792 Paine published the second part

Paine's *Rights of Man* 1791-2

of his book that he became unpopular. For then he praised the republican form of government; and people were so alarmed by events in France that they rallied to the established order and the 'good old King'.

The opinions expressed in Burke's *Reflections* on the one hand, and in Paine's *Rights of Man* on the other, reflected the two extremes of English thought. The bulk of the nation, disgusted by the excesses in France, took Burke's view. In politics, a large majority of the Whig party, led by the Duke of Portland and by Burke, went over to Pitt, and helped to swell the ranks of the Tories. Fox quarrelled with Burke and, together with his young friend Charles Grey, formed a new Whig party of his own in 1792. Charles Grey, a young man of noble family, destined to give England Parliamentary reform forty years later, was the founder of a society called the 'Friends of the People', the object of which was to encourage democratic ideas in England. The action of Fox and Grey in breaking away from Burke, and holding a point of view diametrically opposed to that of most of their own class, was extremely important. It kept alive a liberal-minded spirit at a time when all ideas of liberty were in danger of being swept away in the tide of war.

War was declared in 1793. War meant that the mildest suggestion of reform was labelled 'Jacobin' – something favouring the enemies of England. War meant that Pitt put aside whatever ideas of liberty he had ever held. Something very like a panic seized the rulers of England. During 1793 and 1794, various men were tried for holding democratic opinions which we should now consider very ordinary; people were imprisoned merely for advocating 'representative government'. Two men, Muir and Palmer, were sentenced by the Scottish judge, Braxfield, to transportation to Botany Bay for holding such opinions. Then, in 1794, came the trial of Thomas Hardy, who had founded a working-men's club, called the Corresponding Society. Hardy was accused of treason, and tried for his life. As there was no evidence to convict him, he was acquitted; after this the panic

The Whig Split, 1792

Charles Grey

War (1793) and Reaction

Trial of Hardy 1794

somewhat subsided. But in the same year, 1794, the Government suspended the Habeas Corpus Act, which meant that any suspected 'Jacobins' could be seized and kept in prison without trial. Thus one of the fundamental bases of English liberty was attacked under the stress of the panic caused by the French Revolution.

Habeas Corpus Act suspended 1794

The list of government measures in the last paragraph makes Pitt's government seem very repressive. Fierce laws and exemplary trials, however, were all that the government had to rely on in a potentially dangerous situation. Britain was engaged in a life and death struggle with France, an enemy that might try to utilize the tensions within British society to disrupt the country from within. Against such tactics Britain had little to defend itself with. Admittedly, the government did house troops in barracks near certain large towns, but the country was almost unpoliced. Most government was in the hands of local worthies under very imperfect control from the centre. Many of the most significant initiatives in dealing with the situation were taken at local level.

It was in a distressed county that there originated what became a widespread effort to relieve the labouring population. The Berkshire magistrates met in 1795 at the Pelican Inn, Speenhamland, near Newbury, to discuss the wages of labourers. There had been a poor harvest and since the outbreak of war in 1793 food prices had in any case risen more rapidly than wages. They saw that something must be done to relieve poverty and suffering, and they decided to make up wages out of the parish rates. They drew up a scale by which the parishes had to make up a man's wage to 3s. a week for himself, and 1s. 6d. each for the members of his family. At this time the loaf cost 1s.; if the price of bread rose, the scale was to rise with it. The Berkshire magistrates had reacted to an emergency, but their measures were adopted in many counties and retained over many years. Three unfortunate results became apparent. First, masters were encouraged to pay lower wages, since they knew that the ratepayers would have to make up the deficiency; second, the ratepayers

Distress of the Country

The Speenhamland decision 1795

Its defects

assumed an unfair burden, as the poor rate for the country mounted from £2 millions in 1783 to £6.5 millions in 1813; thirdly, it pauperized the working population by giving them a 'dole' instead of a fair wage. Nevertheless, the Speenhamland system was ended only in 1834.

A few years after this, the Government, still fearing for the preservation of law and order, struck a blow at the factory workers. By the Combination Acts of 1799 and 1800, it was made a punishable offence for workmen to combine with each other for the purpose of demanding an increase in wages. Trades Unions, which were already in existence, were thus made illegal. Two ideas inspired this legislation. First, workmen's unions were regarded as a political danger, for the Government was still nervous of Jacobins. Second, in accordance with ideas of laissez-faire, Parliament considered that the masters of industry must be given a free hand, and therefore that their workmen ought not to combine against them. The Combination Acts remained in force for a quarter of a century.

The Combination Acts 1799 and 1800

Pitt's government is sometimes blamed for its unimaginative approach to Britain's problems and its heavy reliance upon mere repression. Such criticisms seem harsh. Pitt's priority was to win the war against France, not to solve all the problems of the 19th century. The war proved long and hard and there was no guarantee of victory. His freedom of action was always limited, as earlier failures to carry parliamentary reform or free trade with Ireland had shown. His governing coalition was unlikely to withstand the shock of radical initiatives to solve deep-seated problems. When he felt that a radical initiative was unavoidable, as in the case of Ireland in 1800, he had the courage to take it, but it did lead to the end of his ministry.

5. The Romantic Revival

A return to Nature

The period of the French Revolution and the wars which followed it coincides with what is called the 'Romantic Revival' in English

JOHN KEATS (1795-1821)
(Portrait *c*. 1822 by William Hilton)

literature, a period second in importance only to the Age of Shakespeare. It derives its character from the fact that English poetry then recovered its naturalness and its delight in simple everyday things. The poets of the age were in revolt against the formality of the 18th century; the Romantic Revival was a return to Nature.

This revived interest in Nature was intimately connected with the stirring political events of the time. Wordsworth, the prophet of the age, spent his young manhood in the stormy times of the French Revolution; Keats, Shelley, and Byron all grew up in the shadow of the great French war.

Robert Burns

The Romantic Revival in England occurred just after the death of the greatest poet whom the sister country, Scotland, had produced. Robert Burns, who died in 1796, was the son of a peasant. But, like many Scottish peasants' sons, he was brought up with a knowledge of literature, especially of the old ballad poetry of the north. The author of 'Auld Lang Syne' and of a dozen other songs equally well known (e.g. 'The Banks o' Doon' and 'Ae Fond Kiss') is acclaimed as the national poet of Scotland. The note of pathos is often found in Burns's love songs ('When I think on the happy days I spent wi' you, my dearie'); and his generous, large-hearted nature could feel even the troubles of the 'beasties' and birds, as well as of men.

Ilk happing [each hopping] bird, wee helpless thing!
That, in the merry months of spring,
Delighted me to hear thee sing,
What comes o' thee?
Whare wilt thou cour thy chittering wing
An' close thy e'e?

Two years after the death of Burns, *Lyrical Ballads* was published. It was the work of two great English poets, William Wordsworth and Samuel Taylor Coleridge.

William
Wordsworth
(1770-1850)

Coleridge
(1772-1834)

*Lyrical
Ballads* 1798

Wordsworth was born at Cockermouth, Cumberland, and went to school at Hawkshead Grammar School, where the tiny schoolroom in which the poet learnt his lessons can still be seen. From school, Wordsworth passed to St John's College, Cambridge, and during one vacation he paid his first visit to France, then in the throes of revolution. In 1795 he met Coleridge, and the two afterwards settled down in neighbouring Somerset villages to produce, jointly, a book of poems called *Lyrical Ballads* (1798).

According to the Preface of this book, the poets' object was 'to choose incidents and situations from common life, and to relate and describe them . . . in a selection of language really used by men'. This was the object which Wordsworth pursued throughout his life; simplicity, both of subject-matter and language, was the key-note of his writing. It is the setting forth of these views which makes the publication of the *Lyrical Ballads* an important landmark in English literature. Apart from the authors' views, the book would have been important if only for its inclusion of Coleridge's *Rime of the Ancient Mariner*, one of the greatest poems in the English language. The sense of horror which the author conveys in some passages –

> The many men, so beautiful!
> And they all dead did lie;
> And a thousand thousand slimy things
> Lived on; and so did I.

– is only equalled in intensity by the beauty which he portrays in others:

> A noise like of a hidden brook,
> In the leafy month of June,
> That to the sleeping woods all night
> Singeth a quiet tune.

To return to Wordsworth, it is worth while to examine the two most potent influences on his life, because they were typical of the new age that was dawning. First he was deeply influenced by the French Revolution, which he witnessed during his first visit to France. He described this influence in his *Prelude* (written 1799-1805):

Wordsworth's *Prelude*

> O pleasant exercise of hope and joy!
> For mighty were the auxiliars which then stood
> Upon our side, us who were strong in love!
> Bliss was it in that dawn to be alive,
> But to be young was very Heaven!

Influence of the French Revolution

No one will ever understand the impact of the French Revolution who does not appreciate the fact that it was welcomed by youthful, ardent spirits such as Wordsworth's. He lived indeed to see his first hopes for the freedom of mankind crushed; he witnessed the tyranny of Napoleon, and the overthrow of liberty in the land of its new birth.

Influence of Nature

The second influence on Wordsworth's character came from his boyhood; it was that of Nature, as he knew and loved her in the hills and dales of the Lake District. In 1808, when he was thirty-eight, Wordsworth retired to the Lakes, and lived there for the remaining forty-two years of his life. Henceforth he abjured the 'busy haunts of men', and found in Nature all the happiness that life could give.

To appreciate the services of Wordsworth and the 'Lake School', not only to English literature but to English life, it is necessary to understand the entirely different feelings with which the beauties of Nature were regarded in past centuries. John Evelyn, the diarist, when he saw the lovely forest of Fontainebleau (in 1644), thus described it: 'By the way we passed through a forest so prodigiously encompassed with hideous rocks . . . that I think the like is nowhere to be found more horrid and solitary.' Again, Defoe (in 1725) describes Westmorland, which Wordsworth so loved, as 'a county eminent only for being the wildest, most barren and frightful of any that I have passed over in England or in Wales'. That such opinions are no longer held by English people is due in part to the influence of Wordsworth and his contemporaries. His own joy in natural beauty is shown in nearly every poem that he wrote, and especially in the *Ode on the Intimations of Immortality*, and in *Tintern Abbey*:

> How oft, in spirit, have I turn'd to thee,
> O sylvan Wye, thou wanderer thro' the woods!
> How often has my spirit turn'd to thee!

Byron (1788-1824)

A very different character from the quiet poet of the Lakes was Lord Byron. Byron, the spoiled child of Fortune, attained European fame as a poet before he was thirty. In spite of his faults – and they were many – Byron never lost the early enthusiasm for liberty which he derived from the French Revolution; and he died at Missolonghi in Greece, fighting against the Turks for the freedom of the Greece he loved so well. An equally ardent spirit was Percy Bysshe Shelley, who was sent down from Oxford for writing a pamphlet called *The Necessity of Atheism*. Shelley spent a brief, unhappy life in fighting forces too strong for him. His hatred of all forms of tyranny is shown in his political poems of 1818-21; but his lasting title to fame rests on *Prometheus Unbound, Adonais* (an elegy on the death of Keats), and on his many lyrics, such as the *Ode to the West Wind*, and the lyric beginning,

Shelley (1792-1822)

> I dream'd that as I wandered by the way
> Bare Winter suddenly was changed to Spring.

Shelley was drowned off Livorno in 1822, when he was only thirty and at the height of his powers. John Keats, who also died in Italy at the age of twenty-five, was a friend of Shelley and Byron. His chief works are *Endymion, Hyperion, The Eve of St Agnes*, and his wonderful odes, such as *Ode to a Nightingale, Ode on a Grecian Urn*, and *To Autumn*, which are generally reckoned among the loveliest things in the English language. In *La Belle Dame Sans Merci* we get a glimpse of almost uncanny beauty, which recalls some of the passages of the *Ancient Mariner.*

Keats (1795-1821)

A contemporary of these short-lived poets was Sir Walter Scott. His lays and ballads were the outcome of a life spent in deep reading of Scottish history, and of a mind saturated with the legends of the Border. His *Lay of the Last Minstrel* (1805) achieved an immediate success; it was shortly followed by Marmion and the *Lady of the Lake*. In 1814, Scott wrote his first novel, *Waverley*, the first of the long series of the Waverley Novels, by the writing of which Scott strove, in his later years, to pay off the burden of a large debt. Many of the

Scott (1771-1832)

Waverley 1814

Waverley Novels also deal with Scottish history, like *The Heart of Midlothian* and *Old Mortality*. Scott represents two significant trends of the early 19th century. First, there is his interest in the Scottish past, shared by many of his countrymen who were busily appropriating the relics of Gaelic culture, such as tartans, bagpipes and the rest. Second, he helped to achieve a revaluation of the Middle Ages. The 18th century writers had viewed them as an uninteresting period of barbarism, but for Scott their alleged barbarism was part of their appeal. In many of his novels he attempted an imaginative recreation of what he saw as a colourful and fascinating era. After his death Scott's house Abbotsford became a shrine to his memory. He and Burns became modern Scottish heroes who reinforced Scottish pride and the Scots' sense of themselves as a great and special people.

6. Painting in the Romantic Age

The poets of the Romantic age claimed to have rediscovered Nature. Many of the artists of the period had similar aspirations. It is not surprising that the end of the 18th century and the start of the 19th century is a great age of English landscape painting.

JMW
Turner

Perhaps the most successful painter of the period was JMW Turner (1775-1851), a precocious genius who became an associate member of the Royal Academy at the early age of 24 and a full member three years later. He was attracted particularly to what were called the sublime aspects of nature, that is nature as a terrifying and overwhelming force. He painted many scenes of avalanche, shipwreck and storms at sea, which invariably show people as helpless victims at the mercy of awe-inspiring elemental powers. Turner also painted tranquil scenes, but even these are dominated by dramatic natural effects. For example, in his popular work of 1838, *The Fighting Temeraire*, which shows a stately sailing ship of Nelson's navy being towed along the Thames by a steam tug in order to be broken up, the drama is provided by a magnificent sunset.

Turner constantly moved round Britain and later round Europe. With the exception perhaps of Venice, he was not much concerned to convey the special features of specific places. In complete contrast was his exact contemporary John Constable (1776-1837). He wrote: 'Painting is for me but another word for feeling, and I associate "my careless boyhood" with all that lies on the banks of the Stour; those scenes made me a painter, and I am grateful.' The Stour is the river which separates Essex and Suffolk and was used by his father, owner of several grain mills, to transport his produce. The landscape of the river valley and the life along it became Constable's principal subject. He loved it in the same sort of way that Wordsworth loved the Lake District. His great six foot canvases of the period 1819-25, of which the most famous is *The Hay Wain*, depict the features of the river banks in loving detail. In his works men work in harmony with nature, which is rarely a threatening force. Unlike earlier artists, however, Constable evoked the English weather. People complained that when looking at his work, they felt impelled to reach for their umbrellas.

John Constable

Turner and Constable are simply the most famous of the landscape painters of the era. Large numbers of artists worked in watercolour. There arose in some provincial towns groups of artists devoted to the depiction of their town and its neighbourhood. Much the most successful of these local groups was the Norwich School, which flourished from 1803 to 1833. The central figures were John Crome and John Sell Cotman.

There was still plenty of work for portrait painters. The most successful was Sir Thomas Lawrence (1769-1830), to whom Sir Joshua Reynolds said, 'In you, sir, the world will expect to see accomplished all that I have failed to achieve.' Lawrence was commissioned by the Prince Regent to paint all the allied leaders who had contributed to the downfall of Napoleon for a new room in Windsor Castle called the Waterloo Chamber. There they can still be seen: the Pope, the European monarchs, generals like Blucher and, given pride of place, the Iron Duke himself.

Sir Thomas Lawrence

VII

THE GREAT FRENCH WAR (1793-1815)

1. The First Coalition

Pitt and
Peace
February
1792

THE outbreak of the French Revolution, and its progress to the summer of 1792, did not inspire British statesmen with a wish to interfere with the course of events in France. The Germanic powers, as early as April 1792, went to war with the avowed purpose of restoring the French monarchy to its former position. Pitt did not share that aim. As late as February 1792 he made a speech, prophesying fifteen years of peace for Britain, and moved a reduction in the military and naval forces. Exactly twelve months later, Britain embarked on one of the longest wars in modern history.

French
aggression
1792
The Scheldt

It was the events of the last five months of 1792 that caused Pitt to change his mind. In September came the massacres in Paris, which filled most Englishmen with horror and alarm. In November the French troops invaded the Austrian Netherlands (Belgium) and rapidly overran that country, which Britain had formerly fought to keep out of the hands of Louis XIV. In the same month, the Convention issued a decree saying that they would help all nations who wished to regain their liberty. The French, moreover, declared the navigation of the River Scheldt open, any treaties to the contrary notwithstanding. As Britain had, for the benefit of Holland, signed treaties, one as recently as 1788, which gave the control of the Scheldt to the Dutch, she could not approve of the French action. Besides, Antwerp in French hands might prove a serious rival to the Port of London. Pitt therefore gave the British answer to the French claims in memorable words: 'England will never consent that France shall arrogate the power of annulling at her pleasure, and under the pretence of a pretended natural right, of which she makes herself the

EUROPE IN 1798

only judge, the political system of Europe, established by solemn treaties and guaranteed by the consent of all the Powers.'

The execution of Louis XVI in January 1793 inflamed all England against France, and there was now no hope of preserving peace. War was declared by the Convention on Britain and Holland on 1 February 1793. George III wrote to Lord Grenville, the Foreign Secretary, saying that the declaration of war 'is highly agreeable to me'. He went on to say that England would, he hoped, 'curb the insolence of those despots (the French government) and be the means of restoring some degree of order to that unprincipled country, whose aim at present is to destroy the foundations of every civilized state'.

War with France 1793

167

The war which thus broke out continued with two brief intervals for twenty-two years. Pitt's conception of waging it was twofold. First, he used British money to maintain a European coalition against France. He looked to his allies, to whom he paid subsidies in cash, to bear the brunt of the land attack on the common enemy; Britain's military effort was very small. Secondly, he intended to use British naval power to destroy French commerce, to seize French colonies, and to deliver attacks on the French Atlantic and Mediterranean ports.

Pitt's War Policy

The First Coalition (1793-5) consisted of Britain, Austria, Prussia, Holland, Spain, and Sardinia. A small British army, under the Duke of York, was sent to assist the Austrians and Prussians in the Netherlands. The allied efforts, however, were of little avail; the French kept their hold on Belgium and incorporated it into France; and they invaded Holland. The Dutch navy, held fast in the frozen Rhine, was captured by a detachment of French cavalry in 1794. Holland became a satellite of France; the Dutch were forced to change sides and fight against their former allies.

The First Coalition 1793-5

Britain's efforts to aid the Royalists in France were no more successful than the Netherlands campaign. An expedition sent to Quiberon in Brittany arrived too late to help the Royalists there. Then, also in 1793, Admiral Hood entered Toulon harbour at the invitation of the citizens, who were opposed to the Revolution. But a Republican army besieged the town, and the British fleet in the harbour was fired on by Lieutenant Bonaparte's guns, and forced to withdraw. Such was the first round of the fight between Britain and her arch-enemy. At sea, Lord Howe won a five-days' battle usually called the 'Glorious First of June' (1794), capturing six French battleships.

Admiral Hood at Toulon 1793

First of June 1794

Between 1795 and 1797 England was deserted by all her allies. Holland had been forced into a French alliance. Then Prussia made peace by the Treaty of Basle of 1795 in order to turn its attention to the subjugation of the unfortunate Poles. Poland had just been

Prussia and Spain

NAPOLEON BONAPARTE (1769-1821)
(1812 portrait by Jacques-Louis David)

finally partitioned between the robber Powers (Prussia, Austria, and Russia) under the Second and Third Partitions (1793 and 1795). Prussia kept out of the French war for another ten years. The Spaniards also made peace in 1795, and in the following year they decided to change sides and throw in their lot with France. This caused the British to withdraw their Mediterranean fleet to Gibraltar in January 1797.

Bonaparte in Italy 1796-7

Events were thus going badly enough for Britain when a new star appeared on the horizon. Napoleon Bonaparte, a young Corsican soldier, had joined the Republican army shortly after the overthrow of the monarchy. He had taken a prominent part in the siege of Toulon, and later in the quelling of a mob attack in Paris. In 1796 he was put in command of the French 'Army of Italy'. It was in Italy that his astonishing military genius was first demonstrated to the world. Bonaparte first fell on the Sardinians and forced them to make a separate peace in 1796. Then, in a series of brilliant campaigns, he

Defeat of Austria

beat the Austrians and drove them out of Italy. Bonaparte relied chiefly on the power of sudden attacks, delivered by infantry in column formation, and on the use of light field-guns, which could be moved quickly into action. The Austrian generals were no match for him, either in tactics or in the power of leading men to victory. By the beginning of 1797 the Austrians were in full flight across the frontier; Bonaparte chased them over the mountains and forced them to sign an armistice.

Position in 1797

Britain alone

In the year 1797 Britain was faced with a most serious situation. All her continental allies had either been defeated or had withdrawn from the war; the French were masters of western Europe. The naval situation was scarcely less serious, for the fleets of France, Spain, and Holland were now ranged against Great Britain. Admiral Sir John Jervis, however, with Nelson as second-in-command, broke the

Cape St Vincent

Spanish line at the battle of Cape St Vincent in February 1797 and scattered the enemy, removing for the time being the naval threat of Spain. But scarcely had one danger thus been removed, when the whole British naval position in the North Sea was threatened by serious mutinies in the fleet. The grievances of the seamen were real enough: they were badly fed, seldom paid, given inadequate leave and kept at their duty by a system of brutal punishments for which discipline is too mild a word. The first mutiny occurred at Spithead; the government, recognizing that some concessions were necessary, eventually accepted most of the men's demands, and order was restored. A more serious situation, however, was created by the mutiny of the North Sea fleet, under Admiral Duncan, which was blockading the Dutch coast. The mutineers seized the ships and sailed back to the Thames estuary, their headquarters being at the Nore. Duncan, with two ships left, hoodwinked the enemy by sending signals to an imaginary fleet behind. After an anxious month, the men returned to their duties. Parker, the ringleader, and eighteen others were hanged. Duncan continued the blockade of the Dutch coast, and it was not till October that the enemy fleet emerged. An action took place off Camperdown which proved an overwhelming victory for the British: nine out of sixteen Dutch ships were captured and the Dutch navy was devastated. The sailors, who had so recently been mutineers, had amply proved their patriotism, and were pardoned by the Government.

A week after Camperdown, Austria signed the Treaty of Campo Formio (1797) with the French Republic. By this Treaty, Belgium and the Rhine frontier were given to France: it had not received such gains under the greatest of its Kings. At the same time, the dependent republics which the French had set up in Holland, Switzerland, and North Italy were recognized by Austria. Britain stood alone against the victorious Republic, which, only four years before, was thought to be on the verge of destruction.

In one respect, however, Britain had done well out of the war. Her naval superiority had enabled her to attack the overseas possessions not only of France but of the allies of France. The Dutch had suffered heavily in the loss of Ceylon and the Cape of Good

Marginal notes:
Mutinies in the Fleet

Camper-down

Treaty of Campo Formio 1797

British Colonial Gains

The Cape

Revolution in the West Indies

Hope in 1795 and of Demerara in South America in 1796. The Cape was then chiefly important on account of its position on the route to India, but it afterwards proved a valuable colony in itself. Spain lost Trinidad in 1797 and what became British Honduras; the French lost several islands, of which the most important was St Lucia. But a great deal of money and thousands of lives – 40,000 deaths and the same number again rendered unfit for service – were consumed in a useless attempt to conquer the French colony of Haiti on Hispaniola, where a rebellion of the black population broke out. The rebellion was due, in the first instance, to the influence of the French Revolution on the slaves; it spread to several of the other islands, where, however, it was ultimately quelled. But Haiti remained, and remains, an independent republic. The obsession with collecting colonies was a symptom of the belief of British statesmen that the war against revolutionary France was fundamentally similar to earlier 18th century wars, in that it was a war for limited gains which would be ended by an exchange of territory. Colonies might ultimately be traded for French concessions in Europe.

By 1797 an unprecedented situation existed. France had achieved an apparently unshakable domination of western Europe, which had eluded Spain in the 16th century and Louis XIV in the 17th century. On the other hand, Britain had achieved domination of the world outside Europe. The French, the Spanish and the Dutch could no longer defend their colonial empires or maintain their old colonial economic systems. The boast that *Britannia rules the waves* was true, and the events of the next few years proved it so.

2. Britain and the Mediterranean

French control of the Mediterr-anean 1798

At the beginning of 1798 the French troops marched into Rome, whence the Pope, Pius VI, fled; a Roman republic was set up. The French were now in command of all north Italy; Spain was their ally; they controlled the western Mediterranean. It merely remained for

172

them to conquer Naples, and to attack the unwieldy Turkish Empire, and the Mediterranean would become a French lake. An attack on Egypt (nominally a Turkish province) was therefore decided on. Bonaparte, who was given the command, already dreamed of annexing the Turkish Empire, and of advancing, from Egypt, to the conquest of India. 'This little Europe,' he declared, 'is too small for me.'

Britain decided to challenge the French supremacy in the Mediterranean. But the French Egyptian Expedition, eluding Admiral Nelson, sailed from Toulon to the Nile. On the way the French demanded the surrender of Malta from the Knights of St John, and left a garrison to occupy the island. Landing in Egypt, Bonaparte beat the Mamelukes (the military caste which dominated Egypt) at the battle of the Pyramids. While he was celebrating this victory, news arrived that his fleet was gone. Nelson had destroyed it at the battle of the Nile. Sailing into Aboukir Bay (in one of the mouths of the Nile), where the French fleet lay at anchor, on 1st August 1798 Nelson attacked with his terrible gun-fire at close quarters. As usual, Nelson showed extraordinary boldness by attacking from the shore-ward as well as the sea-ward sides, despite the danger of running aground. Nelson achieved the decisive victory he always sought: thirteen ships were taken or sunk; only four escaped.

Malta

Bonaparte in Egypt

Battle of the Nile, August 1798

After this it was evident that Bonaparte would have to abandon the dream of a French Mediterranean, which must obviously depend upon sea-power. But he still had his army, with which to invade other parts of the Turkish Empire. He marched into Palestine, expecting to meet with little resistance, but was held up by the Turkish defence of Acre in 1799. The Turks were assisted in their defence by part of the British fleet, under Sir Sidney Smith, one of Nelson's captains. Foiled at Acre, Bonaparte had to return to Egypt. By this time, news from Europe decided him to desert his army and return home. Sailing secretly with a few companions, he eluded the British fleet, and landed safely in France.

Siege of Acre, 1799

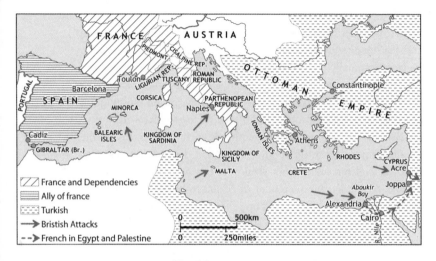

THE MEDITERRANEAN, 1798-1800

A Second Coalition was now in being, consisting of Britain, Austria, Russia, and Turkey. An Austro-Russian army under Suvorov invaded northern Italy and swept out the French. Then it forced its way through the Alpine passes into Switzerland, and was successful until September, when Masséna defeated Suvorov at Zurich. In Naples, earlier in the year, the French had set up a republican government, and there was now further fighting between the revolutionaries and the adherents of the King of Naples. Finally, the republicans of Naples surrendered to Cardinal Ruffo, on the promise that their lives should be spared. Just as this treaty was signed, Admiral Nelson appeared in the Bay of Naples, with the exiled Neapolitan King on board. King Ferdinand IV repudiated the treaty, and, with Nelson's help, proceeded to crush the rebels in a series of cruel executions and imprisonments.

Second Coalition 1799

Nelson at Naples

Meanwhile Bonaparte was received with tremendous enthusiasm in France. He decided that the moment had arrived to assume

Coup d'état of 1799

control of the Republic. He therefore overthrew the government of the Directory by force, an event known as the *Coup d'état of Brumaire*, in November 1799, and set up a new government of three consuls, with himself as First Consul. From the moment when he became First Consul, Bonaparte was the absolute ruler of France, a position which he held for fifteen years. Soon he raised a new army, full of enthusiasm, and ready to follow him to victory. He did not disappoint his soldiers; at the battle of Marengo (near Genoa) the Austrians were again defeated. Shortly after this, Russia and Austria made peace; by the start of 1801 Britain once more stood alone.

Marengo 1800

The British, however, scored two important successes. They took Malta in 1800, which became a British possession till the later 20th century, and they sent an army to Egypt in 1801 under Sir Ralph Abercromby, which procured the surrender of the French army which Bonaparte had left behind. The position, by 1801, was thus similar to that of 1797. The French attempt to break out of Europe into north Africa and the Middle East had failed. Britain was more than ever mistress of the world outside Europe, because it had decisively re-entered the Mediterranean and secured a new base there in the form of Malta. Yet the efforts of the Second Coalition to check France in Europe had proved fruitless. France had again demonstrated its military supremacy and had reaffirmed its control of northern Italy. It was in a position, should it choose to do so, to remodel yet more of Europe.

British take Malta, 1800

France and Britain in 1800

Interest now shifted from the Mediterranean to the Baltic. The Tsar of Russia, Paul I, revived the Armed Neutrality of the North which had been formed during the War of American Independence in 1780 to contest the British claim to search neutral shipping. Russia, Sweden, and Denmark were thus ranged in hostility to Britain and laid an embargo on British shipping. The British Government dispatched Admiral Sir Hyde Parker, with Nelson as second-in-command, to the Baltic to attack the Danes. Nelson engaged the Danish fleet, and disregarded Parker's signal to withdraw. "'Do

Armed Neutrality of the North, 1801

you know what's shown on board the Commander-in-Chief?" asked Nelson. . . "Why, to leave off action!" "Leave off action!" he repeated, and then added, with a shrug, "Now damn me if I do!" He then observed to Captain Foley, "You know, Foley, I have only one eye – I have a right to be blind sometimes." And then, with an archness peculiar to his character, putting the glass to his blind eye, he exclaimed: "I really do not see the signal!'" As usual, Nelson sought a decisive victory and he achieved it. The bombardment lasted four hours, after which the Danes surrendered. All seventeen of their front-line ships in Copenhagen harbour had been destroyed or taken. Meanwhile, a court tragedy changed the policy of Russia, the leader of the Armed Neutrality. The mad Tsar, Paul I, was murdered in 1801; his son and successor, Alexander I, at once came to terms with Britain, and the Armed Neutrality collapsed.

First Battle of Copenhagen, 1801

Shortly after these events, Pitt resigned the premiership for reasons unconnected with the conduct of the war. George III had forced him to break his promise to the Irish Catholics, and Pitt did not consider it honourable to remain in office. On his resignation in 1801, Addington, formerly Speaker, was made Prime Minister; Pitt remained out of office for three years.

Pitt resigns 1801

Addington Government 1801-4

Addington's government decided to make peace with France. The negotiations lasted some months, but, after much haggling, peace was made at Amiens in 1802. Britain agreed to restore all its colonial conquests apart from Trinidad (taken from Spain) and Ceylon (taken from the Dutch). In return, France was to evacuate south and central Italy. Britain assumed that Napoleon would keep the terms of his recent peace with Austria, whereby France had agreed to respect the independence of the republics in north Italy, Switzerland and Holland. In short, the assumption which sustained the peace was that Napoleon had limited ambitions and was prepared to settle for terms which gave him far more than any previous ruler of France had possessed.

Peace of Amiens 1802

A CARTOON OF 1806 BY GILLRAY
Pitt holds the sea for England, while Napoleon helps himself to Europe

3. Land power versus Sea power

The peace signed at Amiens lasted only a year, for it soon became
obvious that Bonaparte's ambitions were not as limited as the British
government had hoped. He became president in north Italy and
annexed Piedmont to France. He intervened in Switzerland. He
acquired Louisiana from Spain, which seemed to mark another
attempt to recreate France's colonial power. Britain, increasingly
suspicious of his intentions, refused to give up Malta; by May 1803
war was again declared. As the country prepared for a second and
even more terrible struggle, Britain was more united as a nation than
ten years previously. Those who had formerly held that the French
Revolution heralded the dawn of European liberty, were now

War renewed
1803

convinced that that very liberty was in danger from the ambitions of the First Consul. This feeling was expressed in Wordsworth's sonnet of 1803 on the precious heritage of British freedom:

> We must be free or die, who speak the tongue
> That Shakespeare spake; the faith and morals hold
> Which Milton held.

Pitt's Second Ministry 1804-6

Though Addington had not been a disastrous Prime Minister, confidence in his ability to lead the country at a time of national emergency was lacking and by early 1804 Addington had lost the backing of the King, of his own cabinet and of much of the Commons. In May 1804 he was replaced by Pitt. That same year in

Napoleon Emperor 1804

December Bonaparte crowned himself Emperor as Napoleon I; he also converted the French conquests in Lombardy into the Kingdom of Italy, with himself as King. Having made these arrangements, he turned to the agreeable task of crushing Britain, as a preliminary to further European conquests. He saw that France, to achieve European supremacy, must first overcome 'these active islanders', as he called the British. Pitt endeavoured to counter his schemes by

Third Coalition 1805

forming the Third Coalition of Britain, Austria, and Russia in 1805.

During 1804 and 1805, Napoleon collected a large army at Boulogne for the purpose of invading England. He ordered the

The Camp at Boulogne 1804-5

construction of a fleet of flat-bottomed boats for the transport of the soldiers. The transports were capable of carrying about 167,000 men, a total that might have proved adequate to overcome the 80,000 regular troops and the many assorted militiamen and volunteers available to the British government, especially since before late 1806 the coastal defences were very weak. The essential preliminary to invasion was to win control of the Channel for about three days. A certain amount of panic was created in England by French preparations, especially as the camp at Boulogne could be seen through a telescope. There, on the white cliffs of France, were assembled the troops sworn to destroy English independence; there, no doubt, paced the dreadful figure of 'Boney', the Corsican ogre, the terrible little man whose soldiers always marched to victory. The British Navy, however, felt confident of its strength. Lord St Vincent (Admiral Jervis) said in the Upper House: 'I do not say, my lords, that the French cannot come. I only say, they cannot come by sea.'

In the early months of 1805 the French carried out the pre-liminaries to the plan for the invasion of England. Napoleon ordered the various French and Spanish fleets – at Toulon, Cadiz, Corunna, Rochefort, and Brest – to elude the British blockade and sail for a secret rendezvous, Martinique. The fleets from Toulon, Rochefort, and Cadiz all ran through the British blockade and sailed for the West Indies. Nelson, on guard in the Mediterranean and so far ignorant of their intentions, followed them in May 1805. When he reached Martinique, he guessed that the West Indies was merely a rendezvous, and that the French intended to attack England itself. He therefore sent a fast brig ahead to warn Lord Barham at the Admiralty, while he himself with the rest of the fleet some days later followed the enemy's armada back across the Atlantic. Lord Barham sent Calder to meet Villeneuve, the French admiral, and an indecisive action was fought off Cape Finisterre. Villeneuve then put in at Corunna and later succeeded in reaching Cadiz, thus raising his fleet from 18 to 33 vessels. Meanwhile, in August 1805 Napoleon heard that the Austrians were mobilizing; he therefore broke up his camp at Boulogne, and transferred his 'Army of England' to Germany.

The Plan of Invasion

The plan abandoned August 1805

The last three months of 1805 witnessed the two most spectacular victories of the whole war on sea and land respectively – Trafalgar and Austerlitz. While Napoleon was pursuing his victorious way across Germany, he ordered his admiral, Villeneuve, to come out and fight. The result was the battle of Trafalgar on 21 October 1805, when Nelson swept on the combined fleets of France and Spain, and vanquished them. The Franco-Spanish fleet was disposed in a huge

Trafalgar 21 October 1805

arc, which Nelson's ships, approaching in two lines, pierced, so destroying the enemy formation and producing the 'pell-mell' battle which Nelson favoured. The expert gunnery and determination of the British fighting at close quarters then won the day. Twenty out of the thirty-three enemy battleships were captured or sunk. While pacing the deck wearing his orders of knighthood, Nelson was picked off by a French sniper aloft up a mast, and he died on board the *Victory*, happy in the knowledge that he was the saviour of his country. In the naval war Trafalgar was decisive; Napoleon was never able to reverse the verdict of that October day, and for the remaining ten years of the war the power of the British Navy was not seriously challenged. At the Guildhall banquet that November, the Prime Minister paid tribute to England's dead hero. Referring to the prestige which the fleet had won, he said: 'England has saved herself by her exertions; she will, I trust, save Europe by her example.'

Death of Nelson

But, even as Pitt spoke, the armies of the relentless Emperor were hacking their way across Europe. One Austrian army was surrounded at Ulm, and forced to surrender. Napoleon entered Vienna. Then, in December, he met the allied armies of Austria and Russia, and annihilated them at Austerlitz. His great victory – as overwhelming as Nelson's though not so lasting in its effects – forced Austria into a humiliating peace and left Napoleon a free hand in Germany. The news of Austerlitz was brought to London, where a sick and ageing man struggled with a burden too hard for him to bear. Pitt was studying a map of Europe when he heard the fatal news. 'Roll up that map,' he said, adding with prophetic insight, 'it will not be wanted these ten years.' Pitt's health was failing even before he received news of the disaster. Years of overwork and excessive drinking had undermined his health, but it seems to have been gastric ulceration that finally killed him. 'My country, how I leave my country!' were his last words in January 1806. Medallions struck at the time of his death showed Britannia weeping and bore the inscription: *Non sibi sed patriae vixit.* (He lived not for himself, but for his country.)

Austerlitz December 1805

Death of Pitt January 1806

HORATIO NELSON (1758-1805)
(1797 portrait by Lemuel Francis Abbott)

Pitt's death opened the way for his great rival Fox to enter the Cabinet. A coalition ministry was formed – the Ministry of All the Talents, it was called, though in fact it was a ministry largely of Whigs – in which Fox held the post of Foreign Secretary for the few months left to him of life. It was this ministry that passed the Act making the slave trade illegal in 1807. Fox died in September 1806 just before the Act was passed, but he helped in its introduction.

Ministry of All the Talents 1806-7

Death of Fox September 1806

Meanwhile, the wisdom of Pitt's remark about the map of Europe was becoming clear. Napoleon expelled the Bourbon King, Ferdinand, from Naples, and set up his own brother Joseph Bonaparte in his stead. His brother Louis became King of Holland. In Germany, after Austerlitz, Napoleon worked his will. French influence was so dominant that all western Germany was formed into

Napoleonic changes in Europe

the 'Confederation of the Rhine' under French tutelage. In August 1806, Napoleon notified the German Reichstag (Parliament) that he no longer recognized the existence of the Holy Roman Empire, which had endured for a thousand years. The Emperor Francis resigned his ancient title, and assumed that of Emperor of Austria, which his family retained till 1918. Apart from Austria and Prussia, Germany lay at the feet of Napoleon. Later in the same year, 1806, Napoleon picked a quarrel with Prussia, and inflicted on it the crushing defeat of Jena. He then entered yet another foreign capital, Berlin, and from there issued the Berlin Decree, aimed at Britain.

End of the Holy Roman Empire 1806

Jena, 1806

By this Berlin Decree Napoleon declared the British Isles to be in a state of blockade, and forbade all commerce between them and France, or the states allied with France. Meanwhile, Napoleon had fought the Russians in a bloody and indecisive battle at Eylau and then defeated them at Friedland. Next year Napoleon made an alliance with the Tsar by the Treaty of Tilsit, of 1807. Alexander agreed to enforce the 'Continental System' – the name given to Napoleon's plan to ruin British commerce and 'cut off supplies to the stomach' of his enemy. 'I have every reason to hope,' wrote Napoleon, 'that this measure will deal a deadly blow to England.' He had some reason for his hope; for he could control the ports of France, Germany, Italy, Spain, and Holland, and he had Russia for an ally. Ruining British trade might bring about internal upheaval, or at least it might destroy Britain's ability to subsidize other states when they fought with Napoleon. The British Government replied by their Orders in Council of 1807. A counter-blockade was declared on the ports of France and her allies, and neutrals were forbidden to trade with Napoleon and his allies. Thus was all Europe involved in the fight to the death between Britain and Napoleon. The British working-class suffered from the high price of bread. But even Napoleon could not manage without British goods, and his own envoys – in spite of the Berlin Decree – smuggled British coats, caps, and shoes for the French army.

Berlin Decree 1806

Treaty of Tilsit, 1807

The Continental System

Early in 1807 the coalition ministry in Britain fell; the Tories came in and stayed in for twenty-three years (1807-30). First came a short but important ministry under the Duke of Portland (1807-9). This ministry included two remarkable men and inveterate enemies, George Canning and Lord Castlereagh. Canning, as Foreign Secretary, received secret information that Napoleon and the Tsar were planning to unite all the navies of Europe, which involved seizing those of neutral countries, such as Denmark and Portugal. Acting with great promptitude, Canning sent Admiral Gambier to the Sound to demand the immediate surrender of the Danish fleet. The Danes naturally refused so outrageous a request, but Gambier bombarded Copenhagen till they gave way. He returned home with the Danish fleet as a prize. Continental countries were indignant at this incident, which the British Government defended on the plea that they had merely forestalled the French. The Baltic was kept out of Franco-Russian control.

Second Battle of Copenhagen, 1807

That all Europe must be involved in the struggle between the two great antagonists – the land-monster and the sea-monster – was soon made plain. In the same year that Britain seized the Danish fleet, Napoleon struck at Portugal, on the ground that the Portuguese were trading with Britain. General Junot's army overran Portugal; it arrived at Lisbon just too late to capture the Portuguese fleet and the King of Portugal and his family, who sailed away to Brazil in 1807 on board a British ship which Canning had sent to the Tagus.

French invade Portugal 1807

Napoleon now controlled Europe from Lisbon to Moscow. His enemies, on the other hand, controlled the seas. In the Mediterranean the British held Gibraltar and Malta, and maintained the exiled King of Sardinia (who had lost Piedmont) and the King of Sicily (who had lost Naples) on the island parts of their dominions. In the outer world, the French, Dutch, and Spanish islands had again been seized since the failure of the Peace of Amiens; Cape Colony was permanently occupied in 1806. Napoleon had abandoned his colonial ambitions in the short term at least by selling Louisiana to the United

States. It remained to be seen whether Napoleon could destroy Britain through his Continental System or whether that very system – with its war against British sugar and cotton, tea and coffee – would raise up enemies against him.

4. The Overthrow of Napoleon

The downfall of Napoleon was brought about by the Peninsular War and the construction at last of a reasonably solid coalition of all the great powers against him finalized by the Treaty of Chaumont of 1814. It will be convenient to follow the war in Spain to its conclusion, before dealing briefly with events elsewhere.

Napoleon attacks Spain, 1808

In 1808 Napoleon decided to overthrow the Bourbon monarchy of Spain. He lured the Spanish royal family into his power, and forced the King, Charles IV, to abdicate in favour of his son Ferdinand. He then insisted on Ferdinand's abdication, and gave the crown to his own brother, Joseph Bonaparte. The result of these manœuvres was not at all what he expected. For fifteen years the French had been invading the territories of their neighbours, and overthrowing, with comparative ease, the governments opposed to them. In dealing with countries like Germany and Italy, which were divided up into small states, there had been little difficulty. But Spain was a nation, not a collection of small states. Its government, it is true, was as inefficient as any in Europe, but the Spaniards were a proud people, ready to defend their independence. Moreover, though there was some sympathy for French liberal doctrines, the *afrancesados* (the French sympathizers) were generally seen as unpatriotic and attacks, particularly on the Church, were widely resented. For the first time in the war, the French encountered something like national resistance. It was found necessary to garrison every Spanish town of any size, in order to keep the government of King Joseph in being.

The Spanish National Rising

It was at this point that the British Government made an important decision. So far the direct British military effort in the war

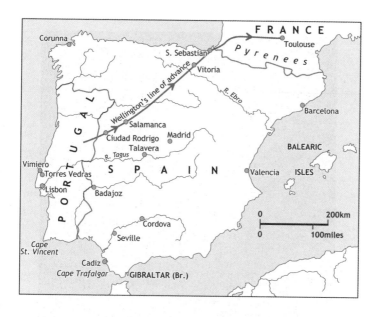

SPAIN AND PORTUGAL, THE PENINSULAR WAR

had been almost entirely naval and colonial; now it was decided to embark on a military effort in Europe on a much larger scale. Canning and Castlereagh (Secretary for War), who agreed in little else, agreed to this. A Spanish alliance was welcomed by English manufacturers, eager to sell their iron and cotton goods to the Spanish colonies in America. From the military point of view, the alliance proved to be decisive: English persistence kept alive the Spanish revolt, and it was the 'Spanish ulcer', as Napoleon confessed, which ruined him.

The Peninsular War 1809-13

An army of 30,000 men was sent to Portugal under a young general called Sir Arthur Wellesley, who had already distinguished himself in India. Wellesley won the battle of Vimeiro, and was then superseded by superior officers arriving from England. Left to

Vimeiro 1808

185

SIR ARTHUR WELLESLEY, 1ST DUKE OF WELLINGTON (1769-1852)
(1804 portrait by Robert Home)

himself, Wellesley would probably have brought about the surrender of Junot's army; as it was, the French, by the Convention of Cintra of 1808, were allowed to evacuate Portugal without further loss. Napoleon himself now came to Spain; he had an army of 250,000 to hold down the country. Sir John Moore, the new British commander, advanced into Spain, and so drew off a large proportion of the French army, and certainly saved Lisbon. Napoleon sent Marshal Soult to chase the English to the north of Spain. Moore was killed at Corunna – they 'buried him darkly at dead of night' – but his army safely embarked on a British fleet at that port in 1809. Later in the year,

The Retreat
to Corunna
1809

Napoleon was obliged to return to Germany to fight the Austrians. He never re-crossed the Pyrenees. Spain he left to his marshals.

Sir Arthur Wellesley was once again given the command in Portugal. In the campaign of 1809, he advanced into Spain and won the battle of Talavera, but was again forced to retreat to Lisbon. Marshal Masséna now took the offensive with the object of driving the 'English leopard' into the sea. But Wellington's (Wellesley had just become a peer) tactics in 1810 foiled him. The English commander constructed lines of trenches across the peninsula on which Lisbon stands. These lines, known as the lines of Torres Vedras, were so well fortified that Masséna found it impossible to attack them. Besides this, Wellington had devastated the country around, so that Masséna soon found his army starving. Wellington, on the other hand, was in an impregnable position behind the lines, with Lisbon as a base; and Lisbon was supplied from the sea. Masséna was forced to retreat with heavy losses in 1811; and the French did not enter Portugal again.

Wellesley in Portugal

Torres Vedras 1810-1

These tactics wore down the French, who were further hampered by their long lines of communication – 500 miles from Portugal to the Pyrenees. The Spaniards waged a guerrilla warfare all the time, attacking French columns on the march and then retiring to their mountains. Napoleon, during the Peninsular War, had to wage two other major campaigns, one against Austria in 1809 and one against Russia in 1812. This made it difficult for him to relieve his harassed troops in the Peninsula. Above all, the supremacy of the British at sea secured their connexion with Lisbon, on which the whole of Wellington's schemes depended.

Difficulties of the French

In 1812 – the year of Napoleon's fatal expedition to Moscow – Wellington felt strong enough to advance into Spain. He began by storming the two fortresses of Badajoz and Ciudad Rodrigo, which commanded the two main roads from Portugal into Spain. Then he advanced as far as Salamanca, where he won a brilliant victory, and entered Madrid, whence Joseph Bonaparte fled. In spite of these

The Advance into Spain 1812

successes, the British commander thought it well to retire once more to Portugal for the winter. But in 1813 he reaped his reward. Starting from Portugal in May, he crossed the Pyrenees within forty days, driving the French before him. The last considerable action in Spain Vitoria 1813 was fought at Vitoria, where King Joseph lost all his artillery and stores; Wellington's campaign of 1814 began in the south of France. But by that time Napoleon was fighting with his back to the wall.

Walcheren Expedition 1809 We must now turn to glance at the rest of Europe during the time of the Peninsular War. In 1809 the British government sent an expedition under Lord Chatham (Pitt's brother) to the island of Walcheren, for the purpose of attacking Antwerp and destroying the French fleet there. The expedition was a dismal failure, and brought about the fall of the Government. Canning quarrelled with Castlereagh over Walcheren, and the two ministers fought a duel; both resigned from the Cabinet. A new ministry was formed under Spencer Perceval Ministry 1809-12 Perceval (1809-12), who was assassinated three years later by a lunatic in the precincts of the House of Commons. These dismal years were also years of economic difficulty, especially in 1808 and between the middle of 1810 and the end of 1811. Napoleon's boycott struck at exports and Britain's own Orders in Council produced difficulties with the USA, which also at times tried to keep out British exports. The worst year was 1811, when exports were at only two thirds of the level of 1810 and Lancashire was reduced to working a three-day week. Bad harvests had also threatened the country's food supply, but fortunately Napoleon bowed to the demand of his farmers that they should be allowed to export their surpluses. Ultimately, Napoleon's economic war was a failure. It was as damaging for France and its empire as it was to Britain and partly for this reason it was never applied for long enough to be truly effective. At no time did British morale look like collapsing. Over time, the British became ever more convinced that Bonaparte was a menace and had to be defeated.

Napoleon, meanwhile, had considerable difficulties with his enormous empire, the populations of which were feeling keenly the

EUROPE UNDER NAPOLEON, 1811

loss of British trade. In 1810 he had to depose his brother Louis, King of Holland, because he refused to put the Continental System into force. In order to control the continental ports, Napoleon annexed to France not only Holland, but the whole German coast up to the Elbe. Soon after this the Tsar followed King Louis' example, and broke with Napoleon. The French Emperor therefore embarked on his great Russian campaign in 1812, which ended in one of the most appalling disasters in military history. The Russians set fire to Moscow, and Napoleon had to retreat across the frozen plains back to Germany; he lost more than five-sixths of his army of 600,000 men.

Retreat from Moscow 1812

Liverpool
Ministry
1812-27

Castlereagh
Fourth
Coalition
1813

In 1812 Lord Liverpool became Prime Minister in England, and Lord Castlereagh Foreign Secretary (1812-22) and leader of the House of Commons (as an Irish peer, he was allowed to be elected for the Commons). Castlereagh was one of the most important figures in British politics for the next ten years. In 1813 he arranged the Fourth Coalition of Britain, Russia, and Prussia, and later Austria, which was destined to bring Napoleon to his knees. The revival of Prussia was followed by the desertion of Napoleon by all the German states. Castlereagh's job was made much easier by the news of Wellington's huge victory at Vitoria in June 1813, which gave the leading statesmen the confidence that French armies could be beaten. Napoleon still won another battle at Dresden, but in October 1813

Leipzig 1813

at Leipzig – the so-called 'Battle of the Nations' – he was decisively defeated. Even then Napoleon might have secured fair terms – he was offered the Rhine frontier. But he obstinately refused.

Allies invade
France

By 1814, as we have *see*n, Wellington was over the Pyrenees; he defeated the French at Toulouse. At the same time the allies – Russians, Germans, and Austrians – advanced into France, and the French, for the first time for twenty years, had to defend their own country. Napoleon fell back towards Paris, but the weight of numbers was too strong for him. Finally he signed his abdication at

Napoleon at
Elba 1814

Fontainebleau in 1814. He was taken to the island of Elba, and the victorious allies set about the difficult business of settling the frontiers of Europe.

Reasons for
Napoleon's
Fal

The defeat of Napoleon was due, in the first place, to the fact that he could never secure command of the sea, and so could never defeat Britain. In the second place, it was due to the failure of his Continental System to achieve its designed end: introduced in order to cripple Britain, it ended by turning Napoleon's allies into enemies and arousing everywhere the spirit of resistance. First Spain, then Holland, then Russia, then Germany – all these countries had revolted against the Napoleonic system. The help given at the critical moment by England to Spain, where the first national rising occurred, was the turning-point. The result was secured by the persistence of the British effort and the final decision by the other great powers that Napoleon's power had to be destroyed.

5. Waterloo and Vienna

The Congress of Vienna, which met to make a general settlement of Europe after the war, began its labours in 1814. Prussia, backed by Russia, fell into controversy with Austria, backed by Britain and more than once it seemed that war might break out between the former allies over Polish and Saxon territory.

The
Congress of
Vienna
1814-5

The Bourbon monarchy was restored in France, with Louis XVIII, a brother of Louis XVI, as King. But while the diplomats quarrelled at Vienna, and while the French people tried the doubtful experiment of a Bourbon restoration, Napoleon intervened. He escaped from Elba and landed in France. The soldiers sent to arrest him joined him instead and Louis XVIII fled from Paris. A few days later the Emperor was back in the Tuileries.

Napoleon
escapes
February
1815

Napoleon's restoration – his Hundred Days – was an anxious time for the allies; the nightmare of Napoleonic conquest once more loomed over Europe. The war against France was renewed; Britain declined to make peace as long as Napoleon remained on the throne. The command of the main allied army, chiefly British and German, was given to the Duke of Wellington.

The
Hundred
Days
(March-
June)

This army assembled in Belgium; Brussels was the Duke's head-quarters. In June 1815 Napoleon suddenly brought his forces up to Charleroi, on the Sambre, about 35 miles south of Brussels. On 16 June the Emperor divided his army into two parts, sending Ney to attack the British at Quatre-Bras, on the Brussels-Charleroi road, while he himself led the attack on the Prussians at Ligny. The battle of Ligny was Napoleon's last victory; he drove the Prussians back, and imagined that they were knocked out of the campaign. On 17 June, Napoleon

The
Waterloo
Campaign

Quatre-Bras
and Ligny
16 June

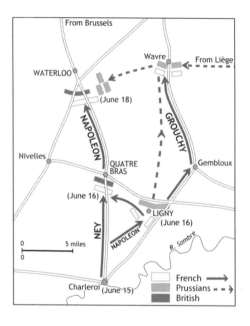

THE WATERLOO CAMPAIGN

joined Ney on the Brussels road. The next morning he began the attack
on Wellington, who awaited him on a ridge in front of the village of
Waterloo. The allied army numbered 67,000, of whom 24,000 were
British; the French had 74,000. Wellington's army occupied a good
defensive position and his object was to hold it until the Prussians could
come to his aid. The French therefore repeatedly took the initiative,
attacking the British positions at farms called Hougoumont and La
Haie Sainte. Attack after attack failed, coming up against the allied
artillery fire and the steady nerves of their infantry who formed
defensive and impenetrable squares when under attack from the French
cavalry. The effect of the French artillery was blunted by orders to the
men to lie down out of sight behind the ridge in front of the army till

*Waterloo
18 June 1815*

the enemy came close. Wellington himself was always at the point of crisis, rallying those pressed back, reacting coolly to emergencies, keeping control of his subordinate commanders. La Haie Sainte fell by the late afternoon, enabling the French to endanger Wellington's centre, but by that time the Prussians were coming on to the field. Blücher, the Prussian commander, had retired northwards after the battle of Ligny. The night of 17 June he lay at Wavre, 13 miles east of Waterloo. Marshal Grouchy had also been sent to Wavre, but he was unable to hold off the Prussian troops. Blücher sent a message promising to come to Wellington's aid, and he fulfilled his promise. Wellington was hard pressed when the Prussians came up, but the arrival of fresh troops turned the scale. About 7 o'clock Napoleon sent forward the Imperial Guard; then he launched his last cavalry reserve. When he knew that Napoleon had put forth his final effort, Wellington ordered the whole British line to advance. The French were routed; the battle was over. 'It has been a damned nice thing,' remarked the Duke afterwards, 'the nearest thing you ever saw in your life.'

After Waterloo Napoleon abdicated a second time, and surrendered to the British. He was taken to the little isolated island of St Helena in the Atlantic, where he died six years later. Napoleon's unquenchable passion for war and restless personal ambition had made him unpopular with many people, even in France, by 1814, but the glory and glamour associated with his career ensured that his high reputation would survive his defeat and continue to haunt the imagination of Frenchmen all through the 19th century and even beyond. He also left solid achievements behind him, particularly his legal reforms, known as the Civil Code, to which much of the rest of Europe had been introduced in the areas incorporated into France or ruled as French satellite states.

St. Helena

The prestige of Britain had never stood higher than in the year of Waterloo. The long duration of the British effort in the war, far surpassing that of her allies, the fame of her great general, the invincibility of her Navy – all combined to enhance the reputation of

The British Army

Britain in the eyes of Europe. The British army, thanks to Wellington's command, had renewed the great traditions of the Marlburian era. Wellington, who was a realist, described his men as 'the scum of the earth, enlisted for drink'; but the iron discipline of the Army – of which the military floggings were a degrading feature – moulded this unpromising material into fine soldiers. The British soldiers who pushed Napoleon's veterans across the Pyrenees were undoubtedly hard and brutal. But they were not permitted to live entirely on plunder, like the French, nor were they so brutal as the Prussian army of occupation in France, whose behaviour disgusted Wellington.

Castlereagh at Vienna

Treatment of France

The services of Castlereagh and Wellington, Britain's representatives at the Congress of Vienna, were invaluable. It was due to them that the allies, particularly Prussia, were prevented from taking revenge on France for the misdeeds of Napoleon. Wellington scorned revenge; and Britain has seldom been represented abroad by a greater statesman than Lord Castlereagh, though his merits were not recognized by the mass of his countrymen. Castlereagh helped to prevent the possibility of a war of revenge by France; he saw that the defeated nation was leniently treated. France was reduced to the limits of her 1791 frontiers and had to pay an indemnity; she lost no territory that had been held by the Bourbons. Britain restored most of the French colonies. Castlereagh was well aware how useful France could be in international affairs as a counter-weight to the eastern powers. Before the deliberations at Vienna were over Talleyrand, the French representative, had proved a useful ally against Russia and Prussia over the affairs of eastern Europe.

Since France had been defeated by a Quadruple Alliance, the Allies inevitably determined the provisions of the peace treaty following its defeat. Each of the four powers wanted its reward. Britain's rewards came in the world overseas. In Europe its main concern was to strengthen the surrounding states against possible future French aggression. This is why the Dutch swallowed Belgium to make a Kingdom of the Netherlands under the House of Orange. Prussia's gains in the Rhineland and Westphahia were not only part of its reward, but also committed Prussia to resist future French attacks on western Germany. In north Italy Piedmont was strengthened by the addition of Genoa and further east Austrian power in Milan and Venice and its influence over restored principalities in central Italy were expected to keep the French out of the peninsula. It was hoped that the restored Bourbon monarchy in Spain would provide a government strong enough to discourage French incursions in the future. The powers hoped in any case that the rule of Louis XVIII in France would prove an antidote to revolutionary zeal. In the east the settlement was shaped by the eastern powers' ambitions. There was no chance of a restoration of Poland: Austria and Prussia regained some Polish territory, but the Tsar was set on having the bulk of the ancient kingdom. He also took Finland from Sweden. Prussia was keen to have the whole of Saxony, but, opposed by the other powers, it settled for half of it.

Of the many conquests which Britain had made all over the world from France and her allies – Spain, Holland, and Denmark – a great part was restored. The French and Spanish West Indian islands of St Lucia, Tobago, and Trinidad were retained. So was Malta, and also Mauritius (in the Indian Ocean). But Java and Sumatra, Holland's valuable East Indian islands, were restored. The Danes surrendered the rock of Heligoland in the North Sea, and a British protectorate was established over the Ionian Islands in the eastern Mediterranean. Britain paid the Dutch three million pounds to keep British Guiana, and six million pounds to keep the Cape of Good Hope; Britain also kept Ceylon. Most of these places – Malta, the Cape, Mauritius, Ceylon, Singapore – were valued as being useful ports of call for the Navy and merchant-ships rather than as possible colonies. Hanover was of course restored to the British King; but this remained a purely personal union.

British Gains in 1815

Summary of the Vienna Settlement, 1815

A. SETTLEMENT OF EUROPE.

1. *Germany.* All Germany, under the presidency of Austria, was formed into the German Confederation (now consisting of thirty-nine states instead of over three hundred and fifty of the Empire before the French Revolution), which lasted till 1866. *Austria* received the Italian province of Lombardy (which she had held before the war) and, in addition, the whole territory of the ancient Italian republic of Venice. *Prussia* received a large part of Saxony (which had always fought for Napoleon) and another large province in western Germany, known as the Rhine Province and Westphalia.

2. *Italy.* All the old states were restored, except the republics of Venice (allotted to Austria) and Genoa (allotted to Sardinia).

3. North Europe. *Russia* received most of Poland, and also Finland from Sweden. *Sweden* was compensated with Norway (formerly Danish) – Norway and Sweden remained united till 1905.

4. Holland and Belgium were joined together as the *Kingdom of the Netherlands*, under a Dutch ruler. This union lasted till the Belgians revolted in 1830.

5. The *Turkish Empire* was not dealt with, but Russia had gained Bessarabia shortly before 1815.

B. BRITISH GAINS IN 1815.

1. In Europe: Heligoland (from Denmark), Malta, and the Ionian Isles (Greece). Hanover was restored to George III.

2. In America: St Lucia, Tobago, Trinidad, British Honduras, and British Guiana.

3. In Africa and the Indian Ocean: Cape Colony, Mauritius, and (in 1824 but arising out of this Treaty) Malacca. Ceylon had been ceded to Britain by the Dutch in 1802 (by the Treaty of Amiens).

Date Summary: The Great French War (1793-1815)

SEA	BRITISH MILITARY EFFORTS	FRANCE AND EUROPE

THE CONVENTION AND THE DIRECTORY (1793-9)

SEA	BRITISH MILITARY EFFORTS	FRANCE AND EUROPE
1793 Siege of Toulon	1793 British expedition to Netherlands	1793-5 Conquest of Belgium and Holland
1794 ⚔ 1st of June		1795 Treaty of Basle (Prussia) Spain makes peace Directory in France
1795 Landing at Cape Town		
1796-7 Ceylon and Dutch East Indies		1796-7 Napoleon's Italian Campaign
1797 (Feb.) ⚔ Cape St. Vincent		Conquest of N. Italy
Trinidad captured		1797 Treaty of Campo Formio
1798 ⚔ Nile	1798-1905 Wellesley in India	1799 Second Coalition
1799 Siege of Acre Nelson at Naples		1799 Napoleon's Coup d'état

NAPOLEON FIRST CONSUL (1799-1804)

SEA	BRITISH MILITARY EFFORTS	FRANCE AND EUROPE
1800 British take Malta		1800 ⚔ Marengo
1801 Armed Neutrality of the North First ⚔ Copenhagen		1802 Treaty of Amiens
		1803 War renewed
		1804 Napoleon Emperor

NAPOLEON EMPEROR (1804-15)

SEA	BRITISH MILITARY EFFORTS	FRANCE AND EUROPE
1804-5 Invasion of England scheme		1805 Third Coalition ⚔ Austerlitz
1805 ⚔ Trafalgar		Napoleon master of Italy and Germany
		1806 ⚔ Jena. Napoleon in Berlin
1807 Second ⚔ Copenhagen		1807 Treaty of Tilsit
British fleet in the Tagus		French invade Portugal
	1808 Wellesley in Portugal ⚔ Vimiero	1808 Joseph Bonaparte, King of Spain
	1809 Walcheren Expedition	1809 ⚔ Wagram
	1810-11 Torres Vedras	
1812-4 American War	1812 ⚔ Salamanca	1812 Retreat from Moscow
	1813 ⚔ Vitoria	1813 Fourth Coalition ⚔ Leipzig
	1814 ⚔ Toulouse	1814 Treaty of Chaumont Allies invade France Napoleon abdicates
	1815 (June) ⚔ Waterloo	
		1815 (Feb.) Napoleon escapes from Elba (Mar.-June) Hundred Days
		1815 Treaty of Vienna

FRENCH GOVERNMENTS		COALITIONS (v. FRANCE)	
The Convention	1792-5	First Coalition	1793-5
The Directory	1795-9	Second Coalition	1799-1800
The Consulate	1799-1804	Third Coalition	1805
The Empire	1804-14 and 1815	Fourth Coalition	1813-5

VIII

IRELAND (1775-1800)

1. Grattan

BY comparison with England, 18th century Ireland was very poor. It lacked wood, coal and iron, commodities that fed the industries of Britain. It had land and cheap labour, but the kind of agricultural improvements which had taken place in England had mostly passed Ireland by. Endemic disorder and random violence did not encourage investment and many of the greatest landowners were absentees, more concerned with immediate income than long term development of their estates. The main change in Irish agriculture was increased cultivation of the potato. Under this crop, the soil was intensively cultivated and supported a much increased population of farmers living near subsistence level. Despite the rights of landowners enshrined in law, the peasants regarded the land they worked as rightfully theirs and they sought to work it in the traditional way without interference. Irish trade had been much hindered by laws preventing it from competing with English interests within the empire: for example, the Irish wool trade was effectively banned. Only Irish linen had been encouraged.

> Ireland in the 18th century

The history of Ireland in the 17th century had left Irish society divided into three main groups. The majority were Roman Catholics whose ancestors had been crushed, first by military conquest, and then by a systematic persecution. Penal laws had been enacted against them. Hundreds of Irishmen, despairing of their own country, emigrated abroad. The King of France had a special brigade, called the Irish Brigade, formed entirely of exiled Irishmen. These men revenged themselves on England by fighting against her on the continent, during the various wars of the 18th century. Some improvement in the position of the Catholics took place towards the

> Irish Emigration

middle of the century, in that some of the laws restricting their freedom were allowed to fall into disuse, particularly those limiting the Catholic clergy. There were still, however, many circumstances which made the Catholics discontented. None could vote, or sit in the Irish parliament, or take part in local government. They were

The Protestant Oligarchy

effectively aliens in their own country. The great mass of them were poor peasants, because the conquests of Ireland by Cromwell and William III had led to the dispossession of Catholic landowners and the transfer of their lands to Englishmen or Scots.

The second important group in Ireland was the Presbyterian population of the north. This community had originated when Scottish colonization of Ulster had been encouraged in the reign of James I in the hope of creating a counterweight to the Catholic majority. The northern Protestants had been reinforced by massive Scottish immigration in the 1690s. The rights of these people to complete freedom of worship were guaranteed by an act of 1719, but they were prevented from taking any part in the government.

The third group was constituted by the members of the Protestant Church of Ireland, organized on the same lines and sharing the same faith and liturgy as the Church of England. The Anglicans constituted a small minority of the total population, but they had a

Religious bigotry

monopoly of political power. In their hands too was much of the land of Ireland, especially outside Ulster, since they were descendants of the beneficiaries of the confiscations of the 17th century. This situation had been brought about because it seemed the best guarantee of continued English domination of Ireland, which in turn seemed vital to English security. Yet England had problems even with this group. They resented the constitutional and economic limitations which England imposed upon them and, unlike the Catholics and

The Irish Parliament

Presbyterians, they had the means of voicing their complaints. That means was the Irish Parliament. This body had 300 members, most of whom sat for rotten borough seats controlled by great Anglican Irish families. The members were organized in interest groups who sold their support to the lord-lieutenant, who represented the King and ran the government of Ireland. If they did not get what they wanted, they were liable to stir up the discontented population in order to increase their bargaining power.

The American war brought a crisis in the relations between Britain and the Anglican landowners of Ireland. The war made Ireland more than usually discontented by producing a depression when Irish exports of woollens and provisions to America or France became classed as illegal trade with the enemy. The Anglicans wanted to assist the empire in its struggle and raised volunteers for home defence, so that the troops in Ireland could be freed for service elsewhere. By 1779 there were 8,000 of them. The politicians at once realized that they could be a valuable weapon in any struggle with the lord-lieutenant.

Lord North had appointed Lord Buckinghamshire as lord-lieutenant. He hoped to change the system in Ireland so that government relied less on bribing the MPs. The leaders of the political interest groups in the Irish parliament disliked this policy and began to ally with the merchants and volunteers against the lord-lieutenant. He decided to appeal to liberal opinion in Ireland by getting North to propose the lifting of all restrictions on Irish trade. North, however, backed away when faced with protests from English interests. The result was a crisis. In 1779 the Irish took a leaf out of the Americans' book by boycotting English imports. The opposition to North in England, men like Rockingham and Fox, encouraged the Irish in their resistance to the government. In the Irish Parliament two powerful orators from the governing group, Flood and Grattan, Henry demanded freedom of Irish trade and they were backed at rallies of Grattan volunteers. The Irish parliament proceeded to use its power of the purse. It refused to underwrite government loans and threatened to withhold taxes.

It was now clear to North that he had to make concessions to Ireland despite English reservations. In 1780 Ireland gained the right to trade freely with the British colonies, freedom of wool and glass exports, the right to share in trade with the Middle East and a bounty on linen exports to England. Most members of the Irish Parliament were satisfied with North's concessions, but Grattan and Flood declared that Irish gains would not be secure unless constitutional changes were made. In this fresh demand, they were supported by the Whigs.

In 1782 Rockingham's Whigs came to power. There was still unrest in Ireland. The delegates of the volunteers meeting at Dungannon voted that Britain should not make laws for Ireland. The Whigs were anxious that Ireland should not go the way of America and believed that winning Irish goodwill should be the foundation of policy. They repealed an Act of 1719, which declared the right of the British Parliament to make laws for Ireland, and they abolished the right of the Privy Council to alter Irish laws, dating from Henry VII's reign. The Irish Parliament showed its satisfaction by voting to raise 20,000 Irish seamen.

Yet difficult issues had been left to the future. How were two independent Parliaments to be co-ordinated? The link between them was the King. He appointed the British ministers, who appointed a lord-lieutenant of Ireland to rule in the King's name. In these appointments, the King respected the wishes of the British Parliament, but he could not respect also the wishes of the Irish Parliament if they were different. In reality, the Irish Parliament was not equal with the British one and Irish leaders would continue to exhibit an opposition mentality, as Grattan showed by refusing office. Sooner or later, the two Parliaments were bound to clash.

Nonetheless, the 1780s were a prosperous time for Ireland. There was a general revival of trade, with particular progress in the linen and glass industries and in sugar refining. The former volunteers had split into conservatives and radicals. Grattan attempted to keep both united. He hoped to bring about parliamentary reform with full emancipation for non-Anglicans, since he appreciated that he could then criticize government measures with more authority. He believed that such reforms would prove compatible with the maintenance of leadership by the Anglican landowners. Not everyone was so optimistic.

2. The Rebellion and the Union

GIVEN the discontents of the country, it is not surprising that the effects of the French Revolution were soon felt in Ireland. There was a widespread movement in favour of the French ideals; and soon a party was formed which demanded far more than Grattan had ever contemplated. The United Irishmen, a society formed in 1791, was anti-English and republican in aim. Its leaders, Wolfe Tone and Lord Edward Fitzgerald, sought to unite the Catholics of the South with the Presbyterians of the North against the rule of England.

The United Irishmen 1791

In the 1780s Pitt had attempted to extend complete free trade to Ireland, but had been forced to give way in the face of determined opposition from English interests. In the 1790s, however, it seemed too dangerous to leave Irish affairs alone. Pitt's aims were twofold. First, he hoped to heal the religious divisions within Irish society by reconciling Anglicans, Presbyterians and Catholics. Second, he aimed to secure co-operation between Ireland and England as it struggled against France. He took a first step towards the realization of his aims by passing the Catholic Relief Act through the Irish Parliament in 1793. Catholics were given the right to vote on the same basis as Protestants. They were given the right to sit on juries, to hold minor civil posts and to hold junior commissioned rank in the army. This was not full emancipation: Catholics were barred from the top places in the administration and could not sit in Parliament.

In 1795, Pitt sent over as lord-lieutenant Lord Fitzwilliam, a Whig who had joined his government at the time of the Burke-Fox split. Fitzwilliam was a man of liberal views; he entirely sympathized with the idea of complete Catholic emancipation, and he led the Irish

Lord Fitzwilliam 1795

to suppose that such was the view of the British government. Pitt probably was already aiming for full emancipation, but he knew that he would meet opposition from the King and probably from the cabinet. He had no alternative but to sack Fitzwilliam and dissociate himself from his plans. The effects of the episode were unfortunate. The enemies of reform in Ireland were alerted, while Catholics and Presbyterians were upset when their hopes of change were dashed.

The United Irishmen now began to correspond with the French republicans, who promised to come to their aid. A French general, Hoche, appeared with a fleet in Bantry Bay, with 15,000 soldiers on board. A storm dispersed the ships, and Hoche failed to land; had he done so, Britain might have found its supremacy in Ireland endangered. Certainly, the officials in Dublin feared that Britain's rule over Ireland was in serious danger from a possible combination of French invasion and Irish rebellion.

Hoche's Expedition 1796

There was formidable revolutionary preparation among the Presbyterians of Ulster. Ordered to suppress it, General Lake had to call on the yeomanry to assist him. These militiamen were ardent defenders of property and Anglicanism. Their disarmament of the Ulster Presbyterians was brutal in the extreme. Floggings were administered on the flimsiest of pretexts: for example, a teacher was flogged for knowing French, since anyone who knew French must clearly be a traitor. Yet the disarmament was effective and the organization of the United Irishmen in the North was crippled.

Meanwhile, Wolfe Tone's effort to include the Protestants in his organization broke down owing to his alliance with the Catholic 'Defender' movement. The 'United' Irishmen became a misnomer; that society, crushed in the North, was now almost entirely composed of Roman Catholics, and hatred of the English was stirred up by the priests. In Ulster, Orange Lodges were formed to combat the danger from Catholics; Protestants all over the country rallied to the government to save the country from a French invasion. Civil war broke out wherever Orangemen and Catholics came in contact. Use

The Orange Lodges

of Protestant yeomanry was extended to the South: suspect Catholics were hunted down in a manner reminiscent of the worst days of Cromwell or Elizabeth. Once again ugly passions were aroused in the name of religion; murders and other outrages were committed by both sides.

The Protestant Yeomanry

The excesses of the Protestant yeomanry provoked the rebellion of '98. The rising was ill planned and soon suppressed. General Lake defeated the main rebel force at Vinegar Hill, County Wexford. Other local efforts, led in many cases by priests, were put down, all with great cruelty. The French sent a small force of 1,000 men under General Humbert which landed in Killala Bay, routed some of Lake's troops at Castlebar, but was finally outnumbered and forced to surrender. Another French expedition was destroyed at sea. On board one of the captured ships was Wolfe Tone, the Irish leader. He was tried for treason, and sentenced to death, but committed suicide in prison. The other major ringleader, Lord Edward Fitzgerald, a former army officer repelled by the excesses of coercion in Ireland, had already been captured fighting, and had died of his wounds.

The Irish Rebellion 1798

Its suppression

When the last Catholic rising had been stamped out, and the last Frenchman captured, Ireland once more lay at the feet of her conqueror. Lord Cornwallis, who had just come over as viceroy, deplored the intolerant tone he found among the English officials at Dublin Castle, and among his own officers. Cornwallis, his Secretary Lord Castlereagh and the Prime Minister Pitt all realized that brutal suppression of rebellion was not sufficient to make the Irish problem go away. They decided to bring about a union of the British and Irish Parliaments, on the model of the union of the English and Scottish Parliaments which had taken place in 1707. Lord Castlereagh was entrusted with the task of putting the Bill of Union through the Irish Parliament. Two methods were employed to induce the Irish Parliament to vote for its own abolition. One was bribery: money was poured out to members of the Dublin parliament; jobs were offered; lavish promises of peerages were made. Pitt's second method was

The Act of Union 1800

persuasion. The insecurity of the Anglicans who controlled the Dublin parliament had recently been made clear by the revolt and so had their dependence on armed force sent from England. Irish Anglicans could no longer afford the constant quarrels with England that possession of an independent parliament led to. The benefits of free trade between Britain and Ireland that would flow from union were also pointed out.

Pitt had a further argument with which to convince reformist doubters about the benefits of a union. Religious passions in Ireland would make it impossible to pass Catholic emancipation through an Irish parliament, whereas in the less charged atmosphere at Westminster a united Parliament would not baulk at such a measure. Moreover, in an Irish context Catholic emancipation was too dangerous, since Catholics would constitute a majority. In the context of a United Kingdom, emancipation could safely be granted.

In 1800 the Bill of Union was introduced by Lord Castlereagh into the Irish Parliament, and carried in spite of Grattan's opposition. In one of his noblest speeches the Irish patriot spoke against the measure, and prophesied that the day would come when Ireland would regain her liberty:

'Liberty may repair her golden beams, and with redoubled heart animate the country . . . I do not give up the country. I see her in a swoon, but she is not dead; though in her tomb she lies helpless and motionless, still there is on her lips a spirit of life, and on her cheeks a glow of beauty:

Thou art not conquered; beauty's ensign yet
Is crimson in thy lips and in thy cheeks,
And death's pale flag is not advanced there.'

Grattan's rhetoric, together with his quotation from *Romeo and Juliet*, makes Pitt seem to be the assassin of liberty, but the Parliament that he destroyed represented only a small minority of propertied Anglicans.

The Bill was passed, and the Dublin Parliament came to an end on 1st January 1801. Ireland was for the future to be represented by 100 members in the House of Commons at Westminster, and by 28 peers and 4 bishops in the British House of Lords. And there was at last to be free trade between the two islands.

The chances that the English and the Irish could achieve reconciliation within the framework of the Union were never good. The Union could not overcome the problem of Ireland's poverty, nor could it make the Irish forget the grievances that had accumulated over the centuries. Yet it rapidly became clear that not even the religious division between England and the bulk of the Irish was going to be bridged. Pitt had been sincere in offering Catholic emancipation, but he found himself unable to deliver. George III considered that to give the Irish Catholics their political freedom would be to violate his coronation oath. Pitt had sometimes managed to bring the King round to his point of view, but on this matter George III felt exceptionally strongly. Moreover, the cabinet was far from united on the matter. Pitt could therefore not proceed. Yet he had given his word to the Irish team of Cornwallis and Castlereagh and through them to the Irish parliament which had dissolved itself. Honour compelled Pitt therefore to resign. This was an age when statesmen were concerned with their honour: Castlereagh and Canning would fight a duel over it. For this reason Pitt gave up at the age of 41 the only job he had ever wanted to do.

Pitt's broken promise

Ireland slid down the agenda of British politicians. Napoleon needed a shorter sea crossing than any to Ireland for his invasion plans and ignored the country. British statesmen concentrated on defeating him. The 19th century was to show, however, that the Union of the Parliaments had increased the capacity of developments in Ireland to disrupt British politics.

IX

THE EMPIRE UNDER GEORGE III

1. India

(i) *Warren Hastings.*

North's Regulating Act, 1773

After Clive's career in India, the whole problem of Anglo-Indian relations entered on a new stage. Before Clive's conquest of Bengal, the East India Company had been concerned merely with matters of trade; now, for better or worse, the servants of the Company had taken over political power. No one, even then, could foresee that the whole of India was destined to pass under British control. But it was already obvious that British responsibilities were too great to be left to the Company alone. Lord North's Government therefore passed the Regulating Act in 1773. By this Act the Governor of Bengal was made Governor-General of all the Company's possessions in India. He was to rule with the aid of a Council of Four, whose vote could restrain his actions. He was also bound to submit his political decisions to the approval not only of the Company, but of the British Government.

Warren Hastings 1774-85

It was under this Act that Warren Hastings, who had already been, for two years, Governor of Bengal, was appointed Governor-General of India. The first in the long line of Governor-Generals, Warren Hastings stands not unworthily at the head of those men whom Britain sent to govern the East. Bred from a boy in the service of the East India Company, he knew more of Indian life and literature than anyone else in the service and believed in making personal arrangements to suit Indian conditions. He had many useful qualities – resourcefulness, courage, and a capacity for hard work – but he was not a good committee man, and it was a committee that the Regulating Act had saddled him with.

Warren Hastings was hampered at every turn by the Council of Four, whom the constitution (under the Regulating Act) obliged him to consult. Three of its members, including Philip Francis, who arrived in India already certain that Hastings was corrupt, were his personal enemies, so that he could seldom obtain a majority vote in the Council for his measures. A crisis arose over the execution of a wealthy Hindu, named Nandakumar, for forgery. The Council sympathized with Nandakumar, and Francis believed (and afterwards asserted) that the Hindu had been put out of the way because he was about to expose Hastings' own misdeeds. In 1776 one of Hastings' three enemies on the Council died, and the situation became less strained. But Hastings and Francis ultimately fought a duel; Francis was severely wounded, and had to return to England, where he did his best to poison every one's mind against the Governor-General.

Hastings and the Council

The main crisis of Hastings' rule arose when France joined in the American War from 1778 to 1783. The danger was that the French would give help to those native princes in India who were hostile to the British power. Of these princes the most formidable were the chieftains of the famous Mahratta Confederacy, and Haidar Ali, the able and warlike ruler of Mysore. The Mahrattas succeeded in defeating Bombay, a defeat which Hastings, overriding Francis, saw must be avenged if British prestige were to be upheld. He strained every nerve to raise money, to find troops and to secure the aid of friendly princes. General Goddard was sent to attack the Mahrattas from the west, while Hastings assaulted them from the east. A highlight was the capture of the supposedly impregnable fortress of Gwalior, 'the key to Hindustan'. The crisis was not yet over, because Madras, which was only nominally under Hastings' control, had antagonized several local Indian states, especially Haidar Ali of Mysore. Haidar Ali was a Muslim adventurer who had usurped the throne of Mysore from Hindu rulers. In 1780 he invaded the Carnatic, which was under British protection, and threatened Madras itself. Hastings, as soon as he heard the news, acted with great vigour:

The Maritime War 1778-83

First Mysore War 1780-2

he sent Sir Eyre Coote with all the men and supplies he could collect
to the Carnatic. Coote, on the scene of his former triumphs, beat
Haidar Ali at Porto Novo in 1781, and so saved Madras.

Suffren and Hughes

Meanwhile, the French had entered the conflict. Admiral Suffren,
with a strong squadron, did his best to cut the British sea
communications with India. He was opposed by Admiral Sir Edward
Hughes. This naval struggle, though fought for three years, was
indecisive. The death of Haidar Ali in 1782, and the end of the
French War in 1783, at last brought peace to India. Thanks to
Warren Hastings, British India had not gone the way of the
American colonies. Instead, without aid from outside, Hastings had
greatly improved the British standing in the sub-continent.

Hastings left India in 1785. On his return home, instead of
receiving the public recognition which his great services deserved,
he had to stand his trial for misgoverning India. The long and

Trial of Warren Hastings

protracted trial of Warren Hastings in Westminster Hall, which went
on, with various postponements, for seven years from 1788 to 1795,
formed one of the most famous scenes in English legal history. The
principal witnesses for the prosecution were Philip Francis and other

Its results

enemies from India. On their side they had the powerful aid of
Edmund Burke, who knew nothing about India, but who had formed
the opinion that Warren Hastings was a tyrant. The old accusation
that Hastings had unjustly procured the execution of Nandakumar
was renewed, and Hastings was accused of corruption. It was true
that he had not prevented Company officials from exploiting their
positions, but he argued that too drastic a policy would simply have
driven them all into revolt. Burke thundered with all his eloquence
against the accused; he said that the acts complained of were 'the
damned and damnable proceedings of a judge in hell, and such a
judge was Warren Hastings'. In the end Hastings was acquitted; he
retired into private life, and lived to the age of 93. False as were most
of the accusations made against him, his trial did good in one way.
Burke's eloquent appeal on behalf of the suffering millions of India,

whom he supposed Hastings to have misruled, helped to awaken a sense of responsibility in Britain towards the peoples under its rule. This sense of responsibility, coupled with the abolition of slavery, did much to mould the character of the Second British Empire which was built up after Waterloo.

(ii) *India under Pitt's India Act.*

When Pitt took office in 1783, it was generally recognized that further legislation was necessary to amend Lord North's Act, under which Warren Hastings had done his best to govern India. Pitt therefore introduced his India Act in 1784. By this Act the position of the Governor-General was strengthened; he was made independent of his Council, which became only an advisory body. In London a special Board of Control (the forerunner of the India Office) was set up to deal with Indian affairs, and through it the government was able to guide Indian policy, with the co-operation of the Governor-General. The Company was to confine itself to commercial affairs, and had no voice in the appointment of the Governor-General. This arrangement lasted till the abolition of the Company in 1858.

Pitt's India Act, 1784

Pitt's first appointment under the Act was Lord Cornwallis, of Yorktown fame, who became Governor-General for seven years (1786-93). He made what is known as the Permanent Settlement of Bengal. He laid down regulations for the administration of justice, and the collection of revenue, which became the model for future British provinces. He took steps to change the ethos of company administration by increasing salaries and reducing perquisites. The freebooting days of Clive were finally gone and the way was paved for the emergence of the Indian Civil Service with its reputation for incorruptibility. Cornwallis also embarked on a war with Mysore, now ruled by Tipu Sultan, the son of Haidar Ali. Tipu was a no less aggressive ruler than his father; in 1789 he invaded Travancore, a state which was under the protection of the Madras government. He

Lord Cornwallis 1786-93

Second Mysore War

was defeated by the British forces, and as a result was forced to cede some small outlying portions of his dominions to the Company. Cornwallis was moderate in victory: his assumption was that major extensions of British-held territory should be avoided.

In 1793 Cornwallis left India, and was succeeded by Sir John Shore, whose five years' rule (1793-8) was an uneventful period. After him came the Marquis Wellesley, whose vigorous personality at once stamped itself on Indian affairs. Wellesley realized that Britain could not rule part of India peacefully without dominating the whole, and he therefore determined to change the British Empire *in* India to the British Empire *of* India. He was probably influenced too by the impending revolution in British trade with India. The expansion of the Lancashire cotton industry raised the possibility of turning India into a highly profitable market for British goods instead of a place where Indian goods could be procured for European markets. This could be more easily accomplished if Britain became the leading power in India. In London Wellesley had an ally in Pitt's trusted ally Dundas.

Wellesley 1798-1805

Wellesley arrived in India at the time of the French expedition to Egypt, when the success or failure of Bonaparte's schemes still hung in the balance. Tipu Sultan of Mysore, England's sworn foe, had declared himself in favour of the French Revolution: he was 'Citizen Tipu', the ally of Napoleon. Wellesley soon decided that Tipu must be crushed before Napoleon could either send aid or – what was not thought unlikely – come himself to India. Wellesley began with Hyderabad, a large but unmilitary state sandwiched between warlike neighbours, Mysore and the Mahratta chieftains. Wellesley offered the British alliance to the Nizam of Hyderabad, with the alternative of war. The Nizam was easily persuaded to abandon the French alliance, to disarm his French troops, to keep an army under British officers, and to join with Wellesley against Tipu and the Mahrattas. The alliance with the Nizam was thus made the key-stone of Wellesley's policy in southern India. It was the first of these

Citizen Tipu

The Nizam

The Subsidiary Alliance Policy

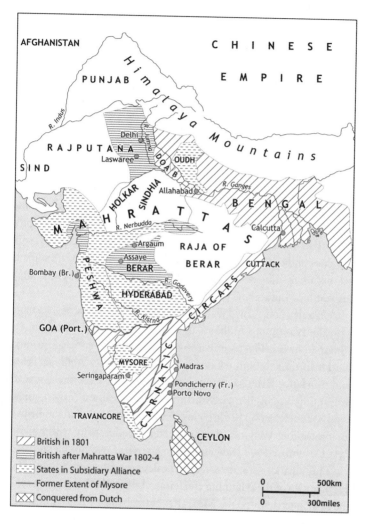

AFGHANISTAN

CHINESE EMPIRE

PUNJAB

Himalaya Mountains

R. Indus

RAJPUTANA

Delhi

DOAB

OUDH

SIND

Laswaree

HOLKAR

SINDHIA

Allahabad

R. Ganges

BENGAL

M A H R A T T A S

R. Nerbudda

Argaum

Calcutta

RAJA OF BERAR

Assaye

BERAR

CUTTACK

PESHWA

Bombay (Br.)

R. Godavery

HYDERABAD

CIRCARS

R. Kistna

GOA (Port.)

MYSORE

Madras

Seringaparam

CARNATIC

Pondicherry (Fr.)

Porto Novo

TRAVANCORE

CEYLON

⧄ British in 1801
☰ British after Mahratta War 1802-4
⋯ States in Subsidiary Alliance
— Former Extent of Mysore
⊠ Conquered from Dutch

| 0 | | 500km |
| 0 | | 300miles |

INDIA UNDER WELLESLEY

subsidiary alliances by means of which he and his successors entered into a league with half of India for the purpose of conquering the other half.

The Mysore War, which shortly broke out, did not last long. The campaign was conducted by Sir Arthur Wellesley, the Governor-General's younger brother (afterwards the victor of Waterloo), who easily beat Tipu's army in the field, and besieged his capital, Seringapatam. British cannon battered down the walls, the troops entered the town, and Tipu was killed in the fight. After this the danger from Mysore was over. Wellesley annexed the eastern coast-line and other parts, so that Mysore was reduced to half its former size. He restored the ancient line of Hindu rajahs, whom Tipu's father had deposed; and the restored rulers became, like the Nizam, the allies of the Company. Shortly after this in 1801, the Carnatic was put definitely under the rule of the Governor of Madras, so that all the south of India came under British control.

Wellesley now turned his attention to northern India, and formed, with the Nawab of Oudh, an alliance similar to that already made with the Nizam. The Nawab also ceded a tract of territory known as the Doab directly to the Company. Soon after this Wellesley came into contact with the Mahrattas, whose chieftains were then engaged in fighting among themselves. In 1802, the Peshwa, their nominal head, was defeated in battle by his neighbours, and fled to the British for protection. Wellesley thereupon concluded a treaty with him on 31st December 1802 and engaged to go to war with his enemies.

This alliance soon involved Wellesley in a war with Sindhia and Holkar, two of the Mahratta chieftains. Arthur Wellesley again took the field, and defeated the Mahrattas at the battle of Assaye in 1803, despite odds of ten to one against him. At the same time General Lake attacked Sindhia, whose territories lay next to those of Oudh, and took from him Delhi, the capital city of India. After the storming of Delhi, the British took possession of the person of the Great Mughal, who had long been the prisoner of the Mahrattas, so that

Marginal notes:

Third Mysore War, 1799

Conquest of Mysore, and of the Carnatic

Treaty with Oudh

Treaty of Bassein 1802

Mahratta War 1803-5

Capture of Delhi, 1803

the Mughal now exchanged masters. One more battle – Laswaree – sufficed to complete the ruin of Sindhia. He also submitted, and surrendered a large slice of territory round Delhi. The other Mahratta chief, Holkar, who had so far stood aloof from the war, now tried conclusions with the British. He was more successful than his fellow chieftains, and inflicted one severe defeat on the British forces. It was this military reverse, together with the cost of the operations, which led to Wellesley's recall in 1805. The British government had become alarmed at the lengths to which his policy was leading them.

Holkar

Recall of Wellesley 1805

Wellesley, in his few years of power, had laid the foundations of British India. The map shows his work in consolidating the British possessions in the Peninsula – north, east, and south. He had struck the first great blow at the Mahratta power, which one of his successors was to complete by the final humiliation of that once-powerful confederacy. Henceforth the British were the unquestioned masters of India, with forty millions under their direct rule. For good or ill, Wellesley's work was done; his successors had to live up to the position which he had created, and from which there could be no going back. Whatever may be thought of Wellesley's high-handed methods, it must be admitted that his work brought peace to India. *The Pax Britannica*, which he inaugurated, depended upon the defeat of the military states, like Mysore, and the absorption of the weak by alliances or direct annexation. The success of his policy meant a new empire for Britain in the East, and a new market for British manufactures.

His work
The Pax Britannica

2. Canada

The present Dominion of Canada has grown out of the small province which Britain conquered from France in 1763. This province consisted of a strip of territory on either side of the St Lawrence, from Lake Ontario to the mouth of the river. It contained

British North America in 1763

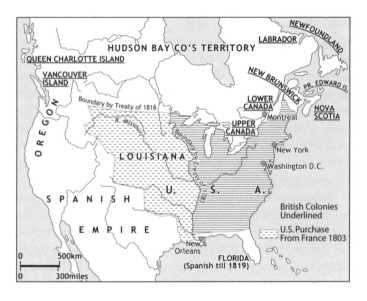

NORTH AMERICA AT THE BEGINNING OF THE 19TH CENTURY

only about 70,000 colonists, all Frenchmen. Two hundred miles east of Canada lay another ex-French colony, Acadie or Nova Scotia, which had been ceded to England at the Peace of Utrecht (1713). Here the population was mixed French and British, the French predominating. To the north and west of Canada lay the vast undefined territory of the Hudson's Bay Company, sparsely peopled by hunters and fur traders.

Sir Guy
Carleton
Quebec Act,
1774

The problem of dealing with the French-speaking, Catholic inhabitants of Canada was solved by a great British administrator, Sir Guy Carleton, afterwards Lord Dorchester, who twice held office as Governor of Canada. Carleton's work was to reconcile the French population to a foreign rule. He achieved this by showing respect for both the customs and the religion of the Canadians, and by

216

persuading the British government to pass the Quebec Act of 1774, by which freedom of worship was guaranteed to Roman Catholics in Canada.

The extent of Carleton's success was shown by the fact that the Canadians remained loyal to him during the American War, when he was able successfully to repel the invasion of Canada by the American revolutionaries. Immediately after the war a new problem arose. About 100,000 former residents of the American Colonies fled from their homes, and took refuge under the British flag. They were known as the United Empire Loyalists, and their crime, in the eyes of their fellow countrymen, was that they had declared themselves in favour of the continuance of British rule. In 1783, when victory had crowned the efforts of the revolutionaries, they were not at all disposed to show mercy to the Loyalists, who were hounded out of the United States. The victims fled to Nova Scotia, and from there founded the separate province of New Brunswick. Others settled among the French in Canada, but more still penetrated the forests to the north-east of Lake Ontario, and settled a new province – Ontario – between the Great Lakes and the Albany River. *United Empire Loyalists*

New Brunswick

Ontario

There were now two maritime colonies (Nova Scotia and New Brunswick) and two inland colonies, Ontario and Quebec, known respectively also as Upper Canada and Lower Canada. The problem which faced the younger Pitt, as Prime Minister, was to reconcile the varying interests of the French and British in the two Canadas. He decided that the demand of the British in Upper Canada for a representative form of government – a free Parliament on the English model – could not be refused. But the French Canadians were suspicious of that institution, Parliament, which they described as *une machine anglaise pour nous taxer* (English machinery for taxing us). Nevertheless, Pitt decided to try the experiment of colonial Parliaments in both the Canadas. But he did not consider it wise to unite the two provinces under one rule, since he thought that the two races would be certain to quarrel. So his Canada Act of 1791 provided *The two Canadas*

Pitt's Canada Act 1791

both Upper and Lower Canada with a Lieutenant-Governor and a Council. Each province was also to have an elected Legislative Assembly, which should vote taxes and pass laws subject to the approval of the Lieutenant-Governor and Council. By this means the demands of the British in Ontario were satisfied, while the French in Quebec learned to adapt themselves to a British institution. This compromise worked well for nearly half a century, during which time the population of Ontario rose from 10,000 to 400,000. Large numbers of British people emigrated to the new lands of the West, which the pioneers were opening in the virgin forest of North America.

The
American
War of 1812

Just as Anglo-French Canada had remained loyal during the War of American Independence, so the two Canadas stood the shock of the second war, during the conflict with Napoleon, between Britain and the United States. This war, which broke out in 1812, was concerned with the old questions arising out of the British naval supremacy. By the Orders in Council, Britain had forbidden neutrals, including America, to trade with the French Empire. Britain also claimed the right to search American vessels for deserters from the British Navy. The Americans were angry with both France and Britain. But France's diplomacy was more skilful, and the British fleet came into conflict with the U.S.A. vessels more frequently, so the U.S.A. declared war on Britain and the conflict thus began lasted two years. At first it was waged on or near the Great Lakes. There were one or two American raids into Canada, and skirmishes between flotillas on the Lakes. The fall of Napoleon in 1814 resulted in the Peninsular veterans being sent out to America, after which the British position improved. In 1814, in revenge for the burning of Toronto, the British raided the American capital, Washington, and burnt all the public buildings and the President's house, which was whitewashed to hide the marks of the flames, whence its new name the 'White House'. Despite this exploit, there was a stalemate in a war which Britain had never wanted to fight and which gravely injured the trade of New England. Peace was signed between the American and British representatives at Ghent in 1814; but the news did not reach America soon enough to prevent a British attack on New Orleans in January 1815, which was repulsed, with great loss, by an American army under Andrew Jackson. The peace made no significant changes, and showed the futility of the war; but it is significant that in the Crimean War – the next considerable war of the century – Britain abandoned its excessive claims against neutrals.

Peace of Ghent 1814

3. Australia

Australia takes its name from the Terra Australis Incognita ('Unknown Land of the South'), which the 16th century map-makers regarded as a huge continent in the southern seas. Such a continent as they imagined did not exist; but the voyage of Tasman and other Dutch navigators in the 17th century proved the existence of parts of north and west Australia, and of Tasmania.

Terra Australis Incognita

It was left to an Englishman of the 18th century to make the most important discovery of all. Captain James Cook, who had been with Wolfe's expedition up the St Lawrence to Quebec in 1759, was appointed in 1768 to command a scientific expedition to the South Seas. On board were Sir Joseph Banks, a prominent member of the Royal Society, and other scientists. Cook sailed first to Tahiti, then made south for New Zealand (already discovered by the Dutch), where he circumnavigated the islands. From New Zealand the expedition sailed westward and so came in 1770 to the hitherto undiscovered eastern coast of Australia. Cook's skilful navigation enabled the ships to sail the whole length of the coast-line, in spite of the perils of the Great Barrier Reef. Sir Joseph Banks was much struck by the profuseness of the vegetation in New South Wales, as Cook named the southern part of the country. One spot Banks named Botany Bay. The explorers imagined that they were seeing the land in the dry season. In fact, it was the rainy season and at other times

Captain Cook

Three Pacific Voyages 1768-79

Botany Bay 1770

the vegetation looks shrivelled and mean. The false idea was created that Botany Bay and the surrounding area would prove a paradise.

Cook made two more voyages to the Pacific, and was killed by some natives at Hawaii in 1779. Sir Joseph Banks urged the Government to profit by his New South Wales discovery, and to send out an expedition to colonize the country. But Pitt and his Home Secretary, Lord Sydney, did not favour the plantation of new colonies. They were impressed, however, by the possibilities of Australia as a convict settlement, now that it was no longer possible to transport felons to the American colonies. They hoped too that the convicts might develop two strategic commodities: Norfolk Island pines for masts and flax for canvas and rope. In January 1788, therefore, after an eight month voyage, Captain Arthur Phillip landed in Botany Bay with the first batch of English prisoners for New South Wales. He had with him about 1,000 men, women and children and 500 head of livestock and poultry.

Foundation of New South Wales, 1788

Botany Bay proved no longer to have the meadows which Cook had seen; so the new settlement was centred instead upon Port Jackson, a sheltered deep water port, afterwards renamed Sydney (in honour of the Home Secretary), a few miles north of Botany Bay. Conditions at first were not good. The early harvests were scanty and the convicts were dependent on meagre rations sent out from England. The prisoners were guarded by soldiers, and for the first twenty years of its existence the new colony was run on the harsh lines of more than military discipline. Phillip sent the worst characters to a new settlement in Norfolk Island in the Pacific; another prisoners' colony was also made in Tasmania in 1804. Most of the men and women had been transported overseas as punishment for crimes of theft, for the British felony laws were at that time the harshest in Europe. Of every twenty convicts, thirteen were Englishmen, six were Irishmen and one was a Scot. Many of the felons made very suitable colonists and by the twenty-fifth anniversary of the foundation of the colony, it was thriving.

The Settlement

In addition, a thin but increasing stream of free emigrants reached Australia. The discovery (in 1813) of a pass over the Blue Mountains, leading to the Bathurst Plains beyond, was important for the future development of the colony. The country beyond the mountains proved to be among the finest grasslands in the world, and the introduction of sheep, some from George III's own farm, founded the prosperity of Australia. Henceforth the immigration of free colonists largely increased. The real history of Australia began with its sheep-farmers and with its intrepid explorers.

Date Summary: The Revolutionary Era (1783-1815)

WILLIAM PITT–PEACE (1783-93)

BRITAIN	AMERICA AND INDIA AUSTRALIA	EUROPE
1783-1801 Pitt's first Ministry		
1784 Dr. Johnson *d.*	1784 India Act	
1786 Commercial Treaty with France	1786-93 Cornwallis in India	
	1787 Constitution of U.S.A.	
	1788-95 Trial of Warren Hastings	
	1789-97 Washington, President U.S.A.	
	1788 Foundation of N.S. Wales	
		1789 FRENCH REVOLUTION
1790 Burke's *Reflections on Fr. Rev.*	1790 Nootka Sound	
1791 WESLEY *d.*	1791 Canada Act	
1792 United Irishmen Whig split Shelley born		1792 France at war with Austria and Prussia September Massacres ⚔ Valmy

WAR – PITT AND NELSON (1793-1806)

BRITAIN	AMERICA AND INDIA AUSTRALIA	EUROPE
1793 War with France		1793-5 Second and Third Partitions of Poland
1794 Habeas Corpus suspended Gibbon *d.*	1793-5 First Coalition	
1795 Keats born	1795-6 British take Ceylon and the Cape	1796-7 NAPOLEON in Italy
1796 Burns *d.*		
		1797 ⚔ C. St Vincent ⚔ Camperdown
1798 Irish Rebellion *Lyrical Ballads*	1798-1805 WELLESLEY in India	1798 ⚔ NILE
1799 Combination Acts	1799 Conquest of Mysore	1799-1800 Second Coalition
1800 ACT OF UNION (BRITAIN AND IRELAND)		
1801 Pitt resigns		
1801-4 Addington Ministry	1803-5 Mahratta War	1802 Treaty of Amiens
		1803 War renewed
1804-6 Pitt's second Ministry		1804 Napoleon Emperor
		1805 Third Coalition
		1805 (Oct.) ⚔ TRAFALGAR
		(Dec.) ⚔ AUSTERLITZ
1806 Pitt *d.*		

WAR–CANNING, CASTLEREAGH, AND WELLINGTON (1806-15)

BRITAIN	AMERICA AND INDIA AUSTRALIA	EUROPE
1806-7 Ministry of All the Talents	1807 Britain ends SLAVE TRADE	1806 End of Holy Roman Empire Berlin Decree
1806 Fox *d.*		
1807-9 Portland Ministry Canning Foreign Sec.		1807 Treaty of Tilsit England seizes Danish fleet French invade Portugal
1807 Orders in Council		1808 Napoleon attacks Spain
		1808-14 PENINSULAR WAR
1809-12 Perceval Ministry		
1812-27 LIVERPOOL MINISTRY Castlereagh Foreign Sec. (to 1822)	1812-4 Anglo-American War	1812 Retreat from Moscow
		1813 German rising against Napoleon
1814 Scott's *Waverley*	1814 Treaty of Ghent	1814 Treaty of Chaumont
		1815 Napoleon's Hundred Days ⚔ WATERLOO TREATY OF VIENNA

1 For fuller details of the Great French War, *see* Chart, p. 198

X

AFTER WATERLOO (1815-30)

1. Cobbett's England

THE conclusion of the Napoleonic War found Great Britain the unchallenged mistress of the world's seas, and among the first of the Great Powers of Europe. At the same time, the work of inventors and mechanics, coupled with great natural resources in coal, had put Britain easily ahead of all foreign competitors in the industrial era which was just beginning. In spite of these facts – in spite of its political power and industrial wealth – there was a great deal of misery in Britain; the forty years after Waterloo was a time of recurrent economic difficulty for much of the population.

After Waterloo

There were several reasons for this unhappy state of affairs. It was an age of transition in some industries from one type of economic organization to another, and so great a change inevitably brought hardships. The introduction of machinery in the textile industry was accompanied by much misery. The mechanization of spinning in the later 18th century had enormously increased output and had thereby created employment for hundreds of thousands of handloom weavers. After 1815, however, the power loom began to spread and the wages of the handloom weavers were forced down as they vainly attempted to compete. Only in the 1850s did handloom weaving finally disappear. There were difficulties of a similar kind in the nail-making industry of the Black Country, though far fewer people were affected. In the countryside the main problem was that the rural population was increasing more rapidly than the number of jobs. The result of the superabundance of labour was low wages and these hurt farm labourers all the more because enclosure had reduced their opportunities for grazing animals or foraging on the common or waste lands. The misery of many rural dwellers was noted by

The revolutions in industry and agriculture

contemporary observers such as the journalist and agitator William Cobbett, who published his *Rural Rides* in 1825. He observed 'the house, with rotten thatch, broken windows, rotten door-sills' which remained as 'the dwelling of a half-starved and ragged family of labourers, the grandchildren, perhaps, of a decent family of small farmers that formerly lived happily in this very house'. Yet the problem was not that the number of small farmers had fallen, but that the small farmers had too many sons for them all to have any hope of inheriting a viable small farm.

Peace but not plenty

In addition to these major causes of disturbance in the labour market, the period immediately following Waterloo brought difficulties of its own. Peace, which was supposed to bring plenty, had brought instead worse distress. Three hundred thousand ex-soldiers and sailors, suddenly became unemployed, and sought work among a community which had no further need for their services. Steel and iron workers, gunsmiths, food contractors, and clothiers, all suffered from the coming of peace. At the same time, thousands of farmers went bankrupt, when the price of corn plunged, owing to a bumper harvest in 1813 and then in 1814 the competition of imported foreign corn, available again after the end of Napoleon's Continental System. The economic distress rapidly issued in popular agitation, which revived fears of a French-style revolution in Britain. The British government – under Lord Liverpool (Prime Minister from 1812 to 1827) – and the British Parliament followed the same course of action as Pitt in the 1790s and relied heavily on repression to deal with the crisis.

The Corn Law of 1815

Parliament in 1815 was a Parliament of landowners, and landowners were dependent on farmers who could pay their rents. It was not surprising therefore that the complaints of the farmers were taken seriously and that the government attempted a remedy. After the first downfall of Napoleon (1813-4) and the collapse of his Continental System, German and other foreign corn began to come into Britain. The price of British corn fell rapidly. British farmers suffered in consequence, and many were ruined. In 1815, therefore, Parliament passed a Corn Law, which stated that no foreign corn should be imported into the country until British corn reached the price of 80s.(£4) a quarter. Thus the British farmer was protected by law from foreign competition, but the price of the quartern loaf rose from 10d.(about 4p) to 1s. 2d.(about 6p) at a time when the ordinary farm labourer was earning only 8s. a week. It should be remembered that, with a population of 19 millions for Great Britain and Ireland, it was still just possible to feed the United Kingdom with British-grown corn, though it became less and less possible as the years went by and the population steadily increased. From the start the Corn Law was controversial. Petitions against it poured in from the provinces and angry mobs in London expressed their feelings more violently. The selfishness of landlords was blamed for the legislation and some drew the conclusion that Parliament should be reformed in order to achieve the fair representation of other interests.

A large proportion of the people of England in 1815 had an income below that required to meet essential living expenses. Under the Speenhamland system the parish rates had to make up to the labouring population the deficiencies in wages, but, even so, parish relief was often insufficient to keep a labouring family from near-starvation. The Game Laws preserved the well-stocked estates, swarming with pheasants, partridges, and hares, for the use of the owners, and visited with ferocious punishments the poacher who was caught. In 1816 a law was passed punishing with seven years' transportation any man found *in possession* of a net for taking rabbits.

Poor Law

Game Laws

The Game Laws are a fair example of the criminal code contained in the Statute-Book in 1815. More than 200 offences, mostly forms of stealing, were punishable by death. True, the juries refused to convict for such crimes as stealing apples, so that many of the so-called crimes received no punishment. But the actual results were bad enough. Sir James Mackintosh, who devoted a large part of his life to the question of the criminal code and its reform, told the House

The Penal Code

of Commons in 1818 that 101 persons had suffered the death penalty for forgery alone in the last seven years. Seventy-five thousand persons were transported to Botany Bay between 1787 and 1836, some, no doubt, for serious crimes of violence, but most for offences such as sheep-stealing. The record of crime mounted up after the end of the war. In 1805 only 4,600 persons were committed for trial of whom 2,700 were convicted; in 1819, 14,000 persons were committed and 9,500 convicted.

The demand for reform

The cry for reform, which had been smothered during the Napoleonic War, gradually grew more insistent. There were various kinds of reform, each of which had its own particular advocates. The followers of Wilberforce still pressed for the abolition of slavery; men like Sir Samuel Romilly and Sir James Mackintosh devoted themselves to pressing the reform of the criminal code on a reluctant Parliament. Others like Francis Place, the London tailor, agitated for the repeal of the Combination Laws, which made workmen's trades unions illegal; others, again, pressed for the relaxation of the laws against Roman Catholics. But one and all were united in their demand for the reform of Parliament itself, for it was felt that the old unreformed Parliament was the root of most of the evils of the time. Change the constitution of Parliament, and the laws would soon be changed too.

In the years following Waterloo, the radical cause gradually gained adherents in England. *Radical* means desirous of change that is fundamental, literally from the root. (*Radix* is Latin for *root*.)

The Radicals

Radicalism was hardly represented in the aristocratic, landowning Parliament, but it had a vigorous following outside the walls of Westminster. One of its chief leaders was Major Cartwright, well into his seventies, who went about founding 'Hampden Clubs'. Their object was equal political rights for all men and their main area of strength was Lancashire. Other leaders of working men included Thistlewood, who afterwards took to more desperate courses, and Hunt, the mob orator. There were middle class radicals too. The man who, more than any one else, influenced the advanced thought of that generation was Jeremy Bentham, who was already sixty-seven in 1815. Bentham had been early trained in legal studies, and he regarded the whole structure of English society with the precise mind of a lawyer. His test question, with regard to any law or institution was: What is the use of it? Examined by this standard, Bentham found that many laws ought to be abolished, and many institutions reformed. His *Catechism of Parliamentary Reform* (1817) exposed the absurdities of the existing system of representation, and argued that a more democratic form of government would help to produce the 'greatest happiness of the greatest number'. This book had a considerable effect on thinking people; and Bentham's arguments did much to bring about the gradual reform of English institutions.

Bentham

Bentham influenced the thinkers of his day; the man who stirred the masses was William Cobbett (1762-1835). A Surrey man of peasant stock, Cobbett had passed his youth in the army, where he rose to the rank of sergeant-major. At one time a supporter of Pitt, he turned, about the time of that statesman's death, into a bitter opponent of the government and of the landed interest. His newspaper, the *Political Register*, first issued in 1802, became the main organ of radical opinion in England. In 1816, Cobbett published his paper at 2*d.* (1p). instead of 1*s.* 1/2*d.*(5p); he avoided the stamp duty on newspapers by omitting all items of news. The paper was widely sold, and often read aloud to the illiterate masses.

Cobbett

Cobbett had an exceptional command of terse, vigorous English; he had also an exceptional capacity for hatred. He hated the landowners and clergy, because he said they impoverished the people by rents and tithes; he hated manufacturers, because they were depopulating his beloved countryside; and he hated rotten-borough owners, because they controlled the whole system, as represented by an unreformed Parliament. Cobbett lumped all the objects of his hatred together and called them 'The Thing'. How intensely he loathed 'The Thing' can be read in his *Rural Rides*, his description of journeys on horseback

'The Thing'

through southern England. Cobbett hated towns, which he called wens – London was the Great Wen – as he believed them to be sucking the life-blood out of the country. Watch him pass through Wiltshire and enter a couple of towns which were also rotten boroughs: 'I could not come through that villainous hole, Calne, without cursing Corruption at every step. . . . In about 10 miles more, I came to another rotten hole, called Wootton Bassett. This also is a mean, vile place, though the country all round it is very fine.'

Another violent hater of the existing system was the poet Shelley, who, in the three or four years following Waterloo, issued a number of political poems, most of them inciting the English people to rise against their masters. Shelley's generous soul burned with rage at the spectacle of so much unhappiness all around him; he would have welcomed a revolution, as we can see in his '*Men of England*':

Shelley
(1792-1822)

> Men of England, wherefore plough
> For the lords who lay you low?
> Wherefore weave with toil and care
> The rich robes your tyrants wear?
> Wherefore, Bees of England, forge
> Many a weapon, chain, and scourge,
> That these stingless drones may spoil
> The forced produce of your toil?

2. Post-War Agitation and Repression (1815-21)

The
Liverpool
Ministry
(1812-27)

The Premiership of Lord Liverpool lasted fifteen years from 1812 to 1827. His first years saw the triumph over Napoleon and the making of the Treaty of Vienna. His peace-time ministry can be divided into two periods: the period of popular agitation which was met by government repression between 1815 and 1821; and the quieter years when a number of younger reforming ministers came to the fore between 1822 and 1827. Liverpool was, according to one of his junior ministers, 'one of the best tempered men living' and this quality enabled him to hold together a cabinet composed of men of widely differing views and clashing temperaments. He was the first Prime Minister after 1714 to use the label 'Tory', but not all his ministers were happy with the name. He much admired the Younger Pitt, but he did not try to keep the various departments of government on a tight rein, as Pitt had. Instead, individual ministers were allowed a great deal of autonomy.

The four chief ministers during the earlier period were Lord Castlereagh, the Duke of Wellington (from 1819), Lord Eldon, and Lord Sidmouth. The first two were largely responsible for the overthrow of Napoleon, and played their part in the resettlement of Europe which followed; but, as Castlereagh was the spokesman for the government in the House of Commons, he was given credit for all its misdeeds – a fact which prevented his countrymen from appreciating his great services to Europe. Lord Eldon, the Lord Chancellor, stood firmly against change; Sidmouth (formerly Addington, Prime Minister 1801-4), the Home Secretary, was entrusted with carrying out most of the repressive acts of the Government.

Castlereagh, Wellington, Eldon, Sidmouth

In 1816 the Government announced that the income tax, which had been introduced as a war measure, would be reduced from a 10 to a 5 per cent tax. Brougham, a Whig leader, who believed that the income tax was an unwarrantable interference with British liberty, raised an agitation for its complete withdrawal. The Commons supported Brougham and the government had to give way. Hence Britain was denied the most obvious method of reducing her enormous debt – 860 million pounds, nearly all incurred by the expenses of the late war.

The Income Tax Riots, 1817

Meanwhile, the state of the country was alarming the ministry. There was much rick-burning and machine-breaking; radical agitation was very active. In November 1816 there was a large radical meeting in Spa Fields, London, which was broken up by the authorities. Early in 1817 a window of the royal coach was shattered by a shot or stone aimed at it. The occupant of the coach was George, Prince of Wales, and Prince Regent of Great Britain for the last ten years (1810-20) of his father's life; for George III was now mad, blind, and deaf. Few princes have been more heartily disliked by their subjects than the Prince Regent. But stones thrown at the royal coach were a sign, the ministers thought, of a widespread disaffection. In 1817, therefore, they suspended the Habeas Corpus Act. At the same time they passed the Seditious Meetings Act, which required that licences should be obtained from magistrates before public meetings were held.

Habeas Corpus suspended 1817

While seriously disturbed by the activities of the radicals, the government was further alarmed in 1817 by the news that a large body of handloom weavers were marching from Manchester to lay their grievances before their rulers. These men were known as the Blanketeers, because each man carried a blanket to sleep in. Sidmouth caused their leaders to be arrested; the march broke up, and the men got no farther than Derbyshire. But the ministry had not heard the last of Manchester. In 1818 there were strikes of spinners and weavers, but the employers made no concessions and in the very depressed year 1819 the weavers turned back to the search for a political solution for their problems. In 1819 a very large meeting – 50,000 to 80,000 people – assembled in St Peter's Fields, Manchester, to listen to 'Orator' Hunt. The magistrates panicked and sent in the local Manchester yeomanry to arrest Hunt and disperse the crowd. Believing the yeomanry to be in danger, the magistrates ordered the regular troops to charge. The result was a dreadful stampede, in which 11 persons were killed and about 500 wounded so badly that they had to be taken to hospital. The Manchester 'Massacre', nicknamed Peterloo in mockery, aroused considerable indignation in the country. The government, without waiting to discover whether the magistrates had acted wisely or not,

Manchester

The Blanketeers 1817

Peterloo 1819

wrote to congratulate them on their action. Any criticism might have led to a failure of nerve of local authorities, which were the country's first line of defence against a collapse into anarchy. The fact that the victims were quite unarmed, and had assembled for a peaceful purpose, provoked much sympathy for them in the country at large.

The government's main concern was to enforce order, and for this purpose they passed the Six Acts later in 1819. Of these Acts, the first two forbade all unauthorized military training, and empowered magistrates to search private houses for arms. The Seditious Meetings Act made the assembling of more than fifty persons illegal; this Act was in force for five years. The Blasphemous and Seditious Libels Act was intended to curb the freedom of the press, while the Newspaper Stamp Duties Act was aimed particularly at Cobbett, and imposed a duty of 4d. on all cheap pamphlets, whether they contained 'news' or not.

The Six Acts, 1819

The general effect of the Six Acts was to curb the power of the popular press, and to make popular assemblies illegal. The passing of this legislation drove some of the radicals to desperate courses. Thistlewood and others formed a plot – the Cato Street Conspiracy – to murder the whole Cabinet one evening while they were at dinner. The plot was betrayed, the Cabinet saved, and the conspirators executed; this failure did much to discredit the extreme radicals.

Cato Street Conspiracy, 1820

Just before the discovery of the Cato Street Conspiracy, the reign of George III came to an end. Shelley in 1818 had written of

Death of George III 1820

An old, mad, blind, despised and dying King –
Princes, the dregs of their dull race, who flow
Through public scorn, – mud from a muddy spring.

When death at last removed the pitiful figure of the third George, the nation accepted, with little enthusiasm, the transformation of the Prince Regent into King George IV. George was notorious for his mistresses and his debts, not to mention his corpulence, which had

George IV (1820-30)

earned him the title 'The Prince of Whales'. He was widely denounced for his faults and mercilessly ridiculed. Yet he also made of the British monarchy a much more splendid affair: Windsor Castle and Buckingham Palace, already made into important royal residences under George III, acquired under his son their modern appearance. Holyroodhouse was refurbished in Scotland. George was less successful at maintaining the dignity of the monarchy. George had scarcely ascended the throne, when he involved himself and his government in a scandal. His Queen, Caroline of Brunswick, was living apart from him, their marriage having been a fiasco from the start. George was determined that she should not be recognized as Queen and attempted to rid himself of her by divorce. He induced the Government to bring a Divorce Bill for that purpose into the House of Lords. The Queen was accused of misconduct and unfaithfulness to her husband, and though these charges may have been true, it was nauseating that they should have been brought by such a man as George IV. Lord Brougham defended the Queen with spirit and success; this fact, together with the agitation outside in the Queen's favour, induced the ministers to drop the Bill. Their own part in these unsavoury proceedings added greatly to their unpopularity and ministers' windows were broken by the London mob. Yet the Queen Caroline affair was soon forgotten, especially once she had died in 1821, and Liverpool's ministry survived.

The Royal
Divorce Bill
1820

In 1822 Lord Castlereagh, the chief spokesman for the government in the House of Commons, committed suicide. When Castlereagh's body was brought for burial in Westminster Abbey, the populace turned out to see the last of the hated minister. Horrible cheers greeted the funeral procession as it passed through the streets of London. After Peterloo, Shelley had written his *Mask* (our spelling would be *masque*) *of Anarchy*, in which Castlereagh was blamed for the events in Manchester.

Death of
Castlereagh
1822

232

I met Murder on the way –
He had a mask like Castlereagh,
Very smooth he looked, yet grim;
Seven bloodhounds followed him.

Evidently, the London populace shared Shelley's view, unfair though it was.

Castlereagh's rival, George Canning, was about to sail for India to take up the duties of Governor-General when the suicide occurred, but Liverpool at once offered him the Foreign Secretaryship and the leadership of the House of Commons. Canning accepted these posts, and the government was reconstructed. Sidmouth retired from the home Office in favour of Robert Peel and Huskisson became President of the Board of Trade and a member of the cabinet. These men were likely to take more notice of public opinion than their predecessors had done. They were fortunate in that economic conditions improved and staving off threats to order was no longer the government's chief concern.

3. The Tory Reformers (1822-7)

George Canning, the new Foreign Secretary and government Canning spokesman in the Commons, was one of the most brilliant men whom that age produced. A man of imperious will and abounding energy, he swept the more hesitating members of the Cabinet off their feet, while his own devoted adherents, mostly younger men, believed him to be the saviour of England. The obliging Lord Liverpool let him have his own way. To the masterful mind of Canning, the state both of England and of Europe called for action. At home he was convinced that the day of reform was, in many matters, long overdue; he carried the Cabinet with him, some with enthusiasm, others reluctantly. In one matter, however, Canning was resolutely opposed to the demands of the radicals – he did not believe in Parliamentary

Reform. He foresaw that it would lead, in time, to democracy, and he disbelieved in democracy; he thought that reforms should be imposed from above. In his dealings with the Powers of Europe, Canning's conception of British interests was similar to that of Castlereagh, but unlike his predecessor, he liked to appeal to British public opinion and often flavoured his speeches with a strong dash of liberal rhetoric. Hence, his policy seemed more different from Castlereagh's than it really was.

Peel

Canning's two most prominent colleagues in the Cabinet were Robert Peel, the Home Secretary, and William Huskisson, the President of the Board of Trade. Peel was the member for Oxford University, in those days the stronghold of reaction, though Peel himself was far from being a reactionary. He was the son of Sir Robert Peel (the first baronet), a Lancashire cotton manufacturer. The elder Peel had made an enormous fortune in cotton, had sent his son to Harrow and Oxford, and marked him out for a political career. Peel belonged, therefore, by birth if not by education, to the new manufacturing classes rather than to the landed aristocracy. His chief work as Home Secretary was to take up from the Government benches the task which men like Romilly and Mackintosh had long been working at in a committee of 1819: the reform of the penal code. It is noteworthy that Peel wrote to and consulted, not only Mackintosh, but Bentham, who was regarded as the father of all reform. Peel introduced five statutes abolishing the capital punishment for over 100 offences; before he left office in 1827, nearly 300 Acts, laying down harsh punishments, had been wholly or partially repealed. Peel also took a step towards reform of the prisons by making them subject to regular inspections by local magistrates reporting to the Home Office.

Reform of
the Penal
Code 1823-7

Huskisson

William Huskisson, President of the Board of Trade, was an enthusiastic follower of Canning and enjoyed a greater measure of that statesman's confidence than Robinson, the Chancellor of the Exchequer. Both Canning and Huskisson were disciples of Pitt, and set themselves to carry out the economic policy which Pitt had begun, but which the long war had interrupted. Huskisson began by lowering or abolishing tariffs on various imported articles. He was the first minister in the 19th century to advocate free trade; his reforms, followed up later by those of Peel and Gladstone, continued the swing of the pendulum – begun by Pitt – away from the policy of Protection.

Beginning of Free Trade 1823-7

Canning and Huskisson next turned their attention to the colonies. Only a few years before, a minister had declared that the colonies existed solely for Britain's benefit: that Britain retained a complete monopoly of their trade in return for defending them. This was a defence of the Old Colonial System which had already led to the loss of America, and which the old school of Tories were ready and anxious to continue. But Canning and Huskisson set themselves to overturn the Old Colonial System by altering the economic regulations which governed it. The Navigation Acts – passed under the Commonwealth and Charles II – were still in force in 1822; next year Huskisson considerably modified them. For the first time in history, foreign countries were allowed to trade direct with the British colonies. But trade between Britain and her colonies was still confined to British ships, and could not be carried on in foreign vessels.

Canning, Huskisson, and the Empire

Huskisson was a man with a vision of the empire. His policy was a complete denial of the doctrine that the colonies were the chattels of Britain; he encouraged them to believe that their interests and those of Britain were one. He encouraged emigration, and even helped intending colonists with public money. He adopted the system of colonial preference, by which the colonies were given preferential treatment by the British tariff system as against foreign countries. Colonial preference lasted until Britain abandoned tariffs altogether (under Gladstone in the 1850s). By all these means, Huskisson, with Canning's backing, showed that Britain cared for the welfare of the colonies as well as for its own. This policy strengthened the moral bonds between Britain and the colonies, and it entitles Canning and

Huskisson to be considered among the founders of the Second British Empire.

One important reform of these years was not due to the government, but to the labours of a remarkable man, a tailor named Francis Place, who devoted the latter part of his life to politics and to social reform. He was a master of the art of collecting evidence in support of his case; and for years he laboured to get the Combination Acts repealed. These Acts, passed by Pitt during the French War (1799, 1800), forbade any combinations of workmen for the purpose of raising their wages, and thus made trade unions illegal. In fact, the Acts were never vigorously enforced. There was a large amount of union activity in the years when the Acts were nominally in operation and if it confined itself to economic ends and was peaceful, it was usually tolerated. Employers rarely wished to exacerbate industrial relations by invoking the Acts and prosecutions were expensive and not always easy to achieve. In 1824, Place judged that, now the new ministers were in office, it was a favourable time to get the Acts repealed. He prepared his evidence, portraying the Acts as interference by the government in industrial relations which actually encouraged unions. Place's case was considered before a Committee of the House of Commons, and finally (through his friend Hume, a radical M.P.) he had the satisfaction of seeing the Acts abolished in 1824. At once there was a rash of strikes, taking advantage of the boom conditions of 1824-5. The Government then became nervous, and brought in another Bill to restrict strike action by trade unions, though the brief depression that set in at the end of 1825 did more to curb the unions, which were robbed of their bargaining power by unemployment.

During the last five years of Liverpool's administration, tensions among the groups of politicians who made up the Tory party intensified. In 1827 an event occurred which split the Tory party in two. Lord Liverpool had a paralytic stroke; his mental powers were impaired, and he was forced to retire. George IV offered the

Francis Place

Repeal of the Combination Acts 1824

End of the Liverpool Ministry 1827

Premiership to Canning, who accepted it. Throughout the period of his ministry, Liverpool had kept Catholic emancipation as an 'open question' in the cabinet. That meant that cabinet members could hold differing opinions on the issue and vote according to conscience if there was a vote on the matter in Parliament. On the other hand, no minister would take any initiative on the question. The new Prime Minister, Canning, favoured Catholic emancipation, with the result that Wellington, Eldon and Peel at once resigned. Canning therefore formed a ministry of his own followers among the Tories – Huskisson became leader of the House of Commons – and some of the Whigs. The official leader of the Whigs, Lord Grey, remained aloof and hostile, from motives of personal dislike. But Canning was dying when he took office and before the summer was over he was dead. The incapable Robinson, lately Chancellor of the Exchequer, now Lord Goderich, tried to carry on the Whig-Canningite Ministry, but resigned in a few months; he never met Parliament. The King then sent for the Duke of Wellington, who consented in January 1828 to form a Ministry.

Canning Prime Minister (April-August 1827)

Goderich Prime Minister (1827-8)

4. Wellington (1828-30)

The Duke of Wellington, whose great reputation had been made on the battlefield, was in some ways the ideal Tory leader. He did not understand the need for reform, and he looked on radicals and reformers in the manner of a sergeant-major inspecting a squad of awkward recruits. But, in spite of his reactionary tendencies, the Duke was destined to disappoint the High Tories. He was not their servant, and he dared to oppose them if he thought it his duty to do so. The rulers of England in those days were men who believed that their first duty was not to show loyalty to a party or a sectional interest, but to carry on the King's government. It was once suggested to Canning that he could not govern England without the aid of the aristocracy. Canning haughtily replied: 'I will not act (as I never have

Wellington Prime Minister (1828-30)

acted) as the tool of any confederacy, however powerful.' These words might equally well have been spoken by Wellington, or by Peel.

The Duke began by trying to re-unite the Tories, old Tories, and

Canningites
leave the
Ministry
1828

Canningites, but it was soon seen that he could not work with the latter; Huskisson and his friends were dismissed within three months. Henceforth, the Duke presided over the last ministry of old Tories that ever ruled England. Huskisson, who was killed by a railway train in 1830, never rejoined them; the other Canningites joined the Whigs, and produced two future Prime Ministers of England, Melbourne and Palmerston.

Wellington's right-hand man was Peel, who again became Home

Metropolitan
Police Force
1829

Secretary and leader of the House of Commons. In 1829 he introduced the measure by which, perhaps, he is best remembered. He saw that the growing city of London required a new and better organized police system, and he therefore founded the Metropolitan Police Force. Later, many of the features of that Force were extended to other forces that were set up all over Britain. The new police, armed only with truncheons, proved equal to their task of enforcing order. Ultimately, by the second half of the century, governments came to feel much more secure in the face of threats to law and order thanks to the existence of the police forces. The repressive measures of Liverpool's government in the period 1815-20 had been due largely to its weakness, its nervous awareness of how ill-prepared it was to meet any serious threat. Once a professional police force was in being, governments no longer had to depend on spies, who tended to exaggerate threats, or on troops whose appearance at trouble-spots was liable to be provocative. Unpopular at first, the Police Force – nicknamed 'bobbies' or 'Peelers' after the Home Secretary – eventually became one of the institutions of which Britons were proud.

Repeal of
Test and
Corporation
Acts, 1828

One question with which the Duke's ministry was soon confronted was that of the religious inequalities which still existed. In 1828 Lord John Russell, one of the younger Whig leaders, brought in a Bill to repeal the Test and Corporation Acts, passed in Charles II's reign, which restricted most government positions and membership of town corporations to Anglicans. The government did not oppose Russell's Bill, which was carried by a large majority. Henceforth, the laws preventing Nonconformists from taking up office were removed. The change was symbolic rather than real, since for many years an annual Indemnity Act had in effect suspended the laws discriminating against Nonconformists. Even after this, the Roman Catholics, both in England and Ireland, were refused admittance to the universities, to the Bar, and to Parliament. The situation created by the anti-Catholic laws affected relatively few people in England; in much of Ireland they affected most people.

Before Pitt had passed the Act of Union (1800) between England and Ireland, he had held out the promise that the laws against Irish Catholics would be repealed, but the action of the King, George III, and opposition from many politicians had caused him to break his promise. For twenty years after the Union, the Irish suffered in silence. Then a Catholic leader arose: Daniel O'Connell, an Irish lawyer. It was O'Connell who founded the Catholic Association to extort justice from the British Government. O'Connell deliberately appealed to the religious passions of his countrymen; he enlisted the help of the priests to band the people together, and to demand justice.

Ireland

The Catholic Association 1823

In 1828, Wellington appointed an Irish Protestant landlord, Vesey Fitzgerald, President of the Board of Trade. Fitzgerald had to seek re-election – for County Clare – but was opposed by O'Connell himself. Though Fitzgerald was personally popular, O'Connell was elected by the enthusiastic Irish Catholics. But as a Catholic he could not take his seat in the House of Commons, unless the law were to be altered. The Chief Secretary wrote to Peel saying that the expulsion of O'Connell from the House of Commons would be the signal for a general rising in Ireland; the Lord Lieutenant also wrote to ministers saying that they *might* have time to alter the law 'before we begin to fight'. What might happen if a general election had to be

The Clare Election 1828

called and dozens of Catholics were elected did not bear thinking about. Wellington hesitated no longer. His first duty was to maintain the King's government and he believed he could do so only if the law was altered. So, under the threat of revolution, Wellington and Peel in 1829 passed the Act of Roman Catholic Emancipation both for England and Ireland. To Peel fell the unpleasing duty of proposing in the Commons the very measure against which he had often spoken in the past. The older Tories, who would not listen to reason, said that the Duke had betrayed his party; they heaped insults on Peel, which that statesman bore in silence.

The year 1830 was an exciting one, both at home and abroad. The demand for Parliamentary reform, which the Duke still steadily opposed, grew stronger; Cobbett rode about the country addressing enthusiastic meetings. Then, in June, George IV died unlamented, and was succeeded by his more popular brother, William IV. The death of the King in those days necessitated a general election. Before it could be held, news arrived of another revolution in France. Charles X and his reactionary minister, Polignac, had been driven into exile in July 1830, and a more moderate government was set up under King Louis-Philippe (1830-48). Englishmen felt that the time had come for a great change in their own country. Then in August, just as the elections were being held, there was another revolution, this time in Belgium, where the populace rose against their Dutch rulers.

The Duke was not perturbed by this outbreak of revolutions. He met the new Parliament in November. Earl Grey, who had supported the cause of reform for forty years, rose once more in the House of Lords to suggest an alteration in the Parliamentary system. Wellington replied in a speech which did more credit to his tenacity than to his political judgment.

'He was fully convinced (he said) that the country possessed a Legislature which answered all the good purposes of legislation, and this to a greater degree than any legislature ever had answered in any country whatever. He would go further and say that the Legislature and system of representation possessed the full and entire confidence of the country – deservedly possessed that confidence . . .'

The Duke's Government did not long survive this speech; it was defeated by a combination of the High Tories (whom he had offended over Roman Catholic Emancipation), the Whigs, and the Canningites. The most unpopular man in England in November 1830 was the victor of Waterloo. Grey formed a government composed of Whigs and Canningites. Before the new Government could embark on its work of reform, however, it was faced with a serious agricultural revolt, which took place at the very moment of the change of ministry in November 1830. In their treatment of this revolt, the Whigs behaved more in the spirit of Eldon and Sidmouth than in that of enlightened reformers. The revolt broke out in Wiltshire, Hampshire, and Dorset, where the wretched labourers, stung to fury at long last by a combination of injustices – game laws, death and transportation for sheep-stealing, and work on 7s. a week – rose against their masters. Even at the height of their fury they shed no blood; but they burnt ricks and broke into houses. This was enough – more than enough – to alarm the government. A Special Commission of judges was sent down to Salisbury, Winchester, and other towns; at Salisbury 34 men were sentenced to death and 33 to transportation for life, besides numerous lesser sentences. No more than six or eight men were actually hanged; but 400 were transported to Australia from the villages of southern England in the first month of the reform ministry. The Whigs reaction to the disorder no doubt reflected the fact that they too were landowners, but in any case they could not afford to convey the impression that they were soft in defence of property if they were to govern through a Parliament representing the propertied.

Resignation of Wellington November 1830

Agricultural Labourers' Revolt 1830

5. The World after Waterloo

Castlereagh and Canning

English foreign policy from 1815 to 1830 naturally divides itself into the same two periods as does domestic history: the years when Castlereagh was foreign secretary, 1812-22, and the years when Canning was, 1822-7. It was Canning who gained the reputation of being the leader of a liberal policy in Europe: the champion of Greece and of the South American Republics. Canning seemed different from his predecessor because he insisted on letting his dislike of the Congress system be known and because he used radical-sounding language to rally public opinion behind him. Though the rhetoric of the two men was very different, their conception of British interests was remarkably similar.

Castlereagh and U.S.A. 1817-8

Castlereagh's chief success was achieved in the critical years 1815-8. He played a large part in making the Vienna settlement, which was not vindictive to the defeated enemy, France. And Castlereagh scored another important success across the Atlantic. He arranged with the United States of America, with whom peace was concluded in 1814, that the rival navies on the Great Lakes should be scrapped (1817). Next year, he settled the Anglo-American frontier, hitherto determined only as far as the Great Lakes. By the agreement of 1818 the frontier was continued as far as the Rockies, along the 49th parallel of latitude. This frontier, as well as the waters of the Great Lakes, was undefended by either nation – a great triumph for the policy of peace and mutual trust, which, unfortunately, was not imitated by the nations of Europe.

The Holy Alliance 1815

Great Britain in 1815 found itself on the side of the victorious monarchies of the Continent, Austria, Russia, and Prussia. These Powers had been Britain's allies in the struggle against Napoleon, but British opinion was not at all in favour of the royal absolutism which obtained in eastern Europe. Englishmen celebrated their freedom of opinion and expression, which they considered was far greater than any liberty enjoyed by the Germans or the Russians. The

Tsar, Alexander I (1801-25), a firm believer in the Divine Right of monarchs, suggested the so-called Holy Alliance between the rulers of Europe, which was drawn up 'conformably to the words of the Holy Scriptures which command all men to consider each other as brethren'. Castlereagh described the Holy Alliance as 'a piece of sublime mysticism and nonsense'; he refused to let the Prince Regent join it. He feared that the Tsar might use his Holy Alliance as an excuse to interfere all over Europe.

The real leader of Europe in the generation after Waterloo was not the idealistic Tsar, but Prince Metternich, Chancellor of the Austrian Empire. Metternich's chief aim was to crush revolution, whenever and wherever it appeared. In Austria itself he crushed everything that might lead to revolution. He muzzled the press; he crowded the gaols with political prisoners. His example was followed in Prussia, and in most of the petty states of Germany and Italy. But this was not enough for Metternich; he wished to put the whole of Europe under the same iron discipline. Revolution, he considered, was an infectious disease, and must be suppressed everywhere. Conscious of Austria's relative weakness, he proposed that the four chief Powers who had beaten Napoleon, and who had signed a Quadruple Alliance (1815) – Britain, Austria, Russia, and Prussia – should liaise to stamp out revolution. Metternich was able to manage the Tsar, in spite of his idealism; the real trouble was Britain. For though Castlereagh disapproved of most revolutions, he was not willing to rule out political change everywhere on principle and he did not want the Congresses of the chief Powers to turn into a kind of world government. He foresaw that if the Congresses attempted to run the world, they would end up causing more conflict, not less. For the first ten years after Waterloo, a number of Congresses were held between the Great Powers; France was allowed to join after 1818. Castlereagh made British reservations about the Congress System clear as early as 1820 and after 1822 disagreements among the other powers prevented any continuation of the System without Britain.

Metternich

The Congress System

Castlereagh was suspicious of the Congress System; in 1820 he flatly declared that Britain would in no circumstances lend her aid to the forcible suppression of revolutions in foreign countries. Castlereagh was succeeded by Canning, who went farther. At the moment of his accession to power, a European Congress was meeting at Verona to consider the Spanish problem. The Spaniards had risen against King Ferdinand VII, and had established a constitution to limit royal absolutism for the future. Metternich wished the Powers to act jointly in announcing their disapproval of the Spanish revolution; in that case, said Canning, Britain would not take part. Eventually France acted alone, sent an army, and restored King Ferdinand. Canning protested at this exercise of French power, but he could not counter 100,000 French troops.

Canning's annoyance at the spectacle of French troops crossing the Pyrenees – which revived memories of the Peninsular War for most Englishmen – led directly to his decisive American policy. The Spanish colonies in America had all revolted against the government of Ferdinand VII, and now refused to return to their allegiance. Ferdinand asked for a European Congress to be summoned; in 1824 Canning refused to send a British representative. After the French invasion of Spain, Canning feared that France might attempt to profit from a revived Spanish American empire. At stake was the valuable prize of trade with the ex-colonies. Hence, Canning gave the French and Spanish Governments to understand that if they attempted to reconquer Spanish America, they would be opposed by the British fleet. President Monroe of the U.S.A. followed this up with his famous 'Doctrine' that 'the American continents . . . are henceforth not to be considered as subjects for future colonization by any European Powers'; and that if the latter interfered in America, North or South, they would incur the hostility of the United States. At this stage in its history, the USA had no means of enforcing the Monroe Doctrine, but the British fleet was strong enough to prevent any challenge to it. Canning and Monroe between them thus gave the

Canning and the Congresses

Spain 1822

Canning and South America 1823-4

Monroe Doctrine 1823

death-blow to the wider schemes of the 'Holy Alliance' Powers, who wished to re-establish monarchical rule in America. 'Contemplating Spain as our ancestors had known her' (said Canning in the House of Commons), 'I resolved that if France had Spain, it should not be Spain with the Indies. I called the New World into existence to redress the balance of the Old.' By the time Canning gave this speech, he had already recognized Colombia, Mexico and Buenos Aires as independent republics in order to secure their co-operation in protecting British trade.

In 1826 Queen Maria succeeded to the throne of Portugal and ruled as a constitutional monarch. When Spain threatened to intervene to restore a more conservative regime, Canning sent 4,000 troops, not so much because he liked the constitution as because he wished to maintain a traditional sphere of British influence.

Before he died, Canning took one other important step which had the effect of breaking up the 'Holy Alliance' of the other Powers. The bone of contention was Greece. The Greek War of Independence (1821-9) was fought to expel the Turks from what had once been the home of European culture. The spectacle of the modern Greeks fighting for their freedom against the Turks aroused the generous enthusiasm of many Englishmen, educated in the classical tradition of ancient Greece. Lord Byron died of disease there, at Missolonghi (1824), fighting in the cause of freedom. Canning, like Castlereagh before him, at first attempted to prevent European intervention, since Russia might be able to profit from it to strengthen its position in the eastern Mediterranean. The intervention of the Egyptians on the side of the Turks and the accession of a new Tsar, Nicholas I (1825-55), anxious to champion the Orthodox Greeks and to strike a blow at the decaying Turkish empire, forced a change of policy. The only way of exerting influence over Russia seemed to be to join it. Canning, therefore, disregarding the protests of Metternich, arranged for the British, French, and Russian fleets to be sent to the Levant. The hope was to force an

Greece
1821-9

armistice, but the actual result, which took place just after his death, was the battle of Navarino, when the Turkish and Egyptian fleets were sent to the bottom. Britain then did lose control of events. French troops completed the conquest of the Morea on behalf of the Greeks, the Russians marched on Adrianople, and in 1829 the Turks had to acknowledge Greek independence. Greece had its freedom, but British statesmen feared that a high price had been paid in terms of an increase in Russian power in the area.

Battle of Navarino 1827

A year later in 1830 the ultra-conservative government of Charles X of France gave way to the more liberal rule of his cousin Louis-Philippe. This was a blow to the cause of absolute monarchy, which disturbed Metternich. Then came the revolt of the Belgians. Belgium had been placed, in 1815, under the rule of the Dutch king; the revolt of 1830 therefore upset the arrangements made at Vienna. Metternich considered that the Great Powers were being openly flouted. It fell to Lord Palmerston, foreign secretary after 1830, to co-operate with France in securing the independence of Belgium.

Belgian Revolt 1830

By 1830 the Congress System, as interpreted by Metternich, had broken down. In many places the conservative cause had been upheld: in Spain; in Italy, where Austria put down revolts in 1820-1 and in 1830-1; in Poland, where the Tsar crushed a rebellion at the end of 1830. Yet these victories had been achieved not by the powers acting together, but by individual powers acting alone. In several places Austria had been unable to prevent change: Greece and Belgium had both won their independence, the ex-Spanish colonies had defied their former masters, and the reactionary King of France had been bundled off his throne. British statesmen like Canning were prone to express approval of constitutional regimes, but they did not do much to bring them about, or to promote national independence movements. Their concern was with British interests, which they understood as preventing French expansion into the Low Countries, preventing Russian expansion in the eastern Mediterranean, preserving British spheres of influence in countries like Portugal and

Europe in 1830

upholding British trading interests in areas like Latin America. Their attitude to forms of government or issues of national independence was determined by pragmatic considerations. British interests were of overriding importance to them and that is why the foreign policies of Castlereagh and Canning are so similar.

DATE SUMMARY: AFTER WATERLOO (1815-30)

THE OLD TORIES (1815-22)

1812-27 LIVERPOOL MINISTRY

1815 CORN LAW Quadruple Alliance

1817 Habeas Corpus Act suspended
   Blanketeers

1818 Dover-Calais Steamer

1819 Peterloo
   Six Acts

1820 George III *d.*

1820-30 George IV

1820 Cato Street Conspiracy

1815 HOLY ALLIANCE

1818 Anglo-American Treaty

1819 Voyage of the *Savannah*

THE TORY REFORMERS (1822-8)

1822 Shelley *d.*
   Canning Foreign Sec.; Peel Home Sec.

1823-7 Reform of Penal Code

1823 Navigation Acts modified

1824 Combination Acts repealed

1825 Stockton and Darlington Railway

1827 Canning Ministry

1827-8 Goderich Ministry

1821-9 Greek War of Independence

1822 Congress of Verona

1823-4 Canning and S. America

1823 MONROE DOCTRINE

1824-6 First Burmese War

1825 Tsar Alexander I *d.*

1827 Navarino

WELLINGTON (1828-30)

1828 Repeal of Test and Corporation Acts

1829 Metropolitan Police Force
   Clare Election
   Catholic Emancipation

1830-7 William IV

1830 Liverpool and Manchester Railway
   Huskisson killed

1829 W. Australia

1830 French Revolution

1830-48 Louis-Philippe, King
   of the French

1830 Belgian Revolt

CONCLUSION

Throughout the years from 1714 to 1832 the Hanoverian dynasty occupied the English throne. They presided over a state which enjoyed an extraordinary run of successes.

The first great achievement was the birth of a new British nation during these years. The British state came into existence when the Act of Union of 1707 united the English and Scottish Parliaments. Making the British nation took longer. Between about 1750 and the accession of Queen Victoria in 1837, the Englishmen, Scots and Welshmen who shared the island of Britain acquired a new shared identity as Britons superimposed upon their English, Welsh and Scottish identities. That they all lived in the same island gave this new identity an appearance of naturalness and even inevitability. That all three peoples were overwhelmingly Protestant helped to give them a sense that they shared a common destiny, especially since their external enemy was usually Catholic France. From the reign of George III, the monarchy provided a symbol of unity. Whatever his shortcomings in other respects, George IV gave the monarchy a Scottish dimension through his visit to Edinburgh in 1822 and his interest in the picturesque legacy of Scotland's highland past. Acquisition of a British identity did not mean that older identities were weakened. In the case of the Scots, their sense of belonging to one historic nation was much increased at this time as lowland Scots appropriated the kilts and tartans of the highlanders.

The development of a British identity among all the peoples of the island owed much to the wars of the 18th and early 19th centuries. The extraordinary run of victories against external enemies, and particularly against the traditional enemy France, fostered pride in the British state which had won them. Success in war is the second major achievement of the British state in the Hanoverian period. By the time the Napoleonic wars concluded, Britain had helped to destroy French hegemony and create a Europe where power was distributed among four major states which seemed likely to check and balance each other. The other main fruit of Britain's success in war was its position of exceptional dominance in the world. It was left as the only considerable west European colonial power. At Vienna in 1815, other western European colonial powers recovered or retained only what Britain allowed them to have. The British navy ruled the oceans. The areas under British rule were already large; much larger still were the vast areas whose trade was largely in British hands.

British trade flourished because of Britain's third great achievement: the economic transformation achieved by the inventors and businessmen known as the first industrial revolution. The start of this change is usually dated to the end of the 18th century and it gave British industry the lead in the production of textiles and iron goods. The Scots and the Welsh shared in the British industrial revolution and the British empire can fairly be called an Anglo-Scottish empire.

Yet the legacy of the Hanoverian years was not wholly benign. The formula of Parliamentary Union, tried with such success in Scotland, was tried also in Ireland. By 1832 the demand for repeal of the Union was already insistent. Between the Irish and the peoples of Britain yawned a religious and political chasm, but that was hardly new. The divergent economic development of the two islands in the Hanoverian period added another fatal difference. Whereas by 1832 Britain contained an industrializing society, most of Ireland contained few but impoverished peasants. Despite experiencing severe strains, it was already likely that Britain would be able to sustain its vastly increased population and even begin to raise its living standards. It was already unlikely that the Irish would be able to avoid demographic catastrophe.

In the Hanoverian period, the British social and political system had proved astonishingly resilient, partly because the ruling elite had been so successful at winning its wars, thereby proving its competence. There had always been room within the elite for rising men of talent and the political system was not insulated from public opinion. Even so, the system that had served well a society based on agriculture was certain to need considerable adjustment if it was to be suitable for an increasingly urban and industrial society. In the years after 1815 there were ever louder demands for change and the governments of the 1820s were not oblivious to them. Yet the process of adaptation had not gone very far. The difficult task of adapting British institutions to meet the needs of a new kind of society was the most important unfinished business which the Hanoverians bequeathed to their posterity.

INDEX

INDEX

INDEX